Feminist Technosciences

Rebecca Herzig and Banu Subramaniam, Series Editors

Reinventing
Hoodia

**PEOPLES, PLANTS, and
PATENTS in SOUTH AFRICA**

LAURA A. FOSTER

UNIVERSITY OF WASHINGTON PRESS

Seattle and London

Copyright © 2017 by the University of Washington Press
Printed and bound in the United States of America
Design by Thomas Eykemans
Composed in Chaparral, typeface designed by Carol Twombly

21   20   19   18   17   5   4   3   2   1

University of Washington Press
www.washington.edu/uwpress

Portions of this book were previously published in Laura A. Foster, "The Making and Unmaking of Patent Ownership: Technicalities, Materialities, and Subjectivities," PoLAR: Political and Legal Anthropology Review 39, no. 1 (2016): 127–43, and Laura A. Foster, "Decolonizing Patent Law: Postcolonial Technoscience and Indigenous Knowledge in South Africa," Feminist Formations 28:3 (2016), 148–173. Reprinted with permission of John Wiley and Sons, and Johns Hopkins University Press.

Library of Congress Cataloging-in-Publication Data
Names: Foster, Laura A., author.
Title: Reinventing hoodia : peoples, plants, and patents in South Africa / Laura A. Foster.
Description: Seattle : University of Washington Press, 2017. | Series: Feminist technosciences | Includes bibliographical references and index. | Description based on print version record and CIP data provided by publisher; resource not viewed.
Identifiers: LCCN 2017010452 (print) | LCCN 2017024609 (ebook) | ISBN 9780295742199 (ebook) | ISBN 9780295742175 (hardcover : alk. paper) | ISBN 9780295742182 (pbk. : alk. paper)
Subjects: LCSH: Materia medica, Vegetable—South Africa. | Medicinal plants—South Africa.
Classification: LCC RS182.S6 (ebook) | LCC RS182.S6 F67 2018 (print) | DDC 615.3/21—dc23
LC record available at https://lccn.loc.gov/2017010452

The paper used in this publication is acid-free and meets the minimum requirements of American National Standard for Information Sciences—Permanence of Paper for Printed Library Materials, ANSI Z39.48–1984. ∞

To San peoples,
and to those who seek to decolonize knowledge
and build alternative belongings

Contents

Acknowledgments

This book is the product of a collective intellectual and political journey that I have shared with many people over time. It began more than twenty years ago while I was taking an undergraduate women and law class at Georgetown University, where I engaged with the law and against the law by considering how it could be deployed, changed, or even abandoned to ensure a more socially just future for those historically considered less worthy of legal protection and rights. I honed this critical engagement with and against the law while attending the University of Cincinnati (UC) as a graduate student in law and women's studies. I owe a tremendous debt to the courageous vision and work of Barbara Watts, Robin Sheets, and many others at UC who helped establish the very first MA/JD in Women's Studies program, from which I was the first to graduate. While I was in law school, Dorothy Brown, Gabriel Chin, Bert Lockwood, and Barbara Watts taught me to apply a critical lens to all areas of the law. My professors in the UC Department of Women's, Gender, and Sexuality Studies (WGS) were instrumental in helping me develop that lens. Patricia Hill Collins taught me that social justice inquiry starts with formulating critical questions, while Lisa Hogeland stressed that social change requires both liberal and radical politics. After my graduation, Anne Runyan also reminded me that WGS remained my home as I struggled with the politics of being a practicing attorney.

I would not have been able to write this book without the experience of being a corporate lawyer because it taught me how power truly functions, but it is my doctoral training in the Department of Gender Studies at University of California–Los Angeles (UCLA) that gives this project its theoretical, methodological, and political depth. This book developed out of research informed by colleagues who courageously supported my desire to push the field into ever more expansive inquiries into where power resides, such as intellectual property rights. Richard Abel, Carole Browner, and Christine Littleton promoted this project from its beginnings and urged me to produce rigorous intersectional work. I owe a special thanks to Sandra Harding who is my model for doing rich intellectual and political work while enjoying life at the same time. I am indebted to her for asking me just the right questions, pushing me to find my own voice, and reminding me to keep family and friends first.

The field of women's, gender, and sexuality studies is indebted to those who came before and those who come after. It is a privilege, honor, and responsibility to earn an advanced degree in this emerging field. The National Women's Studies Association was founded in 1977 and Emory University offered the first doctoral degree beginning in 1990, so there are very few role models for how to navigate the life of a graduate student and faculty member trained in this field. Although it shares many attributes with other interdisciplinary programs, it also has distinct histories, genealogies, politics, and futures. This book's analysis is a testament to the possibilities of this field and how it enables entirely new sets of inquiries and frameworks to emerge. For that reason, I am grateful for those who came before to establish this institutional home, to those who struggle to maintain it, and for those who dream its enduring possibilities.

There are many at UCLA who share this vision of the field and who greatly influenced this book. I would like to thank several supportive faculty members in the UCLA Department of Gender Studies, including Sondra Hale, Douglas Kellner, Rachel Lee, Beth Marchant, Kathleen McHugh, Abigail Saguy, Nadera Shalhoub-Kevorkian, Jenny Sharpe, Sharon Traweek, and Juliet Williams. I am also thankful for several graduate school colleagues who both intellectually inspired me and held me accountable to doing social justice work, including Azza Basarudin, Gwen D'Arcangelis, Evangeline Heiliger, Sharmila Lodhia, Loran Marsan, Saru Matambanadzo, Jennifer Musto, Katie Oliviero, Khanum Shaikh, and Anna Ward. I owe a special thanks to Tina Beyene, who has been on this journey with me for the longest time as a colleague at both UC and UCLA; many of our conversations over the years are reflected in this book. The story of Hoodia demonstrates the need to recognize the multiple contributions that go into producing knowledge, so I also thank Van Do-Nguyen, Richard Medrano, Samantha Hogan, and Jenna Miller-Von Ah for their tireless administrative and emotional support.

Interdisciplinarity and intersectionality require intellectual engagements across numerous relations and domains of power, which also means physically traversing multiple academic units. Specifically, this project was shaped in powerful ways by spending five years working closely with the UCLA Institute for Society and Genetics (ISG). I am deeply grateful to ISG for several years of intellectual support, financial resources, interdisciplinary training, and friendships that have continued to nurture and sustain me. Thanks especially to Olivia Banner, Ruha Benjamin, Soraya de Chadarevian, Carrie Friese, Sally Gibbons, Debra Greenfield, Chris Kelty, Russell Korobkin, Hannah Landecker, Ed McCabe, Linda McCabe, Aaron Panofsky, Lindsey Smith, Ana Wevill, and Norton Wise for their endless support. I was also privileged to work with the Tribal Learning Community and Educational Exchange at UCLA School of Law, which enabled me to collaborate on a project with the Indigenous Peoples' Council on Biocolonialism. In doing this work, I am forever grateful to DeAnna Rivera (Taíno), Debra Harry (Northern Paiute), and Le`a Malia Kanehe (Kanaka Maoli) for helping me design this research project and its commitments to learning from San peoples. Furthermore, to the undergraduate students in my 2007 *Bioprospecting and Patent Law* class who greatly inspired me and made important contributions to the early stages of this project, in particular Carrie Holmes, Irene Targaryan, Jillian Theil, and Jennifer Truong.

This book would not be possible without the assistance of several colleagues and friends in South Africa who have provided me with support, encouragement, and friendship while I was doing this research. First, thank you to the many people, especially San peoples, who shared their stories about Hoodia with me over many wonderful meals, cups of tea, desert walks, and unforgettable dances. I am also grateful to them for reading drafts, approving quotations, and providing generous feedback on the research and writing of this book. Collin Louw and Arrie Tities in particular have shared numerous insights with me on San histories, for which I am forever grateful. I also received much support from the faculty, staff, and students at the Centre for African Studies at the University of

Cape Town and the South African Research Chair in Property Law at Stellenbosch Law School, two places that provided nurturing academic homes for this work. I am grateful to Brenda Cooper, Harry Garuba, Lilian Jacobs, and AJ (André) van der Walt for allowing me to be a part of these critical spaces. I am also thankful to several colleagues, such as Roger Chennells, Wilmot James, and Rachel Wynberg, who have offered many insights into this project and into South African politics more generally. I have also had the honor of working with Natural Justice, a nongovernmental organization in Cape Town led by a dedicated group of lawyers, researchers, and indigenous peoples who work closely together on issues of indigenous peoples' self-determination. Thank you to Kabir Bavikatte, Lesle Jansen (Khoisan), Harry Jonas, Catherine Traynor, and Johanna von Braun for their inspiring political work. I have also had the distinct pleasure of working with the faculty, staff, and students of the Intellectual Property Unit at the University of Cape Town Faculty of Law. Thank you to Caroline Ncube, Andrew Rens, Tobias Schonwetter, Nan Warner, and Phyllis Webb for creating a space where critical examinations of intellectual property are strongly encouraged. Several individuals in South Africa have also provided much assistance in writing this book. My gratitude to Michael Theron for helping me translate informed consent documents from English to Afrikaans. I also owe a special debt of gratitude to Debbie Collier, Adam Haupt, Julian Jonker, and Monica Tabengwa for their encouragement and warm friendship over the last several years and for reminding me of the importance of, difficulty of, and joy in doing this work. Traveling to and from South Africa while leaving two young children behind is never easy, but thank you to Terry, Jess, and Bongi for providing me a home away from home in Cape Town and for sharing many memorable meals.

In writing this book, I have benefited from numerous conversations across diverse fields. I would like to thank my feminist science studies colleagues Aimee Bahng, Rajani Bhatia, Sara Giordano, Jennifer Hamilton, Clare Jen, Carole McCann, Anne Pollock, Deboleena Roy, Banu Subramaniam, Kim TallBear, and Angela Willey for providing feedback on this project and for creating such a supportive intellectual community. I am also grateful to several colleagues in socio-legal studies who have made suggestions and provided encouragement, including Andrea Ballestero, Dan Burk, William Gallagher, Debora Halbert, Ernesto Hernández-López, Jonathan Kahn, and Osagie Obasogie.

The tremendous support of colleagues at Indiana University Bloomington have also been instrumental in shaping this book. My colleagues from the Department of Gender Studies, including Marlon Bailey, Maria Bucur, Freda Fair, Lessie Jo Frazier, Sara Friedman, Justin Garcia, LaMonda Horton-Stallings, Colin Johnson, Jennifer Maher, Amrita Chakrabarti Myers, Stephanie Sanders, Cate Taylor, Nina Taylor, and Brenda Weber, have all encouraged me in some way to push the boundaries of the field. I am also thankful to my colleagues from the IU Science Studies Reading Group, such as Barbara Andrews, Nathan Ensmenger, Allison Fish, Ilana Gershon, Thomas Gieryn, Rebecca Lave, Eden Medina, Christena Nippert-Eng, Selma Sabanovic, Cassidy Sugimoto, and the late David Hakken, who have helped me strengthen my arguments and taught me new ways of doing interdisciplinary work. The faculty and staff of the Center for Intellectual Property Research at IU Maurer School of Law, in particular its director, Mark Janis, have also been tremendously important in encouraging this new field of critical intellectual property studies. I would also like to thank all those colleagues in my women's writing groups over the years for their generosity and accountability. My deep appreciation also to Victor Quintanilla and Alberto Varon for reading multiple drafts of this book and for making me a better writer. Indiana University Bloomington provided generous funding for this project, including a New Frontiers in the Arts & Humanities Major Grant and a Mellon Innovating International Research (MIIRT) Faculty Fellowship.

I have had the distinct honor of teaching and learning from the next generation of graduate students in the field of women's, gender, and sexuality studies, and they inspire me on a daily basis. It has been a pleasure to work closely with Lindsey Breitwieser, Lamont Loyd-Sims, Shadia Siliman, and Amanda Stephens. Teaching with Betsy Jose, Alexandra Marcotte, Kimberly Miller, Lauren Savit, Laura Seger, Gretchen Panzer, and Xavier Watson has been wonderful. This book would also not be possible without the research support of Lindsey Breitwieser, Shahin Kachwala, and my undergraduate research assistants, Jordyn Alexander and Taegan Anthony.

I could not have asked for a better experience in working with University of Washington Press. I am thankful to my copyeditor, Jennifer Comeau. I am also grateful to Larin McLaughlin, Banu Subramaniam, and Rebecca Herzig for having the vision to create a series in feminist technosciences, which itself is an intellectual and political project in decolonizing hegemonic knowledge systems.

A final thanks goes out to my family and friends. To Scott for his inspiration, support, laughter, and openness to the adventure; my young sons, Garrett and Kyler, for their smiles, hugs, and lessons in patience and simple appreciations; my mom, brother, Leslie, Bethany, and Gwen for always listening, even when it wasn't going well; and Tim, Tamra, Regan, James, Erin, and Todd for many wonderful nights of distraction. Having the privilege to write this book was only possible with the help of Tonya and the generosity of the Shariff and Kaur families and Gabby, who loved my children like they were their own—thank you!

Abbreviations

ANC	African National Congress
CBD	Convention on Biological Diversity
CIPC	Companies and Intellectual Property Commission, South Africa
CIPRO	Companies and Intellectual Property Registration Office, South Africa
CSIR	Council for Scientific and Industrial Research, South Africa
DEAT	Department of Environmental Affairs and Tourism, South Africa
DETEC	Department of Tourism, Environment, and Conservation, South Africa
IPCB	Indigenous Peoples' Council on Biocolonialism
NKC	National Khoisan Council
SADF	South African Defense Force
SAHG	South African Hoodia Growers (Pty) Limited
SAHGA	South African Hoodia Growers Association
SASI	South African San Institute
SWAPO	South West Africa People's Organization
TRIPs	(Agreements on) Trade-Related Aspects of Intellectual Property Rights
UN	United Nations
USPTO	United States Patent and Trademark Office
WIMSA	Working Group of Indigenous Minorities in South Africa

Chronology

1931	Union establishes the Kalahari Gemsbok National Park
1932	Rudolf Marloth publishes that his Hottentot guide uses ghaap, or *Trichocaulon piliferum*, for food and water and to alleviate hunger
1933	Alain White and Boyd Sloane expand *Hoodia* genus to include fifteen new species
1945	South African Parliament establishes CSIR
1948	National Party comes to power in South Africa and enacts apartheid rule
1949	Prohibition of Mixed Marriages Act prohibits interracial marriage
1950	Population Registration Act requires citizens to register according to racial classification
1950	Group Areas Act segregates residential and business areas by racial classification
1950	Immorality Act prohibits interracial sexual relations
1950–2001	South African Museum displays San in dioramas as primordial
1961	South African Constitution Act establishes the Republic of South Africa
1963	CSIR begins studying edible indigenous plants in South Africa
1966–89	South African Border War with South West Africa (now Namibia)
1990	Displacement of !Xun and Khwe SADF soldiers to Schmidtsdrift
1980	*The Gods Must Be Crazy* film depicts San as primitive
1985	Vinesh Maharaj begins working at CSIR
May 1992	UN adopts CBD
Dec. 1993	CBD enters into force
Jan. 1994	CSIR files a provisional Hoodia-based patent with CIPRO
April 1994	Formal end of apartheid rule in South Africa with election of Nelson Mandela of the ANC
1994	ANC implements Reconstruction and Development Programme
Jan. 1995	World Trade Organization's TRIPs Agreement comes into effect

Jan. 1995	CSIR files a provisional Hoodia-based patent with CIPRO
1995	≠Khomani San initiate action to reclaim former lands
1995–2004	UN announces First International Decade of the World's Indigenous Peoples
1996	ANC outlines Growth, Equity, and Reconstruction Programme
Mar. 1996	CSIR files a provisional Hoodia-based patent with CIPRO
Apr. 1996	Phytopharm begins trading on the London Stock Exchange at 2.57P
May 1996	Constitution of the Republic of South Africa is enacted
Nov. 1996	Intellectual Property Laws Rationalisation Act is enacted
1996	Working Group of Indigenous Minorities in Southern Africa is established
Apr. 1997	CSIR files a provisional Hoodia-based patent with CIPRO
June 1997	Phytopharm announces partnership with CSIR to develop natural antiobesity treatment
Dec. 1997	South Africa enacts Medicines and Related Substances Control Act to allow importation of generic drugs to assist those with HIV/AIDS
Feb. 1998	Pharmaceutical Manufacturers Association of South Africa and US pharmaceutical companies file joint lawsuit in South Africa for patent infringement and trade violations under TRIPs
Apr. 1998	CSIR files a complete Hoodia-based appetite-suppressant patent with CIPRO
Aug. 1998	Phytopharm announces collaboration with Pfizer to develop and commercialize P57 obesity drug
Oct. 1998	Phytopharm announces that P57 drug candidate has entered Phase I clinical trial
Oct. 1999	CSIR files a complete Hoodia-based appetite-suppressant patent with USPTO
Dec. 1999	CIPRO grants Hoodia-based patent to CSIR
Apr. 2001	David Firn publishes story on Hoodia in *London Financial Times*
Apr. 2001	Pharmaceutical Manufacturers Association of South Africa withdraws patent infringement lawsuit
June 2001	Antony Barnett publishes story on Hoodia in *The Observer*

June 2001	WIMSA authorizes South African San Council to negotiate with CSIR
Apr. 2002	Phytopharm announces the opening of a manufacturing unit in South Africa to grow Hoodia plants
Apr. 2002	USPTO grants CSIR a Hoodia-based appetite-suppressant patent
Dec. 2002	USPTO grants Phytopharm a Hoodia-based patent related to treating gastric acid secretion
Mar. 2002	South African San Council and CSIR sign memorandum of understanding for Hoodia benefit sharing
May 2002	≠Khomani San win land claim and sign the !Ae!Hai Kalahari Heritage Park Agreement
Mar. 2003	San-CSIR Hoodia Benefit Sharing Agreement is signed
Mar. 2003	Phytopharm announces Pfizer's plans to conduct a double-blind, placebo-controlled residential study to clinically validate the P57 appetite suppressant
July 2003	Phytopharm announces termination of Hoodia research by Pfizer
June 2004	South Africa enacts the Biodiversity Act, which mandates benefit sharing
Oct. 2004	USPTO grants Phytopharm a Hoodia-based patent related to treating gastric acid secretion
Nov. 2004	Leslie Stahl, a reporter for CBS's 60 Minutes, reports on Hoodia
Dec. 2004	Phytopharm announces the first stage of a joint agreement with Unilever to develop Hoodia whereby Unilever agrees to commit approximately £6.5 million ($12.5 million) out of a potential £21 million in payments to Phytopharm
2005–2014	UN declares Second International Decade of the World's Indigenous Peoples
2005	Formation of SAHG
Feb. 2006	South African San Council signs benefit-sharing agreement with SAHG
Apr. 2006	USPTO grants Phytopharm a Hoodia-based patent for treating diabetes
Apr. 2006	Phytopharm announces second stage of a joint agreement with Unilever to develop Hoodia whereby Unilever agrees

	to commit a further £3.5 million in payments to Phytopharm
Apr. 2006	Phytopharm shares go up 10.2 percent to 43P
Aug. 2006	*Financial Times* reports that Sandy Morrison, formerly of Unilever, is to join Phytopharm as a nonexecutive director
May 2006	*Financial Times* reports a positive Alzheimer's trial for Phytopharm, and Phytopharm's share price goes up to 56.5P
Jan. 2007	CEO Richard Dixey resigns from Phytopharm
Mar. 2007	South African San Council signs benefit-sharing agreement with SAHGA
May 2007	Phytopharm's share price falls slightly to 49P
Sept. 2007	UN adopts the Declaration on the Rights of Indigenous Peoples
Feb. 2008	South Africa adopts Regulations on Bio-prospecting, Access, and Benefit-Sharing
Nov. 2008	*Financial Times* reports the termination of Hoodia research by Unilever, and Phytopharm's shares fall 42.8 percent to 5P
Apr. 2009	US Federal Trade Commission announces charges against Nutraceuticals International for its deceptive advertising of Hoodia products
Apr. 2009	Advertising Standards Authority of South Africa announces charges against Planet Hoodia for its deceptive advertising of Hoodia products
Oct. 2010	USPTO grants Phytopharm a patent for production of Hoodia plant extracts containing steroidal glycosides
Nov. 2010	Phytopharm announces its termination of Hoodia research and transfer of licensing back to CSIR
Apr. 2011	USPTO grants Phytopharm a patent on Hoodia plant extract with improved flavor
May 2011	South African patent office renamed as CIPC
June 2013	US Supreme Court rules in *Ass'n for Molecular Pathology* v. *Myriad Genetics* that a naturally occurring DNA segment is a product of nature and cannot be patented

Sept. 2013	Phytopharm stock sells at 50.1P upon announcement of merger with IXICO
Oct. 2014	UN Nagoya Protocol on Access and Benefit-sharing enters into force
Mar. 2015	South Africa makes Draft Protection, Promotion, Development, and Management of Indigenous Knowledge Systems Bill available for public comment
May 2015	South Africa enacts Amendments to the Regulations on Bio-prospecting, Access, and Benefit-sharing
Sept. 2015	South Africa makes Draft Traditional and Khoi-San Leadership Bill available for public comment
Apr. 2018	CSIR Hoodia-based appetite-suppressant patent set to expire in South Africa and United States

Reinventing Hoodia

Introduction

Peoples, Plants, and Patents in South Africa

> We are the people of stories.
>
> —LYS KRUIPER (≠KHOMANI SAN)

IN MARCH 2003, INDIGENOUS SAN OF SOUTH AFRICA SIGNED A HIS-
toric benefit-sharing agreement with scientists from South Africa's Council for Science and Industrial Research (CSIR), who they claimed had filed
a patent on San Hoodia knowledge in 1998 and aimed to profit immensely
from it as an antiobesity drug. As a heterogeneous group, San did not all
agree, but they had strategically come together through their own South
African San Council to negotiate benefits, protest patent ownership, and
establish pathways for demanding formal recognition from the government.[1] In an official signing ceremony at the Molopo Lodge in the Kalahari
Desert, Petrus Vaalbooi (≠Khomani San Bushman), then the chair of the
council, signed the agreement dressed in traditional San clothing, thereby
reinforcing San peoples as modern political subjects and enacting a new
moment in South Africa's postcolonial, postapartheid politics and its
shifting notions of belonging.

In addition to San claims to self-determination, at the center of the
agreement were two material-discursive meanings of a succulent plant
called *Hoodia gordonii*—Hoodia as a molecule patented by CSIR scientists
as an appetite suppressor, and Hoodia as a plant found in nature and
known by San peoples for generations as a source of food, water, and
energy and as a means of easing breastfeeding and treating gassiness in

babies.[2] Scientists from CSIR sat alongside the attending Indigenous San peoples to witness the signing of the agreement, while global news media stood nearby broadcasting one of the first instances in which scientists had agreed to share benefits with indigenous peoples after patents had been issued. At the signing, Kxao Moses, chairperson of the Working Group of Indigenous Minorities in South Africa (WIMSA), praised CSIR scientists for agreeing to give San peoples across Southern Africa a portion of revenues received from the joint development agreements between CSIR and its global commercial partners Pfizer (of the United States) and Phytopharm (of the United Kingdom). Specifically, CSIR had agreed to give 6 percent of their revenue share from the sale of Hoodia and 8 percent of milestone payments CSIR was to receive when certain benchmarks were reached in the research process.

At the same time, Moses condemned a different but related herbal supplement industry that gave the plant a third meaning—as a cultivated herbal supplement. Several companies from the United States to South Africa had begun selling dried Hoodia as a weight-control supplement just after CSIR and its partners had announced plans for Hoodia as an anti-obesity drug. This led to high demand for Hoodia plants and concerns over its endangerment.[3] This booming industry had developed alongside and separately from that of Hoodia as a pharmaceutical. Assuming that CSIR patents did not apply to their dried Hoodia products, these companies did not obtain licensing fees to offer it for sale. In his speech, Mr. Moses was less concerned with the economics of this situation than with how these companies were using San images without their consent. Hoodia herbal supplement companies were marketing Hoodia-based weight-loss products over the Internet by contrasting disturbingly familiar colonial images of seemingly white, thin female bodies with those of male Indigenous San hunters dressed in loincloths and carrying bows and arrows. Reinventing meanings of Hoodia to fit market models, they also advertised Hoodia both as patented and as the ancient knowledge of male San hunters, in both cases excluding San women from histories of Hoodia and reinforcing hierarchies of gender, ethnicity, and race. Advertising Hoodia as both an ancient "Bushmen's Secret" and a modern patented invention, these companies constructed Hoodia not only as a natural and pure botanical, but also as scientifically innovative.

A few years after the San-CSIR signing ceremony, the South African San Council also negotiated a second agreement, this time with the Hoodia growers in South Africa who were supplying plants for that herbal supplement industry. In 2007, a small group of South African Hoodia growers who had collectively organized as the South African Hoodia Growers Association (SAHGA) agreed to grant San peoples across Southern Africa a levy of 24R per dry kilogram of their future Hoodia exports. San peoples therefore became stakeholders not only in the making of Hoodia at the scale of molecule patented by CSIR scientists, but also in its use as a cultivated herbal supplement. Although the signing of this second agreement brought further recognition to San peoples, they continued to wait for benefits from the San-CSIR agreement.

This delay was due in large part to Pfizer's dropping its plans to develop Hoodia as a weight-loss drug in 2003, a decision that spurred CSIR and Phytopharm to form a new partnership in 2004 with the British and Dutch-based multinational consumer goods company Unilever, which hoped to make Hoodia into a food, such as a yogurt drink, that would help consumers reduce their weight. Despite the fact that an equivalent of millions of dollars had already been invested into Hoodia research and development, the historic San-CSIR benefit-sharing agreement had yet to produce the financial windfall that San peoples had hoped for when they celebrated at the Molopo Lodge. Furthermore, the likelihood of actually receiving monetary benefits from the agreement diminished as the boom of the Hoodia herbal supplement market began to slow, and Unilever announced in late 2008 that it was also terminating its plans to develop Hoodia products. So although the historic San-CSIR agreement had brought global recognition to San peoples and reinforced a new South African politics of multicultural difference, in terms of financial benefits, San peoples received only 569,000R ($70,000) from CSIR, which was significant but still small in comparison to the amount of money invested in Hoodia research.[4]

In this book, I tell the story of how Hoodia was reinvented through patent ownership, pharmaceutical research, indigenous peoples' self-determination efforts, contractual benefit sharing, herbal supplement industries, and bioprospecting legislation. I show how these forces constructed, mobilized, and unequally valued three different meanings and materialities of the same plant: as a molecule, as cultivated, and as from nature. Specifically, I examine how San peoples, CSIR scientists, and Hoodia growers made claims of attachment to these different materialities of Hoodia to assert belonging through securing rights to patent ownership and benefit sharing. At the same time, I also examine how these multiple modalities of Hoodia materiality provoked and reinvented the very forces that had sought to contain them. The way Hoodia plants evolved in patchy spatial distributions, grew too slowly when cultivated, and interacted with the human body as steroidal glycoside molecules shows how forms of nonhuman matter can enact moments of fissure within these relations of power even as they are constituted by them. I use the terms *invention* and *story* not to imply fabrication but to enable an exploration of how, as Nick Shepard notes, "there is nothing natural or inevitable about the production of knowledge" and, I would add, about the valuing of nonhuman matter.[5] My analysis thereby adds to the literature challenging normative constructions of science, law, market, and nature as "natural" and contributes to the growing body of work about San, Hoodia, and bioprospecting in South Africa.[6]

In tracing these reinventions of Hoodia, the following chapters also reveal how, in the words of Carrie Friese, "nature is being actively made" and how those multiple meanings of nature profoundly shape how various groups of people, and especially indigenous peoples, belong and become in the world.[7] Demonstrating that struggles over patent ownership, benefit sharing, and indigenous peoples' knowledge can be understood more broadly as a story of belonging in South Africa, the book argues that San peoples, CSIR scientists, and Hoodia growers made unequal claims for belonging through attachments to differentially valued materialities of the same plant in ways that simultaneously contested, reinforced, and reconfigured colonial histories and apartheid pasts while establishing new, albeit limited, possibilities.

A Feminist Decolonial Technoscience Approach

This exploration of what Hoodia struggles can tell us about shifting notions of belonging in South Africa sets out to demonstrate possible sites of intervention within patent law and consider better ways of doing and governing scientific research through benefit sharing, and also to develop new approaches and concepts for a feminist decolonial technoscience analysis of contemporary science projects and their colonial legacies. Building on the groundbreaking insights of feminist science studies scholars, it strives to advance the development of a more robust feminist science studies that takes seriously the insights of feminist, postcolonial, and indigenous theorizing by examining the intersectional politics of gender, race, indigeneity, and their colonial histories related to contestations over Hoodia.

Critical science studies and socio-legal scholarship produce valuable understanding of struggles over patent ownership and contractual benefit sharing but continue to leave several questions unaddressed. Scholars have argued that patent ownership curtails the sharing of scientific materials and processes,[8] threatens the resources of indigenous peoples,[9] and is based on western notions of property rights that conflict with indigenous peoples' ways of knowing.[10] Scholars have also addressed contractual benefit sharing by situating it as a capacity-building project for the third world,[11] as a strategy for indigenous peoples to contest patent ownership by adopting and transforming Western property logics,[12] as a form of politics that constitutes new publics and collectives by changing relations between scientists and indigenous peoples,[13] and as a potential site of inequality for indigenous peoples.[14] Scholars in South Africa in particular, such as Elan Abrell, Kabir Bavikatte, Gino Cocchiaro, Adam Haupt, Harry Jonas, Caroline Ncube, Andrew Rens, and Tobias Schonwetter, have also begun to develop critical frameworks for interrogating intellectual property rights in South Africa.[15] These are valuable critiques that challenge normative framings of patent ownership as a set of objective legal rules, but they leave unexamined the gendered assumptions, variegated colonial histories, and materiality of patented objects that make us think differently about struggles over knowledge and belonging in South Africa and elsewhere.

The feminist decolonial technoscience approach here brings attention to these relations through its interdisciplinary analysis of Hoodia patent law struggles. Feminist science studies scholarship in the United States examines patent law but continues to come up short by focusing solely on gender, thus situating itself as what Sandra Harding calls a "northern feminist science and technology studies" project.[16] The inquiry tends to be on the historical exclusion of women inventors from patent ownership, lower rates of patenting by contemporary female scientists, or the patenting of breast cancer genes.[17] Such scholarly work addresses important issues for women in the Global North and challenges how patenting can privilege male, masculine norms of science but is less helpful for understanding how patent law can devalue indigenous peoples' knowledge, histories, and cultures.

Alternatively, the impact of science and patent ownership on indigenous peoples has been convincingly established by the work of indigenous and Native feminist scholars such as Winona LaDuke (Anishinaabe) and Linda Tuhiwai Smith (Ngāti Awa and Ngāti Porou), who have described patents as tools of imperialism historically used to strip indigenous peoples of their land, knowledge, and heritage.[18] Debra Harry (Northern Paiute) and Le`a Kanehe (Kanaka Maoli) have offered an analysis of how patents similarly function as instruments of biopiracy, and of the potential dangers of benefit sharing, while Victoria Tauli-Corpuz (Igorot) has called on the mainstream feminist movement to take questions of patent ownership and gender more seriously.[19] These scholars' critiques echo those of the widely known work of Vandana Shiva, who has led campaigns to invalidate patents on the neem tree and turmeric seed in India.[20] Indigenous feminist social movements have also identified intellectual property rights as a threat to indigenous women's lives in the 1995 Beijing Declaration of Indigenous Women and the 2004 Manukan Declaration of the Indigenous Women's Biodiversity Network and the Indigenous Peoples' Permanent Forum.[21] Although feminist scholars of science have produced important gendered histories of patent ownership and studies on empowering female scientists to file patents, such indigenous peoples' theorizing of science and patent ownership as connected to colonial histories provides a critical perspective that is more useful to the project of this book.[22]

Feminist postcolonial science studies more generally also offer insights and tools useful to an examination of Hoodia patent struggles in South Africa. Influential theorists such as Sandra Harding, Donna Haraway, Mary Louise Pratt, Sharon Traweek, and Vandana Shiva have produced valuable insights at the intersections of feminism, postcolonialism, and science studies that demonstrate how science projects are embedded in colonial histories in ways that reinforce relations of power.[23] Scholars within women, gender, and third-world development literatures have also generated important critiques of how science has contributed to the exploitation of those in the Global South.[24] Drawing on these earlier insights, scholars of feminist postcolonial science studies have examined the co-constitution of science and society in new ways by taking colonial histories and their contemporary legacies into account,[25] while feminist scholars in South Africa have recently theorized questions of gender and the biological through the lens of human rights.[26]

The field of feminist postcolonial science studies, as Sandra Harding notes, addresses science and technology issues that have had political repercussions for peoples considered "Other" around the world and acknowledges the sciences of non-European cultures.[27] It has proceeded on the assumption, Harding also observes, that gender and colonial relations have always co-constituted each other and that gendered social relations, while essential to recognize, may not always be as salient to a given analysis as race and colonialism; thus, privileging gender as the central category of analysis can actually hinder a postcolonial analysis. Given its disciplinary attachment to the field of postcolonial studies, the term *postcolonial* itself can, however, elide the histories of indigenous peoples and the colonial pasts of Latin America, for instance.[28] Although postcolonial studies shares similar critiques of colonialism and imperialism, its framework is limited in understanding projects of science and technology for peoples in Latin America and Native Nations who have experienced histories and legacies of colonialism very differently from, for example, South Africa.[29] I have therefore argued, along with Banu Subramaniam, Sandra Harding, Deboleena Roy, and Kim TallBear, for the need to deploy the term more broadly as "signifying a temporal moment, political condition, theoretical critique, subjectivity, and counter politic" for examining how contemporary science projects are informed by different colonial and indigenous peoples' histories and legacies.[30]

The feminist decolonial analysis developed here is thus indebted not only to the rich insights of well-known postcolonial thinkers, but also to Indigenous San and indigenous peoples' theorizations of South Africa's multiple histories of colonization that continue to shape their relationships with science and scientists who have affected them.[31] Its use of the term *decolonial* is also broadly informed by Linda Tuhiwai Smith's (Ngati Awa and Ngati Porou) notion of "decolonizing methodologies" and its examination of how legacies of imperialism and colonialism depend on and value certain forms of knowledge and nature over others.[32] As both a methodological approach and engaged politics, a feminist decolonial technoscience grounded in postcolonial and indigenous theorizing becomes urgent for decolonizing the production and ownership of scientific knowledge and its distinguishing of nature.

By examining how multiple ways of knowing and materialities of Hoodia come together unequally, this study aims to reframe patent ownership as it has been understood within racialized, indigenous, and gendered colonial histories and contribute to ongoing projects in South Africa that seek to challenge hierarchies of knowledge and nature, while enabling multiple ways of knowing and being to flourish. Inspired by these ongoing decolonial projects, this ethnographic study of the Hoodia plant and struggles around it focuses on four main concepts or themes: scale, patentability, materiality, and belonging.

Scale

As recent scholars of science and law have argued, because dominant notions of science and law operate along a single dimension of Western thought or the nation-state, attention to scale can provide a useful technique for disrupting these normative understandings and addressing the political concerns of those in the Global South.[33] Answering such calls for more careful analysis of scale, this book mobilizes the notion of scale not only as an important technique for developing an interdisciplinary feminist decolonial technoscience approach but as its primary organizing principle. Unlike Michele Murphy's study of several different feminist technoscientific devices, the focus here is on a single plant and its different modalities of scale (that is, as a molecule, as a cultivated plant, and as a plant from nature). Its comparison is across these variable forms of the same plant, so it also differs from Abena Dove Osseo-Asare's analysis of several different indigenous plants.[34] By examining the plant from the three different materialities or physical scales of the Hoodia plant identified above, I produce a ethnographic account of a plant by offering a thick description that examines how various meanings and cultures of nature are constructed and valued differently through associated struggles over colonial histories, patent ownership, pharmaceutical research, benefit sharing, Hoodia cultivation, Indigenous San self-determination, and South African belonging.

This multiscale examination contributes to rich traditions of intersectionality scholarship by developing a model for doing an intersectional analysis that includes attention to nonhumans and human-nonhuman relationships. Its emphasis on examining formations of power across multiple scales develops a robust feminist politics that aims to contest binary modes of thinking, make connections across sites of inequality, think across multiple ways of knowing and being, dismantle hierarchies of knowledge production, contest the differential valuing of matter, and imagine alternative modes of belonging.[35] In particular, the various physical scales of Hoodia become flexible starting points for examining how various subjects (San peoples, scientists, growers) simultaneously reinvented nature and their attachment to it (patented molecule, solid drug, liquid food, wild plant, herbal supplement) through different yet related ways of knowing (botany, chemistry, horticulture, indigenous knowledge), South African histories (colonization, apartheid, postapartheid, neoliberalism), legal regulatory orders (patents, benefit-sharing contracts, bioprospecting permits), market industries (pharmaceutical and herbal supplement), and their associated gendered and racialized binaries (human/nonhuman, modern/nonmodern, social/biological, nature/culture) in unequal ways. As a heuristic or analytic tool, this intersectional analysis examines power across these scales by attending both to relations of inequality in terms of indigeneity, race, and gender and also to domains of power such as law, science, and the marketplace. As we shall see, such intersectional analysis provides a deeper understanding of the relationships between different materialities of nonhumans (biochemical and physical scale), the valuing of humans over nonhumans (social and political scale), and the balancing of legal rights (scales of justice). Through this interdisciplinary, intersectional analysis, what becomes clear is the importance of asking what and whose epistemologies, ontologies, and ethics come to matter most.

Patentability

Patentability refers to the legal rules that govern patent law and the legal conditions that must be met to obtain patent ownership. Normative understandings of patentability operate on a single scale of the nation-state, which enacts legislation that determines what requirements scientists must follow in order to obtain patent ownership. This book explores how those normative understandings and the teaching of patent law would change if also accompanied by a recognition of how patent laws are embedded in and reinscribe colonial pasts or how indigenous peoples, scientists, and growers give different meanings to a patented object. To explain the main outlines of the normative understanding of patentability and how it obscures the concerns of indigenous peoples, let me tell the story of how the rules and assumptions of patent law were first explained to me in a classroom in a US law school.[36]

As I sat in an intellectual property law class, the professor explained to the large group of students that patents are intended to incite economic innovation by giving patent holders exclusive control over their invention for a certain length of time. *Patentability*, he explained, refers to the legal requirements for obtaining patent ownership, such as novelty, nonobviousness, and usefulness. These legal conditions for patentability, he further expounded, assume a distinction between discovery and invention. Offering a hypothetical example, he asked us to imagine Indiana Jones going into the rainforest and encountering a group of Oompa-Loompas who teach him about an important medicinal plant. Jones takes the plant and his knowledge back to the United States and hands them over to a pharmaceutical company. Scientists in the lab then isolate the precise chemical compounds in the plant that are responsible for its medicinal properties and apply for and receive a patent on those chemical compositions (product patent) and on the processes for extracting them from the plant (process patent). As the professor finished his hypothetical case, he paused and asked us, "So who is considered the inventor under patent law: Jones or the scientists?"

The students then engaged in a lively debate about the fairness of patent law's recognition of the scientists as the inventors because they had transformed nature into something useful and available for the marketplace. Jones, in this account, may have braved the wilds of the rainforest and the Oompa-Loompas, but he had merely discovered the plant. Many of the students objected to the legal nonrecognition of Jones for his arduous journey and skillfully gained knowledge. Why, they asked, did the patent system reward only the scientists and not Jones? Why did the law recognize the moment of invention, but not that of discovery?

But as the students continued their debate, I was stuck by what was left out of this normative narrative and discussion. I imagined how engaging in a feminist decolonial technoscience analysis might have enabled the students to ask more robust critical questions and, in doing so, challenge normative understandings of patent law as objective and as natural property rights. For example, had Jones stolen the plant from the Oompa-Loompas without their consent? Why were Willy Wonka characters being used to stand in for indigenous peoples?[37] I wondered how differently the discussion may have gone had the students been aware of the ways in which, as Vine Deloria Jr. reminds us, actual archaeologists and anthropologists had committed representational and material violence against indigenous peoples, or of the fact that, as Valentin-Yves Mudimbe argues, Africa is itself an invention, constructed through colonial narratives as a place of savagery, violence, and irrationality to be discovered and conquered.[38] Would their opinions have changed if they had understood that patent law's distinction between invention and discovery is embedded within gendered colonial histories, associating the capacity to produce knowledge with white male and masculine norms of reason and rationality and with devaluing the bodily reproductive capacity of women and the menial labor of people of color and indigenous peoples?[39]

I was reminded of this incident years later when I visited the Chemistry Department at the University of Pretoria in South Africa and noticed a sign on a lab entrance door quoting Dr. Sheldon Cooper, a fictional character from the popular television show *The Big Bang Theory*: "Engineering: where the noble, semi-skilled laborers execute the vision of those who think and dream, Hello Oompa-Loompas of Science." In this reconfiguring, the scientists were now the Oompa-Loompas, thereby blurring the lines between science and indigenous knowledge and rendering them as not so different after all. The students in the law school class that day had missed precisely this point: what is important is the history of violence between colonial settlers and indigenous peoples, but also the similarities and connections between scientists and indigenous peoples as they deploy ways of knowing to assert belonging and expertise within a changing neoliberal economy.

Yet such elisions constitute everyday practice in law school classrooms, where students are taught how to dissect legal opinions and statutory language to develop legal analyses that are presumably objective because they flow from legal precedence and reasoning. Patent law is particularly shrouded in this presumption of objectivity, legitimated and protected from critique by its highly technical rules backed by the imprimatur of science. It is no wonder, then, that neither the students nor the professor could engage in a critical, interdisciplinary examination of patent ownership and its distinction between discovery and invention. Law school curriculum and pedagogy had inhibited the bright students and the expert professor from grasping the raced, gendered, and even anthropocentric assumptions of their discussion. The following chapters explore how a feminist decolonial technoscience critique of patent law might bring new resources for understanding and reconfiguring patentability.

Materiality

Materiality refers to matter, the body, or the corporeal; this book also uses the term to refer to the technicalities or specific rules of the body of law. Honoring feminist scholars' long engagement with biology and matter, it draws on the efforts of such new materialist feminist scholars as Stacey Alaimo and Susan Hekman, Karen Barad, Elizabeth Grosz, Vicky Kirby, and Elizabeth Wilson who have urged feminist scholars to engage more deeply with how matter is socially constructed and how it can also construct social worlds.[40] This book thus undertakes what Angela Willey describes as a rich engagement with both the matter and the politics of science, and in this case also those of the law.[41] It thus attempts to model a feminist decolonial technoscience approach to materiality that is also attentive to how human-nonhuman relations simultaneously constitute and are constituted by the constraints and histories in which they are formed.

To that end, it mobilizes two models of materiality, the first of which comes from feminist science studies and investigates how nature acts back upon law and science.[42] This first model expands on theorizing from Alaimo and Hekman's understanding of nonhumans as having an "agentic force" and from Karen Barad's notion of agency as an enactment or doing in order to examine how Hoodia materialities shape the social worlds around them.[43] Specifically, it attempts to uncover how Hoodia plant materialities (e.g., chemicals, seeds, metabolites, spatial arrangements) refuse, change, or even align with the forces that seek to construct them, such as how the plant's complex stereochemistry refused scientists' efforts to commercially develop the plant into an antiobesity product. In doing so, this book urges attention to the *multiple modalities of materiality* that shape and constitute our worlds.

Although this analysis of materialities addresses nonhuman plant matter, it doesn't help explain how forces such as law and science construct the very matter of plants, which is particularly relevant for understanding how postcolonial technoscience projects in the Global South and the Global North are shaped by different legal and political conditions of inequality and possibility. Recognizing the impact of these differences is imperative for developing specific mechanisms for intervening within and against law and science in ways that benefit indigenous peoples. Multiple models of materiality are therefore needed to examine the co-constituted relations of nonhuman matter and the material provisions of the law.

Thus, the book also employs a second model of materiality that examines how the materialities of law produce unequal material effects on humans and nonhumans. This model understands the law as having, in the words of Jacques Derrida, a "force" that is "direct or indirect, physical or symbolic, exterior or interior, brutal or subtly discursive and hermeneutic, coercive or regulative, and so forth."[44] Law's authority according to Derrida is based on the *possibility* of its enforceability, and thus it acts with a force that defines conditions for belonging and becoming that emanate from but also go beyond the text of the law. Socio-legal scholars such as Annelise Riles have also suggested that legal rules, doctrines, and documents act with autonomous force, while Mariane Valverde brings attention to the technicalities of law as resources for theory, but the analysis here more fully develops a model for examining the materiality of the law and the objects of nature it seeks to contain.[45] As this model will show, the materialities of patent law rules, contractual provisions, and legal forms have animated, mobilized, and brought together networks of scientists, indigenous peoples, Hoodia growers, and plants in unequal ways. It is not enough to argue, though, that law constructs nature and belonging; one must delve into the interior spaces of the legal body and its materialities to really understand its power. Delving into the technical rules of patent law and material provisions of benefit sharing contracts will show how the law simultaneously recognized but devalued San peoples and knowledge as well as particular forms of Hoodia. By attending to multiple models of materiality and modalities of matter, a feminist decolonial technoscience approach thus aims to understand nonhuman plant matter in a way that addresses how those historically considered nonhuman—in this case indigenous peoples—continue to struggle for recognition as fully human through claims for legal recognition.

Belonging

My original analysis of the effect of science and the law on belonging in South Africa followed earlier science studies scholars' use of the notion of biological citizenship to understand the co-constitution of science and society, leading me to view Hoodia patent law struggles as sites for understanding the emergence of an "epistemic citizenship" within the global knowledge economy.[46] As I continued to examine this topic, however, the notion of citizenship began to appear too narrow to fully capture the multiple and complex modes of attachment and recognition at work between peoples and Hoodia plants. That citizenship has traditionally been associated with the nation-state and theorized without attention to nonhumans also hindered a broader discussion about relationships between peoples and plants. Eventually, the notion of *belonging* seemed a more expansive and flexible framework for addressing how San peoples, CSIR scientists, and Hoodia growers were making claims to materialities and ways of knowing Hoodia and how those materialities figured within the relationships among these subjects.[47] This framework also allowed me to uncover how the co-constitution of law, science, and marketplace has constructed plant matter and indigenous peoples' knowledge as propertied raw material and how plants and San peoples have also refused and reconfigured these very relations of property.

Belonging as deployed here refers to all facets of the term—to be classified, to be attached, and to be property—to help us understand struggles over Hoodia patents and associated benefit sharing. In so embracing the notion of belonging, I am following in a long tradition within feminist science studies and feminist legal theory. Groundbreaking work by scholars such as Catharine MacKinnon, Kimberlé Crenshaw, Sandra Harding, and Evelynn Hammonds has mapped modes of exclusion in the law or sciences, powerfully demonstrating how those institutions empower or marginalize different groups and how they also offer modes of inclusion and possibilities for belonging.[48] As the following chapters show, San peoples contested the taking of their knowledge by CSIR scientists without their consent and contested their exclusion from the benefits gained from that knowledge, even as they entered into the domain of science with desires for future recognition.

Other scholars who have turned to belonging as a framework for understanding the changing politics of South Africa have offered valuable insights to which this analysis is also indebted. Consistent with Sarah Nuttall's argument that the politics of postapartheid South Africa have shifted from an emphasis on practices of conquest and exclusion to negotiations of belonging and inclusion,[49] the following chapters demonstrate that science and law have become spaces for fashioning belonging to the nation-state, showing how they have brought scientists and indigenous peoples into relationship with each other in new ways that simultaneously empower and disempower San peoples as modern political subjects.

Notes on Methods and Terminology

In addition to requiring new ways of thinking about and conceptualizing the topic, conducting this research also raised issues about practices that have, historically, problematically affected indigenous peoples' struggles over belonging. According to Andrea Smith, academic scholarship has historically constructed Native peoples within an "ethnographic entrapment" where they are viewed as *knowable* subjects with an essential truth to be discovered, rather than as contradictory subjects themselves capable of making important intellectual contributions to knowledge.[50] To mitigate such entrapment, this book is based on an ethnographic study of both San peoples and Hoodia so as to understand San struggles over Hoodia not in isolation but in relation to scientists and growers. This approach also reveals how San have acted and continue to act as dynamic and contradictory political subjects in the South African San Council's ongoing efforts to contest other entities' taking of Indigenous San knowledge.

To mitigate operating as an agent of ethnographic entrapment, I engaged in feminist methodologies of self-reflexivity about my methods and practices, methodologies that are intended to disrupt hierarchies between researcher and researched but that, as Andrea Smith cautions, can nonetheless reinforce structures of domination by positioning the researcher as a self-reflexive white settler against those being researched as complaining ethnic subjects.[51] As a white female researcher from the United States,

I repeatedly struggled with this tension, which I attempted to reduce, if not entirely avoid or resolve, by embracing the practices discussed below.

On Engagement, Accountability, and Reciprocity

I first began my research on Hoodia patent struggles as a women's studies doctoral student in 2005, an interest sparked by receiving advertisements for Hoodia weight-loss supplements in my e-mail in-box. Although I was initially struck by their use of the previously mentioned gendered colonial images to market Hoodia, as I read more about San peoples and Hoodia benefit sharing, I became increasingly interested in how their struggles over indigenous knowledge were related to their contestations over land and recognition in South Africa. I had first learned about histories of San peoples several years earlier in 1998 while working as a human rights law clerk in Botswana as I pursued an MA/JD in women's studies and law. Unity Dow, the first female Judge of the High Court of Botswana, had invited me to work on issues of gender-based violence at her legal clinic in Mochudi, where I researched Botswana and South African law and helped draft legislation to make domestic violence a crime. (In 2006 she would rule on a landmark case granting San peoples the right to live and hunt in the Central Kalahari Game Reserve.) Although this modest knowledge of San histories and South African law supported my interest in continuing research around Hoodia patent law struggles, my limited general understanding of indigenous peoples and issues led me to begin taking classes in American Indian studies while pursuing my doctoral degree. My professor, DeAnna Rivera (Taíno), both encouraged me and introduced me to Debra Harry (Northern Paiute) and Le`a Kanehe (Native Hawaiian), who directed the Indigenous Peoples' Council on Biocolonialism (IPCB) in Nevada and invited me to conduct research for them. Starting my research on Hoodia while simultaneously learning about US Native struggles was tremendously important in helping me understand how various indigenous peoples' contestations over land and knowledge differ greatly.

Beginning my preliminary research in Botswana and South Africa in 2007, I devoted much of my time learning about the histories, heritage, and political mobilization of San peoples across southern Africa while also analyzing South African history and law more broadly. When I returned to South Africa in 2009, colleagues there encouraged me and put me in touch with Roger Chennells, a human rights lawyer who had been working with San peoples and the South African San Council for a number of years.[52] When I met Mr. Chennells for the first time near his law office in Stellenbosch, he interrogated me about my background while speaking about his own work with the council during its negotiations for the San-CSIR benefit-sharing agreement. Our conversation was engaging, and his initial concerns about my intentions seemed to be alleviated by my previous work in Botswana, with IPCB, and as a practicing corporate lawyer. As we continued our conversation, he suggested I first meet with Collin Louw (≠Khomani San Bushman), chairman of the South African San Council, and explained how the council had its own ethics procedures that would require me to sign a Media and Research Contract that formalized expectations for researchers.

Engagement and accountability were precisely what Collin Louw required of me during our first meeting in Upington, South Africa.[53] Our first conversation in 2009 began with his immediately asking me, "Who are you? What do you want? . . . You researchers, always coming around here, asking questions, talking to people, and nothing happens." In this moment of refusal, Louw acted less as a complaining ethnic subject and more as a producer of his own critique of the colonial legacies and violence that researchers had committed against indigenous peoples. Thinking it might ease his concerns, I told him a little about my experience working in southern Africa and mentioned that I had recently learned more about San histories from my conversations with lawyers from Natural Justice, a Cape Town–based NGO that I knew worked closely with the South African San Council. Stressing the need to follow the proper guidelines for working with San peoples, Mr. Louw interjected, saying, "Those guys, they were not here from the beginning, they did not work, you need to talk to the lawyer that had been involved from the beginning." I assured him I had already met with Mr. Chennells and had received the council's Media and Research Contract to discuss and sign with him. Thanking me for going through what he referred to as "the right channels" for engaging with ≠Khomani San, Mr. Louw spoke at length with me about Hoodia and San histories, while offering numerous insights and suggestions for shaping my research project in ways that benefited San peoples. During what was the first of many amiable conversations, we discussed the research contract and I agreed to continually communicate my research, stay in touch, and share benefits with San peoples in the form of research materials and a percentage of any royalties I might receive in the future. I came to understand how through the contract and its guidelines, the council demanded not only self-reflexivity on my part but a commitment to be responsible and to continue my engagement with them.

My purpose in these initial meetings was not just to gain trust or access but also to navigate conditions of ethnographic entrapment and forge more socially just ways of working together. Establishing these relationships was never smooth or immediate, as the San I met justifiably questioned, interrogated, and challenged me about my whiteness, intentions, and political alignments. Although humbly listening, thoughtfully engaging, staying in touch, and continuing to visit over time helped me develop mutual relationships and establish meaningful ways of doing research, ongoing engagement was sometimes complicated by relationships that were always in flux as peoples' lives and their roles in the community changed. Mr. Louw later explained that he had stated the importance of meeting first with Chennells and members of the South African San Council because they had the most extensive knowledge of Hoodia struggles and had been appointed by San to represent them, and because San are understandably suspicious of researchers, and even of newer NGOs such as Natural Justice, that do not have a "struggle history" of working against apartheid. On the other hand, some ≠Khomani San I spoke with were also distrustful of the council, demonstrating that San are by no means a homogenous or unified group and have their own internal debates about who should represent them and how their interests should be represented.

Although my initial visits with ≠Khomani San in Upington and Andriesville were brief, I maintained contact with a few individuals over e-mail and Skype while back in the United States and continued to build these relationships during later visits in 2014, 2015, 2016, and 2017. During my first visit in 2009, Mr. Louw had graciously invited me to meet with a young ≠Khomani San man named Rykes Jacobs, who facilitated my conversations with San by translating from Afrikaans to English, given that only some ≠Khomani San spoke English and the majority spoke Afrikaans. Although it is a limitation of this study that I talked mostly with ≠Khomani San, I did so because many of them served on the South African San Council and thus were active in the San-CSIR benefit-sharing negotiations and because I did not have the resources to extensively travel across South

Africa to meet with other San groups such as !Xun and Khwe or to travel north to meet with San in Botswana or Namibia. I am grateful to the ≠Khomani San who invited me into their homes and introduced me to others in their community, some of whom are referred to in this book.

There were some members in the community I was not invited to meet and others who met me but declined to talk to me, thus enacting what Ruha Benjamin refers to as practice of "informed refusal" in response to earlier research used against the interests of indigenous peoples.[54] Following the researcher guidelines and directions of ≠Khomani San leaders, I spoke only with those whom other ≠Khomani San referred me to, but I also wondered whom, for whatever reason, I was not invited to speak with. And even though I spoke with both men and women, I was critically aware that many I spoke with who had leadership roles tended to be men. Yet those who did speak with me contributed much to my understanding and also made thoughtful suggestions for conducting research with indigenous peoples and writing responsibly about San peoples and Hoodia.

While conducting this research, I took what Nagar and Swarr refer to as "enacting accountability" seriously, meaning that I responded to other needs and interests of San peoples and others I worked with in South Africa.[55] My position in the United States and access to university resources, for instance, allowed me to meet San requests for electronic copies of articles, share my research findings, and review grant proposals. The South African San Council and members of the National Khoisan Council (NKC) also work closely with Natural Justice and its director, Lesle Jansen (Khoisan), who serves as the lawyer for the NKC. In my work with Natural Justice, they have also invited me to write grants, review contracts, lead seminars, and write policy briefs to help change South African legislation affecting indigenous peoples, allowing us to develop ways of working collectively that have continued to this day. Even as my outsider status and distance from South Africa make engagement difficult, such practices are not just about "giving back" but about developing mutually beneficial relationships that amount to what scholars refer to as an "ethic of reciprocity" that recognizes the mutual benefits received by both researchers and researched.[56] Although my relationships with San peoples began within the binary framework of researcher/researched with San as "human subjects" given legal requirements governing human subjects research, over several years our engagement continued more as colleagues who share knowledge, challenge each other, learn from one another, and imagine new research projects in ways that seek to disrupt these boundaries. These practices of accountability and reciprocity have enabled me to find ways of engaging in the rich, messy, and continually *long process* of, in the words of Kim TallBear, finding ways of "standing with" San peoples and producing "faithful knowledges" that are co-constituted with San interests.[57]

On Language and Terminology

While conducting the research for this book, I became critically aware of how important it was for me to also navigate the messy terrain of language and terminology. In the following chapters, therefore, I attempt to pay careful attention to language, even as I recognize that it is always impossible to fully escape its arrangements of power and knowledge and accompanying reinscription of violence.

As previous scholars have noted, the term *indigenous* has often been used in derogatory ways to present peoples with historical connections to preinvasion societies as backward, less modern, and less human.[58] To challenge that historical representation, many indigenous peoples have begun using the term in new and powerful ways, reclaiming it as an umbrella term with a capital *I* to help organize and build global political networks and movements.[59] The United Nations Permanent Forum on Indigenous Issues encourages a flexible, working definition of the term to account for those who self-identify as indigenous, are a nondominant sector of society, and seek to preserve their cultural heritage and ancestral lands.[60] Governmental entities also often define *indigenous* as being first in place (i.e., autochthonous), culturally isolated, and/or economically marginalized, which are important considerations for indigenous people in general but may not resonate with all indigenous groups.[61] At the same time, as Kim TallBear notes, the practice of adding the term *indigenous* to indigenous peoples' people-specific identities (e.g., Maori, Cree, Dayak) can help them organize against the genocidal and/or assimilative practices of the (settler) colonial state.[62] In this book, I capitalize *Indigenous* as a part of the name of specific groups, such as Indigenous San, and lowercase it when referring to indigenous peoples of the world more generally. This is not a practice of mere semantics, but an important political move supporting indigenous peoples' own practices of naming, intended to contest colonial histories of violence against them.

The indigenous peoples in South Africa, as recognized by scholars and indigenous peoples themselves, include San and Khoi. The latter consist of Griqua, Nama, Koranna, and Cape Khoi groups, while San include Khwe, !Xun, and ǂKhomani. Despite their heterogeneous grouping, the 1996 South African Constitution addresses them as "Khoe and San," which homogenizes indigenous peoples and obscures the distinctions between them. At the same time, leaders appointed to South Africa's National House of Traditional Leaders, a group that advises Parliament regarding issues of customary law within their communities, do not formally recognize San and Khoi. Although Nelson Mandela established the NKC in 1999 as a forum for Indigenous San and Khoi to negotiate with the government for formal recognition of their leadership and customary law, Andrew Le Fleur and Lesle Jansen note that progress toward such recognition has yet to be made.[63]

When discussing San as a specific people in the following chapters, I am most often referring to either the South African San Council or the several ǂKhomani San persons in Andriesville and Upington, South Africa, I engaged with. Even the people-specific names of San or ǂKhomani San can be problematic, however, as several of the ǂKhomani San I learned from preferred to self-identify as "Bushmen," seeking to reclaim the term from its discriminatory colonial past (although one ǂKhomani San elder on the South African San Council warned me about using the term for a US audience unfamiliar with contemporary San histories). Given the term's colonial legacy, I generally use the term *San* instead, though I report the use of *Bushmen* by individuals who prefer to self-identify as such. I was also cautioned by some San to avoid references to *Khoisan*, a term commonly used in South Africa to refer to both San and Khoi, homogenizing them into a single group. I also refer to San and other individuals by their real names unless they requested otherwise.

Academics, lawyers, and scientists with whom I spoke about this book during its writing often asked about how to define who should and who should not be considered indigenous. Given that the law forces indigenous peoples and legal officials to ask this question in conflicts over indigenous peoples' rights to land and resources, it did not surprise me. The question is a difficult one in the context of South Africa, where it is complicated by competing claims to indigeneity, multiple layers of colonization, and little precedence for politically organizing as indigenous peoples.[64] Although these questions are salient, it is always important to consider who is asking the question and why, as such discussions are too often structured by relations of power, deflect the conversation away from addressing histories of violence against indigenous peoples, and imply that indigenous peoples are not capable of deciding for themselves who is and is not a member of their community through their own governing practices, internal debates, and efforts toward self-determination.

When speaking with San and others, I respected their decision to withhold or share information with me. As a lawyer, I recognized the fine line between what could be shared with me and what needed to be kept confidential due to ongoing legal negotiations for benefit sharing and San rights. Although all of these conversations shaped my thinking, I chose not to include some things I learned about Hoodia and benefit sharing in this book. I am also aware that some private legal documents and indigenous customary knowledge were rightfully kept from me. This book therefore practices and is subject to the kind of ethnographic refusal Audra Simpson describes as "what you need to know and what I refuse to write in."[65]

Foreshadowing a Feminist Decolonial Technoscience Analysis

Throughout this book, I therefore refuse to accept normative models of teaching, learning, and understanding patent ownership rights and, by extension, the co-constituted relations of law, science, and the marketplace that shape and are shaped by such rights. Returning to the classroom mentioned earlier, the analysis developed here foreshadows how I would teach a class about Hoodia patents. I would demonstrate how colonial histories of the "discovery" of nature and the classification of San peoples as closer to nature have lasting legacies for understanding contestations over Hoodia and belonging. I would show how patent law rules of novelty and nonobviousness value certain forms of knowledge and matter over others, and how patent documents can reveal that San and CSIR ways of knowing Hoodia are more similar than different. I would analyze how

Hoodia plants and molecules can refuse their commercial promises by growing too slowly in the ground or failing to reduce weight. I also would stress the importance of learning from indigenous peoples and nonhuman plants as dynamic subjects in relation to others such as scientists and growers, molecules and cultivated plants, while considering the unequal modes of power that shape those relations.

Furthering this feminist decolonial technoscience approach, I would consider the intersectional politics of gender, indigeneity, race, and nation most relevant for understanding Hoodia patent law struggles. For example, I would address how patent law was historically constructed through patriarchal systems to protect the creative progeny of inventors assumed to be white and male. I would examine how San men and women described using the plant differently, how advertisements deployed gendered and racialized images to sell Hoodia, and how accounts of San male hunters using Hoodia obscured San women's knowledge of the plant. Expanding my analysis, I would devote most of my time to analyzing and reconfiguring the binary assumptions of nature/culture, modern/nonmodern, and human/nonhuman that are foundational to patent law and that also undergird normative relations of gender, indigeneity, race, and nation. I would examine, for instance, how patent ownership applies only to man-made inventions that are markedly different from what exists in nature. I would also examine how San peoples made claims as modern political subjects based on knowing Hoodia as a plant from nature, CSIR scientists represented Hoodia as man-made drug and as a cure from nature, and growers asserted Hoodia as both a natural gift from God and the product of their labor, thus demonstrating how different ways of knowing and forms of matter were valued differently. Continuing this inquiry further, I would show how the actions (and inactions) of Hoodia plants as they evolved over time, grew in the ground, and interacted with human bodies both contested and reinforced the aforementioned binary assumptions. Students might thus grasp how a feminist decolonial technoscience analysis could inform their own critiques of these binary assumptions, which organize their lives and can hinder their full belonging.

As this decolonizing approach is always and already about a promise of futurity, I would encourage students and others to deploy this radical interdisciplinary and intersectional approach with its emphasis on scale, patentability, materiality, belonging, engagement, accountability, and reciprocity to better understand our worlds and to imagine futures where such dichotomous thinking no longer exists and multiple ways of belonging are possible.

Structure of the Book

The following chapters address various scales of Hoodia materialities to examine how CSIR scientists, San, and Hoodia growers "reinvented" Hoodia to make claims for belonging in South Africa. Chapter 1 investigates Hoodia at the scale of colonial scientific object by analyzing how San peoples and Hoodia plants have historically been constructed as objects of science in similar and different ways through colonial practices of discovery and classification. It also contests those histories by examining Hoodia and San peoples as dynamic and changing subjects that shape such histories.

Chapter 2 examines Hoodia at the scale of a plant from nature as it discusses San mobilization against patent ownership and the South African San Council's demands for contractual benefit sharing through San attachments to Hoodia as a plant from nature. It then analyzes how Hoodia plants acted and failed to act in ways that interrupted San claims for benefit sharing. This discussion offers a new understanding of how San peoples navigate belonging in South Africa as simultaneously modern and nonmodern subjects.

Chapter 3 next interrogates Hoodia at the scale of molecule, situating patent law within histories of South Africa by examining how South African CSIR scientists assert belonging through claims to knowing Hoodia as a patented molecule. It also analyzes the structure of patent law more closely by examining its statutory rules and material documents and showing that CSIR and San knowledge of Hoodia are more alike than different, thereby demonstrating that patent ownership is a historical and sociocultural process rather than a set of value-neutral natural rights.

Chapter 4 analyzes Hoodia at the scales of solid drug and liquid food, tracing how scientists from Phytopharm, Pfizer, and Unilever made claims over Hoodia first as a potential drug and then as a food, and how the plant refused to comply with their commercial desires. This examination offers new insights into how scientific research and patent ownership structure human-plant relationships in ways that posit the scientist as a modern subject while reinforcing the notion of indigenous peoples and plants as raw materials.

Chapter 5 studies Hoodia at the scale of cultivated plant. This examination investigates both how Hoodia growers made claims to knowing Hoodia as a cultivated plant through San-SAHGA benefit sharing and how the unpredictability of Hoodia plants limited their assertions of belonging. The scale of Hoodia as a cultivated plant also connects a discussion of San-SAHGA benefit sharing to how other non-SAHGA Hoodia growers marketed Hoodia on the Internet through stereotypical gendered and racialized images of San peoples without their permission.

The epilogue extends this investigation to discuss implications and futures of a feminist decolonial technoscience for critical scholarship, Indigenous San peoples, and South African politics. Through this approach what becomes apparent is how, within our increasingly technoscience worlds, certain forms of knowledge and matter are being valued over others, while notions of difference are becoming strengthened through attachments to particular subjectivities, ways of knowing, and nonhuman matter.

Following the epilogue are two appendixes, one that provides links to various community protocols and research guidelines for working with indigenous peoples and another that offers key strategies for indigenous peoples who may want to challenge a US patent in court. And finally, the endnotes and bibliography should be read as key resources indicating the interdisciplinary scope of this book, honoring the genealogies that shape it, and offering future pathways for further inquiry and politics.

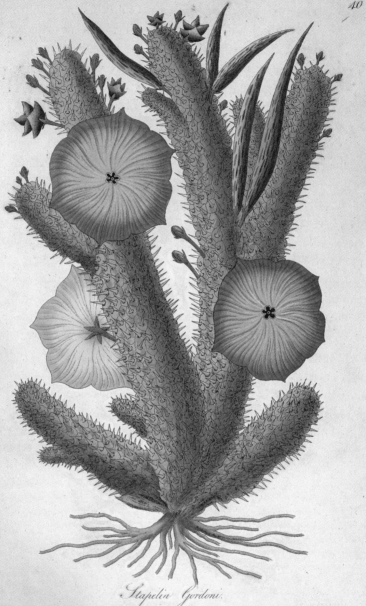

Stapelia Gordoni.

Published as the Act directs, June 10. 1797. by F. Masson.

1

Colonial Science and Hoodia as a Scientific Object

> To talk about one's past makes you human. Your human spirit comes from having a story, from having a history.
>
> —MARIO KAPILOLO MAHANGO (!XUN)

ONE OF THE EARLIEST KNOWN DRAWINGS OF *HOODIA GORDONII* CAN be found in a climate-controlled room in the Bolus Herbarium Library at the University of Cape Town, which holds the colonial-era records of Dutch and British explorers who collected plants in the Cape region. The drawing appears in a book titled *Stapeliae Novae* by Francis Masson, a botanist with the Royal Botanic Gardens at Kew in London, who collected plants in the Cape of Good Hope from 1772 to 1775.[1] Plate 40 of the large brown leather book fills the entire page with a bright, colorful sketch of the plant (here named *Stapelia Gordoni*), the plant's spine-tipped tubular stems standing tall and bearing three circular pink flowers. By identifying Masson as among the first to "discover" the plant, the drawing gives no hint of the plant's precolonial history or San knowledge of the plant.

This chapter's consideration of Hoodia at the scale of a botanical sketch, colonial artifact, and scientific object serves as the starting point of this book's analysis of the ways in which the practices of colonial science constructed both Hoodia plants and San peoples as scientific objects within hierarchical schemes of ordering. By approaching both San and the plant as dynamic and changing subjects, this examination of the complex interplay of science and society provides yet another demonstration that scientific knowledge is not natural and fixed but constructed and continually in flux, and it also contests the conventional histories of San and Hoodia to produce a fuller understanding of contemporary struggles over Hoodia and belonging in South Africa.

While mindful of the risk of reinscribing colonial violence by oversimplifying this long and complex history, in this chapter I aim not to provide a comprehensive history of Hoodia, San peoples, or South African politics but to historicize these subjects as part of a broader interdisciplinary, intersectional analysis of contemporary Hoodia struggles.[2] The discussion here is also informed and motivated by my conversations with San peoples who regularly asked me to share and honor their histories. Despite the potential risk of reductionism or misrepresentation, it remains important to uncover and understand colonial and indigenous pasts because, as Mario Kapilolo Mahango reminds us in the epigraph, having a history is part of what makes you human. In the context of this book, it also plays a vital role in San demands for legal recognition and national belonging.

Historicizing Hoodia: South African Indigenous and Colonial Histories

Representations of San have figured prominently within the historical construction of modern Western science. When developing his hierarchical taxonomies, Carl Linnaeus, the eighteenth-century Swedish botanist and zoologist, classified San and Khoi peoples as the lowest order of humans and thus closer to animals.[3] Until recently, anthropological accounts of San peoples also depicted them as an isolated and unchanging people stuck in a primordial past.[4] This view was promulgated for more than four decades from the late 1950s to 2001 in dioramas of San peoples in Cape Town's South African Museum that displayed them as seemingly frozen in time, thereby preserving, romanticizing, and naturalizing notions of San as closer to nature. This view was even spread internationally in the popular 1980 South African comedic film *The Gods Must Be Crazy*, which told the story of Xi, a San of the Kalahari Desert, who travels to the end of the world to return a Coke bottle in order to restore the primordial life of his people. As we shall see, these understandings of San as ancient and not fully human peoples continue to have a lasting legacy on science projects and real material consequences for San. In the case of Hoodia, to give but one example, Phytopharm executive Richard Dixey told a reporter for the *London Observer* that his company had not originally considered benefit sharing with San peoples because they were "extinct," and, as described in the introduction, Internet ads for Hoodia weight-loss supplements were replete with colonial-era images of San peoples dressed in loincloths and carrying bows and arrows. That the current struggles over the patenting and scientific making of Hoodia are embedded in these cultural understandings of San peoples and the colonial past from which they flow make it imperative to understand South African colonial and indigenous histories. When San peoples made demands for benefit sharing, they were compelled to make their claims within the confines of the law and its acceptable parameters of dissent. This meant strategically asserting themselves as a traditional people with ancient Hoodia knowledge, reinforcing these cultural understandings of San peoples and presenting them as a homogenous group.

Prior to European colonization, various San peoples viewed themselves not as a single group but as distinct and heterogeneous groups who also shared some attributes, customs, and click languages with other indigenous peoples across South Africa.[5] Indigenous San and Khoi peoples, some of the earliest inhabitants of South Africa, developed strong relationships and interacted often. Although San relied more on hunting and gathering and were historically more mobile and less agrarian than Khoi peoples, who often lived in areas with more reliable rainfall that enabled the herding of sheep and cattle, the distinction between the hunter-gatherer San and pastoralist Khoi is a false dichotomy, as likely some San farmed and some Khoi hunted.[6] Even referring to these indigenous groups as "San" and "Khoi" is somewhat misleading, as they organized themselves more closely into familial groups than into collective groups of peoples. Prior to colonization, the groups that came to be referred to as San and Khoi had also developed symbiotic relationships with each other, in which San hunters offered game to Khoi and defended Khoi herds in exchange for milk from their cattle.[7] These mutual relations also produced tensions as Khoi herders and their livestock took over increasing amounts of land, threatening the San hunter-gatherer way of life.[8] In response, some San began to kill Khoi sheep and cattle with poisoned arrows, prompting violent clashes between the two peoples.[9] Over time, the majority of San continued to live as hunter-gatherers in small mobile groups, although several San groups took up more agrarian ways of life and began to assimilate with Khoi herders and farmers.[10]

These histories shape San and Khoi peoples' ongoing political mobilization for rights within South Africa since the formal end of apartheid rule in 1994. San peoples have repeatedly deployed these histories to claim rights in South Africa. South Africa does not formally recognize Khoi peoples (Griqua, Nama, Koranna, or Cape Khoi) or San groups (≠Khomani, !Xun, Khwe) as indigenous peoples or grant them representation in the National House of Traditional Leaders. In making claims for San-CSIR benefit sharing in particular, the South African San Council claimed a distinct history as hunter-gatherers to assert that they were the first people to know about Hoodia in order to assert rights against South African scientists. The assumptions differ, though, when San groups make claims to knowing Hoodia in relation to other indigenous peoples. The San Council of Namibia, for example, recognized San and Khoi as sharing a similar history when the council was negotiating agreements with the Association of Nama Traditional Leaders to form a joint venture in which they would share benefits and knowledge regarding indigenous plants. In advancing their political and economic rights through benefit sharing, San and Khoi aim to strengthen their demands that the government recognize them as indigenous peoples.

San and Khoi peoples' ongoing political efforts to negotiate with the ANC government for formal recognition are also shaped by the histories between them and Bantu-speaking groups who were later classified as Black under apartheid. Between the fourth and the late eighteenth centuries, interactions between San and Khoi changed with the emergence of Bantu-speaking peoples who engaged in mixed-farming practices in the eastern region of the territory.[11] Many Bantu-speaking peoples spoke dialects of Nguni, which is the basis of the modern Xhosa and Zulu languages, and a second language that evolved into what are now known as Sotho, Pedi, and Tswana.[12] Their economies were based on hunting, gathering, and herding, on cultivating crops such as sorghum, and on trading in iron and copper. Although they developed relations with San and Khoi through mutual exchange and trade, as the Bantu-speaking groups' diverse cultures and economies began to dominate southeastern Africa, they began to threaten San and Khoi ways of life.[13] Violent clashes between the groups ensued, and some San and Khoi were forced to assimilate with Bantu-speaking peoples.[14]

The relationships among the indigenous peoples of South Africa were also shaped by colonialism. The founding of the Dutch Cape Colony in 1652 exacerbated existing tensions between San and Khoi. Much of this began through practices of what Winona LaDuke refers to as "the power of naming and claiming" in colonizing indigenous subjects.[15] Early Dutch settlers referred to San and Khoi in a derogatory manner, calling San "Bosjesmen," or Bushmen, meaning low-status people from the bush, and calling Khoi "Hottentots."[16] As Dutch settlers took possession of increasing amounts of land and began growing crops and herding cattle, accelerating tensions led to violent clashes as Dutch took Khoi and San peoples' cattle, exploited divisions among the two groups, and turned their superior weaponry against the indigenous groups, leading to large-scale violence and the death of many San and Khoi.[17] Some San and Khoi survived by fighting back or moving to new lands, while others were forced to work for Dutch landowners under harsh conditions alongside slaves that Dutch brought from southeast Asia to help build infrastructure for the growing colony.[18] This history informed later struggles for rights to Hoodia, with the South African San Council accusing scientists of participating in familiar colonial practices by taking their knowledge without recompense. That Unilever was a Dutch-based company made the connections between Hoodia research and the colonial past even more apparent.

The colonization of South Africa, however, occurred on multiple spatial and temporal scales, as it was ruled first by Dutch and then by British forces starting in 1795 before reverting back to Dutch rule in 1803 and then finally British control in 1806. British forces quickly implemented a systematic plan of conquest over South African lands and peoples that resulted in even more bloodshed and violence. An influx of British settlers in 1820 took over considerable amounts of land and increased farming production, boosting tensions with local Dutch settlers and indigenous groups. British settlers distinguished themselves from Dutch settlers by referring to the latter with the derogatory term *Boers*, meaning farmers, while Dutch settlers referred to themselves with the term *Afrikaners*, the Dutch word for Africans.

More importantly for our current purposes, British land seizures also increased European settlers' control over Khoi and San. The British needed more labor to work their newly obtained lands, but Britain had banned the slave trade in 1807, making it illegal to acquire new slaves. They therefore used Khoi and San as farm laborers and domestic workers alongside individuals who were already enslaved. Although Khoi and San laborers did not always give in easily—for example, they staged a large-scale revolt against their conditions in 1808—by the time a set of 1828 British proclamations forced British settlers to grant equality under the law to San, Khoi, and former slaves, generations of forced labor had increased poverty and landlessness among those groups to such a degree that many had little choice but to continue working on white-owned farms.[19] While England pressured British settlers to follow emancipation proclamations, the settlers found new ways to distinguish white ruling classes from groups of Khoi, San, and former slaves by referring to those groups as "Cape Coloured People," setting a foundation for the eventual system of racial classification and segregation under apartheid. These South African histories continue to shape its politics today, but as South African scholar Premesh Lalu argues, colonialism, postcolonialism, apartheid, and postapartheid are so woven into South African politics and subjectivities that scholars should not view them as linear but rather examine how South Africa has never been postcolonial.[20] By mobilizing against Hoodia patents and demanding benefit sharing, San peoples have challenged these histories and sought to reclaim control over their culture and traditions.

How San struggles against Hoodia patents also constitute a challenge to South African histories is made even more apparent when we recognize that the emergence of patent ownership played an important role in the rise of empire. Following the first patent system in fifteenth-century Venice,[21] early patents were originally considered privileges granted by European states to increase their economic competitiveness. With the advent of the modern legal patent system, beginning with Britain's 1624 Statute of Monopolies and 1710 Statute of Anne, nations continued to use patents to promote capitalist expansion but now legitimated the granting of patents on the grounds of natural rights.[22] Using Lockean philosophies, proponents of strong patent ownership rights justified patents as individual property rights and a natural extension of one's labor.[23] States began to deploy patent ownership to recognize the inherent genius of the scientific inventor—a figure, as feminist scholars have shown, who was coded as heteronormative, white, and masculine.[24]

Patent law was also an important legal mechanism in enabling the colonization of South Africa. As Ikechi Mgbeoji notes, early European patent systems rewarded the first person to introduce an invention into the territory of a nation-state, not the first person to invent it, an approach that greatly facilitated taking resources and knowledge from indigenous peoples in the colonies.[25] Colonial explorers could thus return to their European homelands and apply for patents on others' inventions because the law rewarded not invention per se but the act of making an invention known. Patent systems implemented in the colonies themselves also enabled colonialism. British officials imposed British law on South Africa after reconquering the Cape Colony from Dutch settlers in 1806. In 1860, the British Cape parliament passed the nation's first patent law statute, which was closely modeled on the English Patent Act of 1852.[26] As British forces conquered the remaining territories of South Africa and their inhabitants, they created similar patent statutes in Natal, the Orange Free State, and the Transvaal. After South Africa declared its independence as the Union of South Africa in 1910, the newly formed government consolidated these patent statutes under the Patents, Designs, Trade Marks, and Copyright Act of 1916, modeling it after the British Patents Act of 1907 and thus maintaining its European patrimony.[27] This history of the colonial diffusion of patent law demonstrates that patent ownership is neither natural nor fixed but historical and contingent, and that it continues to shape indigenous peoples' struggles over patents related to their knowledge, resources, and heritage.

Encountering Hoodia: Colonial Discovery and Classification of Hoodia and San

Contestations over Hoodia were also informed by histories of colonial science that involved practices of discovery and classification. As previous feminist scholars such as Sandra Harding, Londa Schiebinger, and Kavita Philip have demonstrated, the rise of science and the logic of empire were inextricably intertwined.[28] This was particularly true of colonial voyages to South Africa, in which, as historian Helen Tilley argues, colonial explorers engaged in early forms of bioprospecting as they transported plants and plant knowledge from the Cape Colony to the British metropole, thereby constructing Africa as a "living laboratory" for conquest and resource extraction.[29] Francis Masson, the earliest illustrator of Hoodia, was one such explorer.[30]

Masson, born in Aberdeen, Scotland, in 1741, collected plants for the Royal Botanic Gardens at Kew and accompanied Carl Peter Thunberg, known as the Father of Cape Botany, on two journeys into the interior of the Cape.[31] A respected botanist, if less well known than some of his peers, Masson published some of the earliest work on Stapeliads in Southern Africa. He corresponded with Carl Linnaeus, sending him Stapeliads and asking him to confirm them as a new genus.[32]

Although Masson was a superb draftsman and produced highly skilled drawings of his specimens, his drawing of Hoodia caused controversy among his peers. According to White and Sloane, botanists found the picture "strange" and "curious," one describing the drawing as "an exaggerated, if not a fictitious representation."[33] Botanists later debated whether Masson's drawing was a copy of one by Colonel Robert Jacob Gordon, a Dutch officer of Scottish descent,[34] whom Masson credited with discovering the plant and for whom he named it.[35] Because early botanical drawings were meant to represent nature and reinforce notions of objectivity by providing accurate sketches of specimens considered objects for scientific study,[36] by questioning the portrayal and authenticity of Masson's drawing, botanists were also expressing doubts about his objectivity and scientific authority. Just as botanists questioned whether Masson or Gordon was the creator of the first Hoodia drawing, Indigenous San more recently asked whether they or CSIR scientists were the first to discover Hoodia's appetite suppressant properties.

But whereas debates over such issues as Masson's use of Gordon's creative work were common within the field of colonial botany, questions about whether he had appropriated and problematically represented Indigenous San and Khoi knowledge were not. This is clear from Masson's unself-conscious descriptions of his encounters with Indigenous San and Khoi in the lengthy travel journals he produced and published in addition to his botanical writings and illustrations.[37] Much like the colonial travel accounts analyzed by Mary Terrall, Masson's travel journals demonstrate the social construction of masculinity and whiteness through colonial writings, and through science more generally, by representing indigenous peoples as savage and primitive and white, male colonial explorers as rational and modern.[38] In his writings, Masson repeatedly portrayed San and Khoi as vicious, savage thieves living like ancient cavemen and more like animals than humans.[39] By depicting San and Khoi as wild, primitive people of the earth in contrast to civilized, modern men of science, he rendered them as outside of history and lacking an enlightened capacity for reason and rationality.

The legacy of such views would linger in later science practices, which no longer depicted San as savage and closer to animals but continued to devalue them nonetheless.[40] Although CSIR scientists were not the first to construct Hoodia and San peoples as scientific objects, their research perpetuated this colonial history through practices of classification or the naming and claiming of nature that, as Foucault has argued, attempted to know the world through reason by classifying objects of nature along a grid of differences.[41] Despite their scientific pedigree and usefulness, however, such classifications and related practices of naming also contributed to social understandings of plants as less than humans and of San as the lowest order of humans. As Anne McClintock contends, they also reflected and reified male desire to control native Others and the feminized spaces of so-called empty lands.[42]

In 1830, Robert Sweet, an English botanist and horticulturalist, was the first to classify the plant Masson had named *Stapelia Gordoni*.[43] Sweet organized plants according to a common system of classification based on morphological criteria such as similarity or difference in flowering and root systems rather than by the well-known Linnean system based on plant reproduction. This latter system, as Londa Schiebinger notes, was highly gendered, as Linneaus labeled plant reproductive parts as "husband" or "wife" and was informed by gendered hierarchies that society used at the time to justify the subordination of women.[44] In following a different classification system, Sweet classified Masson's *Stapelia Gordoni* under a new genus he named *Hoodia*, which he placed within the Asclepiadaceae family.[45] Sweet named his new genus after a Mr. Hood who had successfully cultivated a fine collection of succulent plants in Britain.[46] Masson's original naming of the South African plant after a Dutch explorer and this addition of the name of a British grower of exotic plants is an example of how colonial explorers engaged in practices of domination against indigenous peoples and plants in South Africa through naming, which in turn severed our knowledge of plants from their precolonial histories and obscured San knowledge and expertise.

Also emerging at about the time of Sweet's classification of *Hoodia* were scientific debates over the ordering of people, such as whether humans originated from a single species (monogenism) or from multiple species (polygenism).[47] Linnaeus, who subscribed to theories of monogenism, considered the peoples he called Bushmen and Hottentots to be descended from the same human genus as whites but nevertheless excluded them from the species *Homo sapiens*, instead categorizing them as *Homo monstrosis monorchidei* (monstrous one), a deviant species and the lowest order of humans.[48] Such modes of classification supported and fueled the formation of racial hierarchies that were only heightened by such later public exhibitions in Britain as the display of a group of San Bushmen in 1847 at Exeter Hall in London.[49] Colonial practices of classification thus contributed in several ways to the construction of San peoples as nonhuman and the associated binaries of human/nonhuman, culture/nature, and modern/nonmodern.

The practices of colonial science did not work in isolation, as science and society are always and already mutually co-constituted.[50] Colonial racial taxonomies and discourses of literature, language, and religion informed each other, simultaneously co-constructing San peoples as nonmodern, as in Charles Dickens's description of a Bushman as a "noble savage" and a "wild animal."[51] Even though nineteenth-century German linguists Wilhelm Bleek and Lucy Lloyd produced some valuable studies of San peoples, their representations of their language and culture as primitive contributed to cultural understandings of San as traditional and unchanging.[52] This view was further reflected in and bolstered by the reports of colonial missionaries, who considered San peoples not fully human because of their lack of formal religious practices and belief in God.[53]

At the same time, science and society are not merely co-constituted but also continually in flux. Despite normative social understandings of science as natural, objective, and fixed, the power and authority of colonial practices of discovery resided in their flexibility and adaptability. The scientific classification of Hoodia plants, for instance, changed over time as new epistemologies and technologies enabled scientists to examine plants in greater detail. Nicholas Edward Brown, a botanist at the Kew Gardens in London from 1873 until 1914, was the first to study Hoodia under a microscope, a tool that enabled him to order plants in a more exacting manner and to expand the *Hoodia* genus in 1909 to include seven new species.[54] White and Sloane would later leave *Hoodia* in the Asclepiadaceae family but recognize fifteen distinct species within the *Hoodia* genus and locate it within the *Stapelieae* tribe.[55] Almost a century later, Peter V. Bruyns of the University of Cape Town would deploy molecular DNA technology to identify only thirteen different species in the *Hoodia* genus.[56] As technological apparatuses change, in other words, so do classifications.

Colonial representations of San similarly fluctuated over time. When formal European colonial rule waned and South Africa became the independent Union of South Africa in 1910, colonial settlers' representations of San changed once again to better serve their needs and secure their power. Once colonial settlers had established direct political control over San peoples, they reconfigured their view of San to justify their exploitation of San labor even as they continued to associate San with a prehistoric South African past.[57] During this period, earlier settler portrayals of San as less than human gave way to understandings of them as ignorant and childlike, an improvement perhaps, but one that nonetheless continued to deny their capacity to possess land and livestock. As San were increasingly assimilated as laborers on colonial settler–owned farms, they experienced a further loss of their language and culture. As Andries Olyn (≠Khomani San) has explained, one reason for losing their language "is that there was no chance [on the job] for us parents to sit and talk deeply . . . the Boer watched you," to which Keis Brou (≠Khomani San) added that "they could not, because behind you was the Boer . . . and the Nooi calls, 'Husband, come and beat this maid, she is rude to me.' That's the reason we could not teach our children our language."[58] These shifts demonstrate the material consequences that these co-constructed understandings have on the lives of San peoples.

Hoodia Contestations: Hoodia and San as Dynamic and Changing Subjects

What the above examination of how science and society co-constructed San and Hoodia as scientific objects leaves out is that neither the people nor the plant were merely cyphers to be acted upon but dynamic agents who interacted with and reshaped the social worlds that sought to contain them. A closer examination of Hoodia plants and San peoples reveals that they have found ways to adapt, resist, and provoke change in relation to changing environmental and political conditions, thereby contesting the colonial histories and the patenting of Hoodia properties that left San peoples and Hoodia plants as subjects unaccounted for.

Hoodia gordonii Plants as Historical Actors

Although science and law have constructed plants as mere objects and raw material to be classified or patented, plants, too, have their own histories of becoming. As the evolutionary history of Hoodia plants reveals, they have interacted with and changed in response to the world and thus should be seen as dynamic rather than fixed objects. As the evolutional history of Hoodia traced by White and Sloan suggests, Stapeliads first evolved from semisucculent plants in tropical regions around India.[59] These original ancestors were related to species of the genus *Frerea*, similar to *Carallumas*, which then spread in many directions to more semiarid and drier lands such as Burma, Ceylon, Afghanistan, Persia, Spain, and the Canary Islands.[60] In these drier climates, *Carallumas* became more vivid in color and developed an odor of decaying flesh that attracted flies and insects as pollinators.[61] The plants underwent further dramatic changes as they moved into the drier climates in and around Arabia and Yemen, where new genera of *Carallumas*—including *Echidnopsis, Huernia,* and *Duvalia*—emerged with brighter flowers and new stem formations in response to changing conditions.[62]

After moving farther south toward Lake Victoria, the first species of the genus *Stapelia* appeared.[63] These Stapeliads had changed dramatically from their *Carallumas* ancestors, sharing only the separate lobes of their corona, and flourished in the conditions of the northwestern territory of the Cape Province.[64] Among the many new genera that spread were the *Trichocaulon* and the *Hoodia,* the latter of which was distinguished by its rugged, spiny-tipped stems and circular petals with barely distinguishable lobes.[65] Interacting with flowers and insects over time, the petals of plants in the *Hoodia* generus eventually became more flat and cup-shaped with minute lobes at the tips, and their brighter flowers and stronger odors attracted insects and thereby enabled fertilization.[66] The secondary metabolites within the plants also changed, allowing the plant to survive new diseases and insects it encountered. *Hoodia gordonii*, therefore, has acted and continues to act in independent ways, emerging and changing in reaction to soil, rain, wind, sun, insects, animals, and peoples, thus demonstrating plants as dynamic subjects in relation to humans and environments, rather than as mere nonhuman objects to be acted upon.

South African San Peoples' Histories of Apartheid and Postapartheid Struggle

South African San, too, have acted as dynamic and changing subjects in response to political and economic conditions. The establishment of the Kalahari Gemsbok National Park in 1931 in the northern Cape of South Africa displaced many ≠Khomani San living within the boundaries of the park, who would become further displaced under apartheid rule. South African San peoples were greatly affected by Afrikaners' rise to power in 1948 and subsequent establishment of an apartheid system to maintain white rule—a system that forced them once again to find new ways to adapt and survive. Under the Population Registration Act of 1950, South Africa was divided into three racial groups consisting of White, Coloured, and Native. *Native* applied to a member of any tribe of Africa, whereas *Coloured* meant anyone who was not White and not Native.[67] Bantu-speaking peoples were classified as Native and grouped into "homelands" where "nations" were expected to develop under their authority, but actual autonomy was denied, as governing decisions in the homelands had to be made in close consultation with white officials.[68] The Group Areas Act of 1950 forced the removal of many classified as Coloured and Native into crowded townships with few basic services such as housing, water, and electricity. This forced removal led to the breakdown of extended family support networks, dramatic shifts in women's labor out of the home, and increased costs of living.[69] Government control over education also meant superior facilities for Whites and inferior ones for Natives, who were instructed on their racially inferior status. Coloured schools were also segregated and inferior but were given more government support than schools in the homelands.[70] Classification according to racial type was difficult, however, given the diverse histories of assimilation and interaction among peoples, not to mention the instability of race as a category as government officials classified persons as White, Black, Coloured, and Indian in heterogeneous and arbitrary ways.[71]

Facing continual displacement under apartheid and entirely dispossessed of their land by the 1970s, San spread out across the rural areas of South Africa and often had no option but to provide menial labor on white-owned farms, where farm owners typically subjected them to violence and forced them to speak Afrikaans.[72] As Andries Olyn (≠Khomani San) has recounted, "When I came of age, I was already living amongst the Boers. By that time they had sown us all over the place. They divided us, one working here, the other living there but working here. And you might have been only 12 or 14, but you were given no chance to go to school."[73] Nonetheless, San found ways to assert their identities while working on the farms. Elsie Vaalbooi† (≠Khomani San), for instance, defied being characterized as Coloured under apartheid: "The day they dragged me closer, I had to say what nation I was. I said Bushman. My boss said, 'Nellie, hear what Elsie is saying.' She said, 'No, man, you can't be Bushman, you are a Coloured.'" Vaalbooi† here accounts how she refused to identify with apartheid classifications of San as Coloured, choosing instead to self-identify as Bushman and reconfigure the name from its derogatory meanings.

South Africa's apartheid-era war with South West Africa (now Namibia) from 1966 to 1989 also influenced South African San populations in significant ways, further demonstrating how South African San are quite heterogeneous with distinct histories. During this conflict, the South African Defense Force (SADF) recruited and militarized some San as soldiers, including some from Nyae Nyae in South West Africa as well as !Xun and Khwe living near the Angola border, who fought alongside SADF forces against the South West Africa People's Organization (SWAPO).[74] After hostilities ceased in 1990, San soldiers faced resettlement, and although many Nyae Nyae returned to South West Africa, the SADF relocated several !Xun and Khwe soldiers to the Schmidtsdrift base in South Africa just outside of Kimberly—although whether they went voluntarily is a matter of dispute.[75] Public conceptions changed from an understanding of San as having "innate military prowess" to meet government interests in them as soldiers, to being a "harmless people" to serve local needs as laborers on farms and mines near Schmidtsdrift after the war.[76] Postapartheid South Africa, however, has afforded new opportunities for San peoples to contest these histories and asset their own demands for rights and belonging in South Africa. For example, !Xun and Khwe have collectively organized through their own !Xun and Khwe Trust to negotiate with the ANC government, business entities, and potential donors on behalf of their community.

When apartheid in South Africa formally ended with the election of Nelson Mandela and the drafting of an interim constitution in 1994, new laws in South Africa provided San with an opportunity to demand their right to lands previously taken from them. The new constitution ushered in land-reform laws intended to redress the injustices of apartheid, promote national reconciliation, support economic development, and alleviate poverty.[77] The constitution contained a progressive bill of rights, ensuring some economic rights as well as civil and political ones. Specifically, Section 25 stipulated that individuals had the right not to be deprived of property.[78] In response to these legal and social changes, in 1995 ≠Khomani San initiated a land claim, which they won in 2002 with the signing of the !Ae!Hai Kalahari Heritage Park Agreement.[79] During the negotiation process, ≠Khomani San engaged in powerful if also limited practices of self-determination by establishing a community property association to determine criteria for membership as ≠Khomani San.[80] South African San also joined other San groups to organize more collectively as indigenous peoples. For instance, after a decade of meetings and consultations, they established a nongovernmental organization in 1996, the Working Group of Indigenous Minorities in Southern Africa (WIMSA), to represent the interests of all San across southern Africa.[81] As a regional organization, WIMSA has since formed local San councils in Namibia, Botswana, and South Africa to advocate for San communities. Among the local councils was the South African San Council, formed in 2001 to negotiate for Hoodia benefit sharing with CSIR.

San mobilization has taken many different forms, including San women's organizing in different ways to address the needs and political concerns of San peoples. Discussing San histories without attention to gender necessarily limits an understanding of how uneven San social structures and gendered relations inform contemporary San politics. Indigenous feminist scholars however caution against an uncritical analysis of gender in regard to indigenous peoples. Scholars such as Andrea Smith, Joyce Green, and M. Annette Jaimes argue that feminism, with its attachment to gender, historically has failed to address colonialism and imperialism and has obscured the complexity of indigenous women's lives in relation to—not separate from—indigenous men and sovereignty.[82] An understanding of San histories must therefore address relations of gender but within the frameworks of indigenous peoples' self-determination.

Prior to colonialism, San women held a high social status among their peoples, based on their extensive participation in hunting and gathering food for their families.[83] When colonial settlers compelled San women to work on white farms, they introduced strict gendered divisions of labor that also influenced San relations and led to a loss of social status for San women.[84] Even today, San women in South Africa remain largely relegated to less-valued subsistence farming and domestic roles, in contrast to San men, who tend to participate in wage labor, harvesting for cash income, and in some instances cattle raising.[85] Although San women also experience gender inequality in education and health care and are vulnerable to gender-based domestic violence, they have responded to these conditions with increased mobilization.[86] For example, ≠Khomani San women hold leadership positions and organize gender equality programs; however, Khwe and !Xun women have experienced more difficulty in participating in San governance given the histories of militarization of Khwe and !Xun more generally.[87]

Conclusion

A feminist decolonial technoscience analysis of South African colonial and indigenous histories makes us think differently about Hoodia patents and the colonial sketch of Hoodia by connecting them to histories of South Africa, San peoples, and Hoodia plants. As the later chapters show, struggles over Hoodia patents are embedded within these histories as claims over Hoodia by San peoples, CSIR scientists, and Hoodia growers reinforce and reconfigure these histories in different ways. Considering these histories from the outset provides a means of understanding how postcolonial technoscience projects are never very far from their colonial pasts. These histories become important for understanding how CSIR scientists deployed patents in ways that contested and reinforced these colonial and indigenous histories as they sought to position themselves as producers of Hoodia science. In the next chapter, they become important for examining how the South African San Council's demand for benefit sharing sought to challenge these histories, albeit in limited ways that left San peoples to navigate modes of belonging in South Africa as both modern and nonmodern peoples.

2

San Demands for Benefits by Knowing !Khoba as a Plant from Nature

We are fenced in like cattle in a kraal. . . . We don't know what we can do to hold on to our traditions.

—DAWID KRUIPER (≠KHOMANI SAN)

Some people call me a westernized Bushman. What did those peoples' ancestors wear? Do they still wear that today?

—PETRUS VAALBOOI (≠KHOMANI SAN)

WALKING IN THE KALAHARI DESERT WITH TWO YOUNG ≠KHOMANI San men, I had my first encounter with a !Khoba plant, which was just a few steps from the side of the road, nestled in the knee-high grasslands of the veld. Barely visible beneath a blanket of bright pink flowers in full bloom, the plant's green stalks and sharp spikes provided a source of water and protection from the harsh desert winds and sun. As I met with other ≠Khomani San, they referred to the !Khoba plants growing in the desert as "wild" Hoodia. One of these was Andries Steenkamp (≠Khomani San Bushman), who remarked that !Khoba plants in the veld differed from Hoodia molecules purified in the lab, Hoodia extracts sold in stores, and Hoodia plants cultivated on local farms in that "the strongest one is the one in the veld."[1] As I spoke with members of San peoples, I realized that if I were to understand their struggle to share benefits from CSIR's patents on Hoodia, I first needed to understand San relationships to !Khoba plants.

My first important insight into the ways in which San relationships with !Khoba differed from those of CSIR scientists and their commercial partners came on my initial visit to the four-room office building in Upington that housed the South African San Institute (SASI). As I entered the building, I was immediately struck by a group of five posters representing ≠Khomani San history, knowledge, language, practices, and kinship. The first proclaimed that "trees are our heritage," followed by the other four, which were labeled in turn as "tree of life," "tree of family," "tree of love," and "tree of healing." I found myself thinking about how differently the practices of colonial science had used images of trees to classify and position San at the bottom of a hierarchical, evolutionary tree of life. I thought, too, about the similar tree images used in contemporary population genetics, ostensibly to emphasize a common human ancestry but also, as Kim TallBear points out, visually placing Africa and its people at the bottom of a genetic genealogical tree.[2] By deploying the metaphor of the tree in a different manner to emphasize ≠Khomani San agency, history, connection, heterogeneity, and change, the posters in the SASI offices demonstrated how central the connections between nature and San were to San identities and culture and to San political efforts for self-determination.

The story recounted in this chapter of San peoples' struggle to share in the benefits of the CSIR patents on Hoodia focuses on !Khoba at the scale of a plant in nature. San knowledge of the plant I had seen at the edge of the road served as the legal and political basis of their assertion of a right not simply to benefits but to belonging within the South African nation-state. In a postapartheid South Africa that simultaneously embraced racial difference and national sameness in its vision of a multicultural rainbow nation, the South African San Council based these claims on notions of San as indigenous peoples and their attachment to !Khoba as a plant from nature.[3] As we shall see, their claims were informed by a new South African multinational politics and international debates over the Convention on Biological Diversity (CBD) and its principles of benefit sharing that offered a site for indigenous peoples' claims for recognition. This examination of San claims to the original discovery and knowledge of Hoodia plants reveals that the patenting of Hoodia and struggles over benefit sharing, like many other contemporary science projects, simultaneously empowered and disempowered Indigenous San peoples in new and complicated ways.

Living !Khoba: San Articulations of !Khoba as Nature, Culture, and Natureculture

During that first visit to the SASI offices in 2009, I met with a member of the South African San Council, Collin Louw (≠Khomani San Bushman), who offered to introduce me to other ≠Khomani San who had agreed to speak with me about their understanding of and attachment to !Khoba as a native South African plant. He subsequently arranged for me to travel to Andriesville, a town at the base of the Kgalagadi Transfrontier Park, with a young ≠Khomani San man named Rykes Jacobs, who could introduce me to other ≠Khomani San and help translate our conversations from Afrikaans to English and vice versa. I met with several ≠Khomani San in Andriesville. During our conversations and subsequent visits and e-mail or phone conversations later, I learned that ≠Khomani San sometimes understood !Khoba as distinct from culture and at other times as co-constituted with it. By examining San understanding of Hoodia through what Banu Subramaniam refers to as "naturecultural analysis," what became apparent to me is that Hoodia can be understood as a form of both nature and culture that is inscribed by relations and domains of power.[4] San understandings of Hoodia thus demonstrate how binaries of nature and culture that historically undergird normative notions of ethnicity, race, gender, and sexuality are reinforced and disrupted here in new yet familiar ways through struggles over Hoodia patent ownership.

One of the first of those conversations was with Tommy Busakhwe, a young ≠Khomani San Bushman who had started working at the SASI offices in Andriesville as a San youth organizer in 1998 and in 2003 had become a community development facilitator.[5] Sitting in his office, which was crowded with papers, books, and computers, Busakhwe talked about his work with the institute and his recent experience representing San, whom he called Bushmen, on issues of intellectual property, San heritage, and San-CSIR benefit sharing for several months in Geneva, Switzerland, as part of a United Nations human rights fellowship. Asked what !Khoba meant to him, Busakhwe responded that the "Hoodia plant is very important because our elders had very good knowledge about it. So to me it means our heritage, it means a good future, it means a healthy life to our community. And we must sustain our knowledge about Hoodia and we must sustain our rights toward the use of Hoodia." Busakhwe's understanding of Hoodia as a natural plant connected to the history and identity of San cultures was quite different from the understanding of CSIR and its commercial partners, who viewed Hoodia as patented molecules divorced from San histories and heritage. To Busakhwe, Hoodia was not a potential commodity created through a process of drug discovery informed by progress narratives, but rather a plant from nature that simultaneously stood for an ancestral past, a present heritage, and a future life of San peoples.

A later conversation I had with Katriena Rooi (≠Khomani San Bushman) reminded me of the posters in the SASI offices as we sat in the shade of a tree while she described the relationship between San and the !Khoba plant as like a "mother and daughter or mother and son,"[6] linking plants and San peoples as familial relatives and thus blurring the lines between humans and nonhumans. Rooi's response assigned meaning to !Khoba in terms similar to the understanding of plants among other indigenous peoples, such as Iroquois in the New York/Quebec region who consider corn, beans, and squash the founding "three sisters" of their culture.[7] Her description of !Khoba expressed a similar indigenous epistemology based on understandings of nature and culture as mutually related rather than distinct from one another.

Expressing a similar worldview, some of the other ≠Khomani San with whom I spoke also described the plant as a source of life for them. Andries Steenkamp, for instance, described !Khoba as "life because it comes from nature . . . so that is life. All the plants you see."[8] In speaking about !Khoba as both life and nature, Steenkamp's words testified to the vitality and liveliness of plants, unlike scientific and commercial understandings of Hoodia as raw material, thus distinguishing San claims to knowing !Khoba from CSIR ways of knowing the plant. As I stood with Elizabeth "Bettie" Tieties (≠Khomani San Bushman) in her garden, she crouched down and brushed away a delicate canopy of protective sticks to reveal a small green !Khoba plant with three short stems. Pulling one of its small stalks from the ground, she whittled off its spikes with a dull knife to reveal a bright green watery center. Handing me a small piece to eat, she said of !Khoba that "it is life, it is medicine, [it is] nature,"[9] characterizing it as a living and life-giving plant. In much the same way, oom Jan van der Westruishen (≠Khomani San Bushman), a traditional healer, compared !Khoba to a "bone in the body," an integral part of San peoples' bodies and lives.[10]

These responses demonstrated the deep and even vital connection that San peoples had with !Khoba.

Yet several San also spoke with me about how learning of !Khoba's potential to generate revenue as an antiobesity product had also shaped their understanding of the plant and how they had recently come to place more importance on San understandings of !Khoba in comparison to CSIR ways of knowing the plant. Louw first described !Khoba as a plant from nature given to San as their natural, divine right, declaring, "God created this plant. Yes, we agree on that. But God gave us the knowledge of how to use to the plant." Nonetheless, he claimed, many San had taken it for granted in the practice of their daily lives until it came to be understood as a patented molecule: "Hoodia is now on everybody's lips and minds. It was nothing to us, but now it is, everyone is making money" from it.[11] Louw's comments thus associated San knowledge of Hoodia with nature and CSIR's knowledge of the plant with culture, expressing both an understanding of plants and San peoples as intimately related and a recognition that, to claim legal rights to benefit sharing, San also needed to discriminate between the plant from nature and the plant as patented molecules in the lab.

Sanna Witbooi (≠Khomani San Bushman) made a similar distinction between the !Khoba plant and patented Hoodia molecules based on the different materialities that went into their making.[12] While she was working inside the Bushman Secrets Health Products store, a small SASI-sponsored community project that sold traditional medicines to both ≠Khomani San and tourists, Witbooi explained how she made traditional medicines. She showed me how to use a metal grinder to crush a plant into a fine material, then described how she rinsed the material with water, put it in the sun to dry, and placed the powdered plant material into small plastic bags to sell in the shop. When I spotted small sugar packets next to the grinder and asked her why she put sugar in the medicines, she heartily laughed and told me the sugar was for her coffee. As we talked further, Witbooi argued that her !Khoba medicine was more natural than commercial Hoodia tablets, as it comes "from nature, but the tablets come from the—they put other things inside [besides] the Hoodia plant, so it is not like Hoodia. There is a difference between the tablets and [when] they eat it from the field . . . . So it is also a natural plant, so it is a very good and healthy medicine, the Hoodia." She thus emphasized that

!Khoba is a plant from nature prepared by San peoples in a natural way, free from additives and derived from an interaction with the sun and water. Walking to a tall cabinet to show me an array of medicines gathered from the field and packaged in plastic bottles and small bags, she then pointed to a blood-pressure cuff and stethoscope hanging on the wall as examples of what she said was "Western medicine" and elucidated the importance of both ways of knowing: "There is no difference between the two . . . . If you do not find medicine in the field, you must go to the clinic. If you are very ill, you must go to the shop or pharmacy to buy some tablets or medicine." Witbooi thus distinguished between !Khoba in the field and Hoodia as commercially manufactured tablets that reflected the binary of nature and culture, recognizing the difference between traditional and Western knowledge but the importance of both.

Negotiating !Khoba: San-CSIR Benefit Sharing and Hoodia as Indigenous Knowledge

The negotiations over benefit sharing between San and CSIR were an institutional and legal attempt to acknowledge the value of both these kinds of knowledge and their contribution to the technological and economic development of a new postapartheid South Africa. The negotiations took place within a larger context of international efforts to recognize and fairly compensate indigenous peoples for their discovery of and knowledge regarding native plants. An examination of the history of those negotiations demonstrates, however, that the arguments and terms in which they were framed ultimately advantaged and disadvantaged San peoples in ways that demonstrate the limits of benefit sharing.

Negotiations over Hoodia benefit sharing were set within a new South Africa aimed at reconfiguring the terms of belonging after the end of formal apartheid rule in 1994. Archbishop Desmond Tutu's metaphor of a multicolor rainbow nation became a way of imagining a nation that recognized cultural difference while also promoting a shared identity of being South African. The changing postapartheid landscape in the 1990s, Steven Robins argues, gave rise to revitalization movements by ≠Khomani San to reclaim their heritage, language, and land. Forcibly removed from lands within and adjacent to the Kalahari Gemsbok National Park as a result of apartheid-era legislation, for example, ≠Khomani San capitalized on new land restitution laws and signed a historic agreement with the South African government for land rights. Hoodia negotiations were informed by these efforts at land reclamation and at the same time by a growing global awareness of indigenous peoples' rights to self-determination; indigenous peoples formed networks at the first meeting of the World Social Forum in 2001, and the United Nations declared the First International Decade of the World's Indigenous Peoples (1995-2004). The government of South Africa was also on the verge of passing legislation in its 2004 Biodiversity Act that required the sharing of benefits with indigenous people whose knowledge of local plants and animals had been utilized for commercial purposes, a legislative move that translated the principles of the 1992 United Nations Convention on Biological Diversity (CBD) into South African law.[13] Within this changing national and international political climate, new possibilities for belonging in South Africa emerged for San and Khoi peoples, including benefit sharing as a pathway for further recognition.

Bringing Global Attention to Hoodia Patents as Acts of Biopiracy

Initial mobilization efforts that paved the way for San-CSIR benefit sharing negotiations focused global attention on Hoodia patents as biopiracy against Indigenous San peoples. Rachel Wynberg and David Fig of Biowatch South Africa and Alex Wijeratna of an international nongovernment organization called Action Aid were all actively involved in debates at the national and international level on issues of biodiversity and benefit sharing. After becoming aware of CSIR's Hoodia patents and the CSIR-Phytopharm licensing agreement from newspaper accounts, they urged a reporter named Antony Barnett with the *London Observer* to report on Hoodia as a case of biopiracy with the hopes that public awareness of the issue would compel CSIR to share benefits with San peoples in accordance with South Africa's new legal requirements.

Published on June 17, 2001, the article by Barnett charged that Phytopharm and Pfizer officials, touting the wonders of Hoodia as a "dieter's dream," had enchanted the media and their shareholders while taking advantage of San peoples by stealing their knowledge without their informed consent. He described how San peoples were "expert botanists" who knew much about local plants and had used the Hoodia plant to keep them alive, but now the Western drug industry had stolen their secret to make people thin. Barnett also reported that San peoples were angry about this major act of biopiracy, quoting Roger Chennells as saying, "It feels like somebody has stolen their family silver and cashed it in for a huge profit. The bushmen do not object to anybody using their knowledge to produce a medicine, but they would have liked the drug company to have spoken to them first and come to an agreement." By charging Phytopharm and Pfizer with the exploitation and taking of San peoples' knowledge, the London newspaper deployed the language of biopiracy as an effective political strategy to put pressure on the parties to engage with San peoples for benefit sharing.[14]

The *Observer* article applied further pressure when Barnett reported that Phytopharm executives considered San peoples as extinct, which also demonstrated that Hoodia research was embedded within colonial pasts that deployed similar narratives of extinction. Barnett described how when the *London Financial Times* asked two months earlier whether the company intended to share benefits with the descendants of San people, Phytopharm CEO Richard Dixey claimed, "We're doing what we can to pay back, but it's a really fraught problem, especially as the people who discovered the plant have disappeared."[15] Barnett also reported that Phytopharm officials had become aware that San peoples still existed, quoting Dixey as saying, "I honestly believed that these bushmen had died out and am sorry to hear they feel hard done by. I am delighted that they are still around and have a recognizable community. The ownership of medicinal plants is extremely complex, but I have always believed that this type of knowledge is the most valuable asset of indigenous tribes." Although intended as a defense against charges that his company was engaging in biopiracy, Dixey's comments also revealed how narratives of extinction are still used to subordinate and take advantage of indigenous peoples. To justify the taking and ownership of indigenous peoples' lands, colonial settlers depicted San and Khoi peoples as extinct and therefore the land as belonging to no one.[16] Dixey's comments implied a similar narrative, but this time notions of San as extinct were being used to say that Hoodia belonged to no one, in order to justify the patenting of Hoodia properties and to avoid sharing benefits with San peoples under the CBD. Reporting these particularly incendiary comments by Dixey, the Barnett article provided additional leverage for San peoples to contest Hoodia research.

Making Demands for Benefits from CSIR Scientists

Spurred on by this international attention, San peoples mobilized quickly in June 2001 against the patenting of Hoodia properties. Given the successful ≠Khomani San land claim against the South African government, South African San had existing governance structures in place that enabled them to organize. Their regional San governing organization, WIMSA, immediately authorized the South African San Council and their lawyer, Roger Chennells, to develop a political strategy on how to address CSIR's Hoodia patents. The first decision they faced was whether to challenge the validity of Hoodia patents in court or to demand benefit sharing from CSIR. The South African San Council decided on the latter strategy as a way to bring much-needed financial benefits to San peoples.[17]

With that decision made, the council and its chairman, Petrus Vaalbooi (≠Khomani San Bushman), along with Roger Chennells, approached officials at CSIR to demand benefits for San peoples from Hoodia research. Specifically, they began talks with Petro Terblanche, executive director of CSIR's Bio/Chemtek Unit. According to Terblanche, CSIR executives were initially reluctant to enter into benefit sharing with San because it was very new for the technology-intensive institution to sign agreements with a community.[18] Furthermore, the controversy over Hoodia forced CSIR officials to confront the government research organization's association with the former apartheid-era government. But given mounting pressure from the South African San Council and the global attention on the issue, Terblanche pressed the other CSIR executives to agree to benefit-sharing negotiations with the council.

In her initial meeting with the South African San Council and Chennells, Terblanche reported, she immediately recognized her "unfair advantage of knowledge about intellectual property and license agreements" and that a series of information sessions with San representatives would be necessary before the two sides could enter into fair negotiations over actual contractual terms: "How can I go and negotiate intellectual property rights? How can I go and negotiate royalties and benefit sharing with a group of people who doesn't have the basic understanding of what we're busy with? So Roger and I agreed that we [would] put the San people through a training session, which we funded." The negotiations between CSIR and the South African San Council from June 2001 to March 2003 thus included CSIR-funded information sessions on the scope of Hoodia research and Hoodia patents and visits by several San to CSIR labs in Pretoria to observe how they were processing and purifying Hoodia plants. According to Chennells, these sessions served an important purpose: "We did a lot of training on what is a patent? What is knowledge? Why are we negotiating this thing? What's it about? What's at stake? Who's it for—it's for everybody? So, there [was] a very steep learning curve for the San Council."[19]

But despite the workshops' intention of providing San peoples with important information so they would be better prepared to negotiate, their usefulness was limited in that they were one-sided, directed solely at educating San peoples about the work of CSIR researchers rather than also informing CSIR researchers about the experiences, histories, and heritage of San peoples. As a result, some San expressed frustration over not being heard during the workshops. Andries Steenkamp (≠Khomani San Bushman), for instance, expressed disappointment that "sometimes the meetings did not go nice" and that the CSIR participants failed to "listen carefully" to San peoples' input about their history and demands for recognition.[20]

Once these information meetings were concluded, the South African San Council began to negotiate the specifics of a benefit-sharing agreement with CSIR. As Shane Greene observes, indigenous peoples' mobilization around intellectual property rights raises questions about the role of persons and nongovernmental organizations who act as mediators on their behalf.[21] Because being able to represent one's own community is a central aspect of Indigenous peoples' efforts to gain self-determination, questions of who speaks for whom become especially important. In my conversations with Chennells, he recalled that the members of the South African San Council did much of the negotiating themselves and "did a lot of the talking—most of the talking. I would prepare them, and they would do the talking."[22] For her part, Terblanche felt certain that the representatives of the South African San Council shaped the tone of the negotiations. When she first met Vaalbooi, she recalled, "he said to me, 'You might be a good researcher, but I don't care how much you know, before I know how much you care.'"[23] Terblanche interpreted his remark as stressing the need to frame the negotiations through an ethic of care and concern for Indigenous San peoples—a move that sought to change relations of power and expertise between CSIR and San. However, some San representatives recalled feeling a strong sense of San autonomy during their meetings with CSIR, while others remembered relying primarily on Chennells to shape the benefit-sharing negotiations; thus, the question of who spoke for whom remains contested.[24]

Representing San as Simultaneously Nonmodern and Modern

Obtaining protection through contractual benefit sharing required the South African San Council to do so within the narrow registers of the law, thereby forcing them to assert San peoples as simultaneously modern and nonmodern—a dichotomy that, as seen from the epigraphs at the beginning of the chapter, remains a central tension among ≠Khomani San as they debate the best ways to hold on to traditions or to modernize.[25] The negotiations culminated in a March 2002 memorandum of understanding whereby CSIR recognized San peoples as having first knowledge of Hoodia and then a final, March 2003 San-CSIR contractual benefit-sharing agreement. As mentioned in the introduction, in the agreement, CSIR agreed to give San peoples across Southern Africa 6 percent of CSIR's royalty income related to the commercialization of certain patented Hoodia-based inventions and 8 percent of milestone payments that CSIR was scheduled to receive from Phytopharm at specified stages of the development of Hoodia-based products. Although these amounts were small in comparison to what Phytopharm, Pfizer, and CSIR stood to receive, the South African San Council was satisfied with the terms at the time. Given Phytopharm's projections of potential Hoodia-related profits in the billions of dollars, San representatives anticipated that even these small percentages would bring a windfall of monies to San peoples and thus considered the agreement a victory in their struggle for San self-determination and recognition.

However, as we shall see, the South African San Council was forced to frame its demand for benefits within the narrow confines of the law, thus demonstrating the limits of benefit sharing for purposes of indigenous peoples' self-determination. In her examination of indigeneity in US courtrooms, Jennifer Hamilton argues that the law limits the very language in which indigenous peoples can make claims for recognition.[26] This was also true for San peoples making claims against Hoodia patents. Patent law not only constructs indigenous knowledge as less worthy than

Western scientific knowledge but, according to Hyo Yoon Kang, also manages dissent by "laying out the acceptable parameters of opposition."[27] To secure much-needed benefits for their people, the only acceptable strategy therefore available to the South African San Council as it negotiated the agreement was to deploy San indigeneity in a binary manner that defined San identity as traditional and closer to nature by associating San peoples with !Khoba as a plant from nature, thereby positioning San peoples as simultaneously modern (negotiating within the law) and nonmodern (traditional).

The manner in which the law limited the council's efforts becomes more apparent when considering the actual terms of the San-CSIR agreement. Adopting a model of materiality here that examines the material provisions of the agreement enables a feminist decolonial technoscience analysis that demonstrates how the legal contract acted with a direct, symbolic, discursive, and coercive force that simultaneously recognized San peoples and knowledge while reinforcing them as less modern. The language of the agreement, for instance, acknowledged San as "custodians of an ancient body of tradition and cultural values" associated with "human uses of the *Hoodia* plant" whose ancient knowledge was based on their "interrelatedness with nature in all its forms, over the ages."[28] It also stressed "the importance of the traditional knowledge of the San people," which existed for "millennia" and "predated scientific knowledge developed by Western civilization over the past century." By presenting San as traditional peoples associated with !Khoba as a plant from nature in contrast to modern scientists associated with Hoodia as a cultural invention from the lab, the legal framing of the agreement structured San dissent in a binary manner and constrained the very rhetoric that could be deployed by the South African San Council.

Through the language of the agreement, both San and CSIR ways of knowing became recognized but remained dichotomous. Two protected spheres of value were simultaneously constructed—one a scientifically based commodity and the other traditional knowledge. The agreement also implicitly placed value on the particular materialities of Hoodia associated with such epistemologies: CSIR knowledge of Hoodia at the molecular level was regarded alongside yet distinct from San ways of knowing Hoodia at the molar level as a plant from nature. Acknowledging the relationship between these two enduring incommensurable knowledges, the agreement explicitly asserted the role of San "knowledge [in] leading to new scientific findings, which formed the basis of the patents," implying San knowledge as raw material that must be scientifically proven and reinforcing San knowledge as distinct from CSIR knowledge. Recognition of San ways of knowing also came in the form of educational benefits; for example, the agreement provided for the making of a detailed "Bioprospecting Collaboration" between CSIR and San to conduct bioprospecting in the future together, while also specifying that CSIR would "make the existing CSIR study bursaries and scholarships available to the San Council," allowing members of San communities to benefit from educational opportunities. Financial and educational benefits were to act as recognition of San ways of knowing and redress for taking their knowledge without prior informed consent, but they remained predicated on assumptions of nonmodern versus modern ways of knowing Hoodia.

In return for benefits, the San representatives agreed that San peoples would not claim co-ownership of Hoodia patents or products, assist or work with any third party to develop products or industries that might compete with the Hoodia-based patents or products, approach the patent licensees for additional financial benefits, or contest the validity of the patents themselves. The agreement also required San to help CSIR defend their patents in the case of any third-party claims of infringement and to agree to reevaluate the contract if such challenges were successful. These provisions related to nonmonetary benefits thus required San peoples to refrain from interfering with the patenting and commercial development of Hoodia-based products, and in so doing, simultaneously recognized San peoples as traditional knowers of !Khoba and secured the rights of CSIR scientists to continue their research. Although the agreement recognized both San and CSIR understandings of Hoodia, it failed to reorder material conditions of power by keeping CSIR patent ownership intact.

The speeches given at the formal signing of the agreement also reinforced the agreement's representation of !Khoba knowledge as the traditional knowledge of San peoples. As described at the opening of this book, the formal ceremony included San and CSIR representatives and also several representatives of the state, attending in order to witness the signing and celebrate this important recognition of San peoples in postapartheid South Africa. Some of those who spoke were Kxao Moses, the chairperson of WIMSA, and Ben Ngubane, minister of the Department of Arts, Culture,

Science, and Technology.[29] In his speech, Moses spoke at length about San peoples' histories and their indigenous knowledge of local flora and fauna, reinforcing the notion of San Hoodia knowledge as rooted in the past, while also praising the South African San Council for their successful demand for benefits.[30] Ngubane, too, characterized Hoodia as traditional knowledge, though that of South Africa rather than solely San peoples.[31]

In positioning San as traditional knowers of Hoodia as a plant from nature, the South African San Council proved themselves astute political subjects prepared to demand benefits within a shifting South African politics. The Convention on Biological Diversity mandated the sharing of benefits with indigenous peoples, and South Africa would soon pass similar benefit-sharing legislation in its 2004 Biodiversity Act, signaling its commitment to a transformation politics aimed at being accountable for colonial and apartheid violence against nonwhites. In each of these cases, however, legal recognition of indigenous peoples was based on narrow understandings of them as traditional peoples rooted in the past and in need of protection rather than as dynamic political subjects capable of developing their own strategies for self-determination.

Navigating these narrow legal parameters in making demands for benefit sharing, the South African San Council asserted themselves as traditional, but in doing so, they also signaled that San peoples were savvy political agents engaged in complex decision making and practices of self-determination. As Adam Haupt suggests, the pirating of intellectual property rights not only exploits marginalized groups but also presents those groups with "possibilities for agency."[32] In asserting agency, the council contested both the ownership of Hoodia patents and the colonial history that justified the subordination of indigenous peoples by denigrating them as closer to nature than European researchers, who were viewed as expert producers of culture. In its demands for benefits, the council instead associated itself with tradition and nature to assert San as both expert knowers of !Khoba and modern political negotiators.

As the South African San Council and indigenous peoples around the globe navigate these new rights claims, they are placed in an impossible set of positions. To establish modes of belonging in postcolonial societies, indigenous peoples are forced to mediate between being cast as traditional and being cast as modern, self-determining liberal subjects.[33] They must demand rights as traditional peoples so that past violence against them is addressed, but they must also demand rights as modern peoples so that their present-day struggles are recognized. As indigenous peoples are increasingly forced to make rights claims through means such as benefit sharing, which hinge on the success of the market, they are left to contend with navigating a position as both nonmodern and modern—a position that emerges from the narrow assumptions of the law and the marketplace and, in so doing, forecloses alternative ways of imagining their identities and futures. As Debra Harry (Northern Paiute) and Le`a Malia Kanehe (Kanaka Maoli) also caution, by entering into benefit-sharing agreements, indigenous peoples also end up "accepting western legal frameworks and concepts that do not respect Indigenous laws and customs" and that "may compromise their right of self-determination."[34] Linking San benefits to the uncertainty of the market and making their protection contingent on the commercial success of Hoodia products, for instance, left San peoples to struggle with uncertain financial futures.

Given that benefit sharing afforded San peoples little control over Hoodia production, we can also understand these new rights claims as benefiting nation-states and associated entities more than indigenous peoples. The San-CSIR agreement afforded CSIR scientists the opportunity to confront shameful colonial and apartheid histories against San peoples by asserting themselves both as triumphant patent owners who were protecting the plant from exploitation from entities in the Global North and as benevolent scientists who were willing to share benefits with San peoples. When Unilever terminated its Hoodia research, however, CSIR scientists were no longer accountable to San peoples. Whereas CSIR, Unilever, and Phytopharm had other promising research projects to move on to, the end of their Hoodia research effectively meant the end of benefits to San peoples. Although CSIR researchers expressed a commitment to continuing their Hoodia research, San peoples had no control over the scientists' decision making. CSIR researchers have since tried to secure government funding to develop a fair-trade market for the plant that would put San peoples at the helm, and they went so far as to hold meetings with San peoples to get their input, but by late 2016 little progress had been made, and San peoples remain reliant on CSIR to move the project further.

The disappointment of not achieving the benefits they had expected undoubtedly played a role in the mixed feelings of the individual ≠Khomani San I engaged with, ranging from a deep distrust in such contractual arrangements to optimism about their promise for benefiting San peoples. Reflecting on the agreement, Andries Steenkamp (≠Khomani San Bushman) remembered the signing at the Molopo Lodge as "amazing" and recalled his excitement about the "millions and millions and billions" coming to San peoples and the feeling that "life is going up, not down," an excitement Sanna Witbooi (≠Khomani San Bushman) also recalled.[35] Yet Steenkamp and Witbooi also expressed disappointment that the agreement had yielded fewer benefits than expected, Witbooi going so far as to demand an end to Hoodia research, declaring that the San-CSIR agreement was "a big mistake," that they should "get out of the contract," and that "the !Khoba [research] must stop right now."[36] Arrie Tities (≠Khomani San Bushman) had also become discouraged: "So now it's four years we don't see money. . . . They said, ah, Arrie man, there is no money, there is no money. You must wait. So that is why I have a big concern about the income from the Hoodia."[37] Although Steenkamp acknowledged that the San-CSIR agreement was, "in Bushmen terms, not so good," as it left San peoples without future benefits, he considered it a good model for future relationships between researchers and San peoples. Busakhwe, viewing the agreement's lessons more positively, predicted that "if we arrange ourselves and arrange our intellectual property and arrange our heritage sites and have good relationships with other stakeholders," including the government, "there can be a great future for benefit sharing for us."[38] ≠Khomani San therefore did not all agree on whether the San-CSIR agreement benefited San peoples, but their insights demonstrate both the promise and the limits of contractual benefit sharing.

!Khoba Disruptions: (Mis)Alignments of Indigenous San Peoples and !Khoba Plants

By characterizing San as the traditional first peoples of South Africa and the original knowers of !Khoba plants, the South African San Council's demands fit within an increasing emphasis in South Africa on ascribing belonging to those who claim to be native to the country by asserting the primacy of autochthony, thus reinforcing boundaries between who is native and who is alien.[39] Although their demands were contingent on representing both San and !Khoba as fixed and unchanging, !Khoba plants grew in certain ways that both complicated and supported San claims to benefit sharing. This feminist decolonial technoscience approach draws on Karen Barad's definition of agency as "a matter of intra-acting . . . an enactment, not something that someone or something has" but rather as "a 'doing' or 'being' in its intra-activity,"[40] examining the actions of plants not simply as reactive but as forces that affect social worlds. By analyzing how Hoodia plants act in ways that can both bolster and complicate legal claims, the analysis here examines nonhumans as subjects that act rather than as mere objects to be acted upon, thus expanding on what Alaimo and Hekman refer to as the "agentic force" of nonhumans.[41] This approach therefore deploys a model of materiality that assumes a notion of agency that differs from its historical association with a human subject that acts with autonomy. Without assigning such notions of agency to nonhuman actors, this approach finds that Hoodia's growth patterns across South Africa made San claims for benefit sharing possible while also complicating them.

According to the South African Department of Tourism, Environment, and Conservation, *Hoodia gordonii* is found widely across Southern Africa, but mostly in Namibia and South Africa and to a lesser extent in Botswana and Angola.[42] As the plants grow, they form fleshy, finger-like stems that branch out from the ground and are covered in rows of tubercles with sharp spines. Although they grow in a variety of habitats, they grow more densely in some parts of the region and appear to prefer slopes, ridges, and shale plains. Animals and insects in the region use *Hoodia gordonii* plants for food and moisture and as sites of shelter and shade for breeding. Hoodia's patchy distribution also changes in response to environmental conditions and threats, making where it grows somewhat unpredictable. As a result of this uneven distribution, not all San groups historically used the plant.[43]

The uneven distribution of the !Khoba plant simultaneously enabled and complicated San claims to be the first peoples to discover and use it. During negotiations with CSIR, the South African San Council represented San across Southern Africa not as individuals or groups but as a collective indigenous people. For the purposes of political organizing around benefit sharing, they strategically organized themselves as modern subjects with collective rights to benefits, and thus the materiality of Hoodia's scattered distribution supported their demands as the original knowers of Hoodia. That the range of *Hoodia gordonii* distribution is restricted primarily to southern Africa made it easier for the San negotiators to make their claims as exclusive first knowers of Hoodia.

The full range of *Hoodia gordonii*'s distribution, however, meant that other indigenous groups in southern Africa could also assert rights based on knowing the plant, which could undermine exclusive San claims. As noted, dense patches of *Hoodia gordonii* also extend into the territories of Namibia, where it grows even more abundantly than in South Africa. Thus, both San and Nama in Namibia can claim a rich history of using the plant. As a result, six years after the South African San Council signed the benefit-sharing agreement with CSIR, the Association of Nama Traditional Leaders in Namibia insisted in a joint San-Nama meeting that Nama peoples were also original knowers of Hoodia. The association eventually obtained an agreement with San acknowledging the traditional knowledge of Nama peoples with respect to all indigenous plants in the region, including !Khoba.[44]

San peoples' assertions of belonging through benefit sharing were therefore also contingent on the materiality of Hoodia and its distribution as a species. Because plants engage in actions that make them unpredictable, they do not always easily align with legal assertions, revealing how unstable it can be to attach modes of belonging to the materiality of plants. As South Africa moves forward in emphasizing benefit sharing and as San and other indigenous peoples seek new agreements, the materiality of plants matters for making claims. Although the law constructs indigenous peoples and plants as fixed in place, the materiality of plants is not so neatly fixed and also has consequences for legal claims. The ways in which the unpredictability of Hoodia plants simultaneously enabled and hindered San claims as exclusive traditional knowers of Hoodia demonstrates that plants act in ways that cannot be entirely contained and constructed by legal rights claims.

Conclusion

The South African San Council made claims for benefit sharing based on a particular material-discursive scale of Hoodia—as a plant from nature connected to San histories, culture, and life. Because its claims were structured by discourses of law and science, the council was compelled to represent San as a traditional people closer to nature with ancient knowledge of Hoodia, yet it did so to strategically position San as modern political subjects seeking new pathways to rights, recognition, and belonging in South Africa. In doing so, San peoples simultaneously undermined, strengthened, and reworked binaries of nature/culture and their associated dichotomies of modern/nonmodern and Western/indigenous. Yet these claims were based not only on San peoples' cultural difference as indigenous peoples but also on their attachment to the particular materiality of Hoodia as a plant in nature, and the materiality of that plant both supported and complicated their efforts to obtain benefits. Understanding Hoodia plants as subjects that act back upon the law demonstrates the complex interplay of what is considered nature and culture, propelling us to imagine alternative natureculture worlds that challenge normative notions of nature (natural) and culture (cultural) and the hierarchical processes of naturalization that they engender.

As San and other indigenous peoples continue to make claims for belonging and benefits through their status as first knowers of and attachments to nonhuman plants, it becomes ever more important to understand the implications of claims based on being simultaneously modern and nonmodern peoples, and to recognize the inequality of power relations between San and the scientists and corporations who retain control over research and whose agreeing to share benefits shielded them from further critique. In examining these modes of inequality, the next chapter examines how CSIR scientists made claims for belonging and patent ownership through their authority as scientists and their attachment to Hoodia as a molecule.

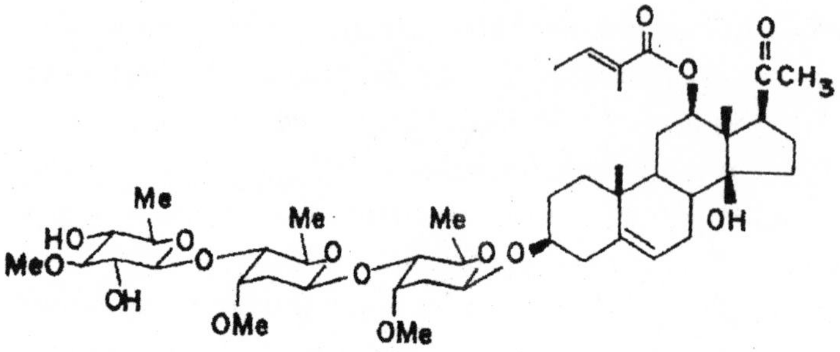

O
O
CCH3
OH
Me
Me
Me
HO
O
MeO
O
O
O
OH
OMe
OMe

3

South African Scientists and the Patenting of Hoodia as a Molecule

> When I dream, my dreams come true. I want to tell you something
> about my father too. His name is Hans Johannes Kock. He lives
> in the "hardeveld" among the medicinal bushes. He carries a lot of
> knowledge about the medicine of the veld. He can also see ahead,
> into his future. He is the only one of the great-great-grandfathers
> that depends on herbal medicine. Therefore I am proud of him,
> my father.
>
> —ANNA-RAADHT WITBOOI (≠KHOMANI SAN)

AS EARLY AS 1994, SOUTH AFRICAN SCIENTISTS WORKING FOR CSIR
filed a provisional patent for a Hoodia-based invention they had made
in South Africa. Via treating the plant with a solvent and purifying its
valuable properties until they became homogenized, they had derived
a chemical extract capable of suppressing appetite. Using filtration and
centrifugation, they removed the solvent from the separated crude extract
and then further isolated the extracted material into a partially purified
active extract by mixing methylene chloride with water. They purified
Hoodia through Waring blenders, rotary evaporators, column chromatog-
raphy, and suitable bioassaying procedures and had used nuclear magnetic
resonance to identify the exact chemical compound within Hoodia that
acts as an appetite suppressant. In doing so, CSIR scientists asserted that

they were expert producers of patented Hoodia knowledge, thus challenging colonial discourses that portrayed South Africa as a site for the mere extraction of raw materials even as they reinforced those discourses by dismissing the product of Indigenous San knowledge as no more than raw material to be transformed and patented without San consent.

This chapter addresses Hoodia at the scale of molecule to examine how CSIR scientists made claims to knowing Hoodia as purified molecules in ways that simultaneously contested, reinforced, and reconfigured colonial histories of South Africa as mere site of extraction and its plants as raw material. It analyzes the chemistry of Hoodia plants but also how the patenting of Hoodia positioned CSIR and its scientists as producers of science while bolstering South Africa's role in the global economy. It also examines the technicalities and materialities of patent law rules and Hoodia patent documents to explain how Hoodia became a patented object and how CSIR patent ownership was constituted. In turn, it analyzes the materiality of Hoodia molecules to show how their complex stereochemistry mattered to CSIR claims to knowing the plant, but at the same time did not align with commercial desires to make it into an antiobesity product. It shows how Hoodia patent ownership differs across multiple scales of nation-state jurisdictions (South Africa and the United States), divergent ways of knowing (San and CSIR), and biochemical states of plants (molecule and plant from nature) while illustrating how patent rights are also contingent on the very material objects they designate as property. Contesting the naturalization of nature as property and by extension the different related histories of the naturalizing of indigenous peoples, women, and people of color as property, the feminist decolonial technoscience here examines the precise material provisions through which the law designated Hoodia as patented invention. Hoodia patent ownership, this analysis demonstrates, does not constitute a Lockean natural property right but results from a contingent and historical process, revealing CSIR and San Hoodia knowledge as ultimately more similar than different. In other words, it shows that the worlds of scientists and indigenous peoples such as Hans Johannes Kock, mentioned in the epigraph, are similarly dynamic and rooted in past histories—an inquiry that dreams along with Anna-Raadht Witbooi for more meaningful futures in which indigenous peoples and their knowledge flourish.

Hoodia Patents and Belonging in South Africa

Although CSIR scientists were the first to transform and patent Hoodia into chemical compositions capable of suppressing appetite, as scientists in a government-funded research organization, they were expected to meet the needs of the people of South Africa rather than stockholders.[1] The CSIR complex in Pretoria includes dozens of buildings situated on an expanse of hillside that to some might appear like a university campus, but it is surrounded by high gates and is tightly controlled. Visitors must pass through an entrance post outside the main gates, where they are photographed, given a badge, and asked to make their computers, cameras, and vehicles available for inspection. CSIR employees and knowledge are therefore rigorously secured and protected. Such security measures are also in place internally. As Andrew Bailey, who worked at CSIR's Bio/Chemtek Division, explained to me, he and others who were not specifically assigned to the Hoodia program were not allowed to enter scientific labs and areas related to Hoodia research without specific permission. "A lot of the work that was done in this bioprospecting unit," he told me, "was secret to protect potential IP (intellectual property). They had special locks on the doors and you couldn't go in. . . . Their servers were separate from the CSIR's main servers just to protect knowledge of [indigenous] communities, and they were very strict about people getting access."[2]

The stated mission of CSIR is to produce scientific knowledge for the benefit of the people of South Africa, but the specifics of this goal have changed over time as CSIR research has shifted in response to government priorities. According to South African scholar Rachel Wynberg, for instance, when CSIR first began studying edible indigenous plants in 1963, using relevant information from colonial botanical guides, it focused on the Hoodia plant because of its promise as a source of food and water for the South African Defense Force, a need that became more urgent while fighting against the South West Africa People's Organization (SWAPO) and the government of Angola from 1966 to 1989.[3] The early research on Hoodia took place within the larger context of CSIR research on nutrition, which examined dietary practices among whites at risk for obesity-related cardiovascular disease and among workers classified under apartheid as Black, Coloured, and Indian who were suffering from malnutrition.[4] A

CSIR report on the early history of its natural products research also identifies Hoodia research as part of its work on the nutritional value of veld foods.[5] What each project attests to, though, is that research on indigenous plants had been hampered by the lack of access to the latest technology during apartheid rule. Hoodia research was relaunched in the 1980s when CSIR was able to acquire nuclear magnetic resonance spectrometry that allowed scientists to identify the exact chemical compounds within the plant that were capable of suppressing appetite.

Interest in this project was also reinvigorated by the arrival of a young scientist, Dr. Vinesh Maharaj. Maharaj began working at CSIR in 1985 after graduating with a Bachelor's of Science degree from University of Durban Westville, a nonwhite institution in South Africa at the height of the antiapartheid movement—a politically significant development given that he was classified as Indian under the apartheid regime.[6] South Africans categorized as Indian were afforded fewer educational opportunities than white citizens during that period, and Black citizens even fewer. Although postgraduate study was hard for nonwhites to obtain, Maharaj had benefited from strong mentoring from the lead chemist of his CSIR lab, who encouraged him to pursue a PhD in chemistry at the University of South Africa and recommended that he study the chemistry of a plant of interest to the Natural Products group, *Trichocaulon piliferum,* for his doctoral work.

Taking his mentor's advice, Maharaj began a decades-long research program at CSIR that would begin with *Trichocaulon piliferum* and eventually shift to *Hoodia gordonii.* In my conversations with him, Maharaj recounted that he had initially studied all of the several *Trichocaulon* species for their appetite-suppressant properties. He said that he had read an article by an ethnobotanist named Marloth who reported that "his Hottentot guide showed him ghaap and told him this is the true ghaap [which] he identified as *trichocaulon piliferum.*" Rudolf Marloth, a colonial settler from Germany who arrived in Cape Town in the late 1800s, had therefore learned about *Trichocaulon piliferum* from indigenous people.[7] As Maharaj continued to read about *Trichocaulon piliferum,* he also came upon a publication by South African botanist Peter Bruyns, who had recently determined that plants in the *Trichocaulon* genus were so similar to plants in the *Hoodia* genus that they should be reclassified as a part of the same genus.[8] As Maharaj read that *Trichocaulon* now belonged to the *Hoodia* genus, he began to investigate the properties of *Hoodia gordonii* and found it had the same compound that he had discovered in *Trichocaulon*. Maharaj therefore investigated the chemical matter of one plant to determine the relevant materiality of another. In fact, CSIR patents do not apply just to molecules and extracts derived from plants from the *Hoodia* genus, but also to those derived from plants from the genus *Trichocaulon*. The history of CSIR Hoodia research at the molecular scale, then, actually begins with the molecules of a different plant.

During our conversations, Maharaj further clarified that he had learned about Hoodia not from San peoples but from these scholarly botanical writings. As he explained, "*Hoodia gordonii*, it may have been 'scientific luck' through the reclassification of the species. We did not approach individuals and ask them, 'Do you use this plant as an appetite suppressant, so that I can research it?' I only looked at *Hoodia gordonii* because of the reclassification." Maharaj elucidated this point not so much to absolve himself from responsibility to San peoples, but rather to demonstrate botanical knowledge production and the contributions of Marloth and Bruyns to his understanding of Hoodia. However, although CSIR's Hoodia research began with Maharaj's exposure to the writings of earlier botanists, those botanists' learning can be traced back to direct interaction with San peoples. Rudolf Marloth had first learned about the plant from those he referred to as his local Hottentot guides, and Peter Bruyns reported learning about *Hoodia gordonii* from early botanical writings by the likes of Marloth, Masson, Brown, and Sloane and White. As the botanical sciences advanced, these botanists operated along a single dimension, the disciplinary dimension of botany, which referenced earlier botanical studies but made little or no mention of how indigenous peoples had initially contributed to those botanical understandings. As the field of botany examined *Hoodia gordonii* as a scientific object of study, it developed its own meanings of the plant, through which the plant was transformed from !Khoba to *Hoodia gordonii*.

By thus connecting his Hoodia knowledge to botany and chemistry rather than to indigenous peoples, Maharaj supported CSIR's claim to knowing Hoodia as a molecule. Even though CSIR eventually acknowledged San as the holders of traditional knowledge regarding *Hoodia gordonii*, they continued to maintain their unique claim to knowledge of the chemical properties of the plant based on Maharaj's identification of the precise molecules within the plant that suppressed appetite. Maharaj also implied that CSIR knowledge of Hoodia as a molecule was distinct from indigenous peoples' knowledge because it flowed from the disciplinary expertise of chemistry and botany rather than from interactions between CSIR scientists and indigenous peoples.

In a similar fashion, CSIR also maintained their distinct claim to Hoodia based on the materiality of Hoodia as a molecule. As Maharaj explained to me, the complex stereochemistry of the active ingredient in *Trichocaulon piliferum* had initially hindered the understanding of the plant's appetite-suppressant properties. Technological advances provided little assistance, but he eventually managed to identify the exact chemical entities within the plant that suppressed appetite. Maharaj told me that he "identified the active compound, which at the time was quite complex, because to elucidate the structure of natural products without the technology can be regarded as complex. However, with the technology that is now available, I wouldn't say it's complex." But it was not enough though to merely isolate the relevant chemical molecules; Maharaj also needed to find a way to synthesize the material to make it more attractive to investors as a potential pharmaceutical. As he noted, "if you cannot produce sufficient quantities, further biological evaluation is limited." Given that *Trichocaulon piliferum* was scarce across southern Africa, an interested pharmaceutical company would want to synthesize the plant to more easily produce its material properties related to suppressing appetite.

What had made the compounds in both *Trichocaulon piliferum* and *Hoodia gordonii* seem so promising to CSIR scientists was that they worked differently from the more commonly known weight-loss supplements containing amphetamines. As Maharaj recounted, "In my early studies with rats being treated with this compound, the rats stopped eating and lost weight. When the compound was taken away after their initial treatments, the rats still did not eat for a few more days until they recovered and started eating normally. In the amphetamine treatment groups, the rats would stop eating, but the moment you took the amphetamines away, the rats would then eat more than what they used to eat." Studying how Hoodia molecules interacted with the bodies of rats, Maharaj commented that there were ongoing studies to determine how the active ingredients suppressed the appetite and whether it might work without affecting the central nervous system, as amphetamines did.

As with the making of all pharmaceuticals, the materiality of Hoodia therefore mattered greatly to its promise as a potential weight-loss drug. Hoodia steroidal glycoside molecules suppressed appetite but, unlike amphetamines, did not cause a spike in the eating habits of the rats. By identifying chemical compounds that not only suppressed appetite but did so in a way that differed from most other weight-loss treatments, Maharaj, in his own words, "made it very attractive to commercial" interests. Yet the way in which the materiality of Hoodia had this effect remained unknown. Despite Maharaj's scientific data showing that purified Hoodia molecules reduced appetite in rats, he could not demonstrate precisely how they did so. In this instance, the science of chemistry could understand nature only partially—knowing *that* it worked but not fully *how* it worked. This knowledge was enough, though, for the purposes of patent law, and so Maharaj and his fellow scientists at CSIR filed a provisional patent in 1994 on Hoodia chemical compositions that they showed were responsible for suppressing appetite.[9]

Of course, the patenting of Hoodia was more than just one individual's story, as it was also a story about CSIR's reestablishing itself as a key institution within a new South Africa and about South Africa's asserting itself as belonging to a new neoliberal global economy.[10] CSIR's core mission had always been innovation even when it served the apartheid state, but the filing of the 1994 provisional Hoodia patent occurred during the nation's intense transition from apartheid to neoliberalism. In the 1990s, ANC's antiapartheid liberation principles were replaced by a neoliberal governing structure that focused less on social welfare and redistribution policies and more on deregulation, privatization, and the market, as embodied in the 1996 shift from its redistributive Reconstruction and Development Programme.[11]

In this shift toward market principles, patent ownership emerged as a strong component of South Africa's neoliberal governing practices and efforts toward economic growth.[12] The same year that the ANC government adopted its GEAR (Growth, Employment, and Redistribution) Programme, for instance, it also passed the Intellectual Property Rationalisation Act, which sought to integrate different intellectual property regimes throughout the country into a more unified system. The year before CSIR filed its Hoodia patent application in 1998, the South African Department of Arts, Culture, and Technology had issued a White Paper on Science and

Technology that stressed the need to align principles of patent ownership with international norms to promote innovation; the following year, the ANC government passed the National Advisory Council on Innovation Act, intended to coordinate a national system devoted to innovation, science, and technology. At the same time, some parties in South Africa sought to condemn patent ownership. The timing of the Hoodia patents correlated with increasing opposition to patent law and neoliberal globalization from South African and international social movements, which in South Africa particularly focused on the patenting of HIV/AIDS drugs and on the World Trade Organization's Agreement on Trade-Related Aspects of Intellectual Property Rights (TRIPs).[13] The patenting of Hoodia in a government-sponsored research institution thus took place at a critical moment in the rise of neoliberal governance in South Africa, when intellectual property rights were both supported and denounced. Hoodia patents offered symbolic as well as economic promise for a country transitioning from apartheid rule by establishing CSIR scientists as makers of innovation, CSIR as a producer of economic growth, and South Africa as a key player in an international neoliberal economy fueled in large part by intellectual property rights.

CSIR scientists, pressured by CSIR and government expectations to transform science into innovation, obtained Hoodia patents and thus gained initial control over its production. CSIR hoped to partner with another company to help in developing their Hoodia-based invention for commercial markets. Maharaj, acknowledging the importance of patents for securing multinational investors, noted the importance of protecting competitive advantage. Obtaining a patent demonstrated the invention's value and legitimated South African scientists as producers of science. By securing patent rights, CSIR scientists sought, in the words of Anne Pollock, to "translate local science into global science" by participating in global knowledge production.[14] Hoodia patents thus enabled CSIR scientists to claim a distinct knowledge of Hoodia as an appetite-suppressant molecule.

By distinguishing themselves as knowers of patented molecules, CSIR scientists asserted that they were producers of science in ways that simultaneously contested and reinforced colonial histories of extraction. One of the legacies of colonialism is that many scientists in the Global North perceive the work of scientists in developing countries as inferior.[15] Obtaining patents enabled CSIR to counter that perception by entering regimes of scientific knowledge production that had historically been closed to them. In particular, Hoodia patents recognized CSIR scientists as knowledgeable experts in the field of antiobesity research and participants in a larger body of Hoodia research, and those patents also generated new relationships between them and Phytopharm, Pfizer, and Unilever, challenging notions of South Africa as a mere site for resource extraction. Yet their patent ownership provided only limited control and authority over their invention. The multinational companies' greater resources and financial investment in the project gave them ultimate control over whether Hoodia-related products would go to market. Thus, when Unilever terminated the project in late 2008, citing safety concerns, CSIR scientists had little say in the decision and never received the royalties they had anticipated.

It is important to recognize, however, that even as CSIR scientists challenged colonial histories by becoming producers of patented Hoodia knowledge, they also reinforced colonial histories and the epistemological foundations of patent law, as Indigenous San recognized when they accused CSIR of practices similar to the colonial settlers' taking of San lands and resources without their consent and without compensation. CSIR scientists bolstered the authority of patent law by maintaining its distinction between discovery and invention, thereby cutting out the network of Hoodia knowledge production by colonial explorers, local botanists, and most importantly San peoples by crediting CSIR scientists as the inventors of Hoodia.[16] Patent law thus made CSIR's ownership appear natural and inevitable, obscuring Indigenous San contributions to Hoodia knowledge production and the history of how their knowledge had been shaped and transformed. By severing the materiality of Hoodia plants from San knowledge, land, and heritage, Hoodia patents therefore privileged CSIR knowledge over San ways of knowing. Reinforcing the binaries of discovery/invention and modern/nonmodern, the patents signified that CSIR's invention of Hoodia as a marketable good was more worthy than San peoples' initial discovery of the plant as a means of subsistence. Although patents on Hoodia's appetite-suppressant properties did not prevent San from using the plant in their daily lives, they harmed San by devaluing their knowledge and reproducing the dichotomous thought that historically had been used to subordinate them.

In addition, the meanings that ≠Khomani San ascribed to patents and intellectual property rights were quite different from those of Maharaj and his colleagues. As Tommy Busakhwe (≠Khomani San Bushman) explained to me, "We do not see our intellectual property as a business, but as our heritage. . . . That is why we are proud of our intellectual properties."[17] Busakhwe thus espoused a broader understanding of intellectual property than its legal definition by defining San knowledge as intellectual property in the sense of heritage. Andries Steenkamp (≠Khomani San Bushman) associated intellectual property with CSIR's research involving Hoodia as a molecule rather than San knowledge of Hoodia as life and from nature, insisting that "you cannot patent a plant because it is life. You cannot patent life." Because San "don't know the molecule in the plant," he continued, they might as well "give the license to the company because he do the research and find the molecule. But I am still hungry [and] the plant is still there, nobody is worried about the plant."[18] Steenkamp asserted that CSIR and San knowledge of Hoodia were distinct and also valued differently. His response is thus a demonstration of how patents' focus on the molecule obscures the plant and San peoples.

Yet scientific knowledge originates not in autonomous scientific experts or even networks of knowledge production, but rather in social worlds of peoples, ideas, nonhumans, and things.[19] As we have seen, the production of Hoodia knowledge did not start and end with CSIR scientists, but rather flowed from the long, tangled histories of what Mary Louise Pratt would describe as a "contact zone" or social space where the cultures of San, British botanists, classification schemes, colonial representations, colonial settlers, Afrikaner farmers, South African scientists, apartheid rule, neoliberal governing, plants, land, and soil all touched in powerful and unequal ways.[20] It was within this zone of contact that CSIR and CSIR scientists deployed Hoodia patents to claim a place of belonging to a new South Africa, and in so doing simultaneously contested, reinforced, and reconfigured the colonial, apartheid, and neoliberal histories that have informed Indigenous San peoples' lives and strategies for self-determination.

Materialities of Hoodia Patents and Postcolonial Moments of Sameness and Difference

Yet an even more complex understanding of the relationships between these different ways of knowing emerges in a closer investigation of what we might term the materialities of legal documents and statutes, which offer an example of what Helen Verran refers to as "postcolonial moments: occasions for theorizing, for telling differences and sameness in new ways." Expanding on Derrida's notion of the "force of law" and what Annelise Riles refers to as "technicalities of law" that act with "autonomous force," this examination demonstrates how patent rules act to value CSIR knowledge over that of San peoples but also reveals how these two forms of knowledge are similar.[21] In so doing, it deploys a model of materiality wherein legal technicalities become, as Mariana Valverde suggests, "resources for theory" to understand relations of law, science, and society.[22] It shows that a consideration of patent ownership at different spatiotemporal scales, including nation-state jurisdictions, divergent CSIR and San understandings, and different modalities of Hoodia materiality, uncovers similarities as well as differences, reveals how the material conditions of law and science co-constitute relations of humans and nonhumans, and pinpoints the precise mechanisms of patent law that provide opportunities for challenges by indigenous peoples.

Patent Ownership in the United States and South Africa

As noted above, South Africa issued a complete patent on Hoodia in 1999 to six scientists from CSIR for inventing Hoodia-related extraction processes and chemical compounds capable of suppressing appetite.[23] In 2002, the scientists proceeded to obtain a patent on the same invention in the United States.[24] Filing patents in different nation-state jurisdictions is a common practice among scientists to ensure global protection for their patents and to satisfy the expectations of potential investors. The CSIR's patent attorneys had to write their patent application for a different nation-state jurisdiction in ways that would make the Hoodia-related invention intelligible and convincing within the patent law of both that nation and South Africa. A comparison of CSIR's US and South African patent applications demonstrates that the foundations of patent ownership are particular to a given culture and society and contingent on the changing priorities and interests of nation-states and peoples.

One notable set of material similarities and differences in the two patent applications is how they frame the requirement of novelty. To obtain a patent under both the US Patent Act (USPA) and the South African Patent Act (SAPA), applicants must demonstrate that their claimed invention is "novel." By designating inventions as novel, patent law constructs and reinforces dominant narratives of modernity that cast progress and what is new in opposition to what is considered traditional and nonmodern. Patent applicants must prove novelty by demonstrating that the object of the patent has not been previously disclosed or anticipated by an earlier "prior art" or "state of art" reference, as discussed below.[25] If a patent examiner finds that a prior art reference fully discloses all the elements found in the claimed invention, the invention is considered anticipated rather than novel and patent ownership is denied.[26] Both laws thereby measure novelty not through some sociocultural sense of what is new and original but through technical rules and interpretations of prior art references.

According to South African law, a state of art reference is one that "has been made available to the public (whether in the Republic or elsewhere) by written or oral description, by use or in any other way."[27] In contrast, US patent law, as amended under the Leahy-Smith America Invents Act of 2013, defines a prior art reference more specifically as something that has been previously patented, described in a printed publication, or made available to the public before the filing date of the claimed invention.[28] The previous version of the US law had made geographic distinctions in prior art, defining it as a reference to a claimed invention known or used by others *in the United States* or as patented or described in a printed publication *in the United States or a foreign country* before the date of invention.[29] By recognizing prior art in a foreign country only if the reference was written in a patent application or printed publication, the former US law made it easier for potential applicants to claim that their invention was novel because an earlier reference that showed how indigenous peoples outside the United States previously knew of or used the invention would not be considered prior art unless the indigenous groups had thought to describe their knowledge in a patent or printed publication. If South African San had tried to challenge the 2002 US patent on Hoodia, they would have had to do so based on the pre-2013 law, by which they would be held to this more difficult standard for challenging novelty and required to show that a patent application or printed publication prior to the date of invention had fully disclosed all the elements indicated in CSIR's claimed invention. Thus, their geographical location outside of the United States would preclude them from supporting their claim with any evidence based on oral communication regarding how they had previously known or used Hoodia.

The different meanings of novelty in South Africa and the United States results not only from differences in statutory rules and interpretations but from the processes of the respective bureaucracies that evaluate patent applications: South Africa's Companies and Intellectual Property Commission (CIPC) and the US Patent and Trademark Office (USPTO). As South African intellectual property expert Andrew Rens explained to me, part of the reason that the scope of patent ownership and novelty differs between the United States and South Africa is that South Africa is a non-examining country, which means that "no review of novelty or other requirements for patentability takes place prior to registration. A lack of novelty can be the basis for a court challenge to the validity of a patent that has already been registered, but then only if those who wish to challenge the patent have the means to launch a court challenge."[30] In contrast, the United States requires patent applications to be examined for novelty prior to approval, which explains why prior art references or "priority data" are listed in the 2002 US Hoodia patent document but not in the South African patent application granted in 1999. Another important distinction Ren pointed out is that given this lack of prior review, the validity of a patent filed in South Africa can be challenged only through a formal court proceeding, which can be costly and thus beyond the reach of many indigenous groups.

As this comparison demonstrates, the material and technical forms of patent law make patent ownership historically contingent and particular. In other words, patent law, rather than representing some universal or natural legal right, is shaped by varied nation-state histories, interests, and governance. The rhetoric of universalism and the harmonization of patents promoted by the United States and global institutions such as the World Trade Organization (WTO) and the World Intellectual Property Organization (WIPO) obscures these particulars of power and how the patent law rules of one country can enable the taking of resources from another. Closer attention to the materialities or technicalities of statutory patent language, therefore, can help us better identify inequalities inherent in existing patent law practices and potential sites for change under the law.

Patent Ownership within CSIR and San Ways of Knowing

The dichotomous legal thinking that privileges CSIR knowledge over that of San knowledge also fails to recognize ways in which these two forms of knowledge are more alike than different. Although patent law implies that indigenous peoples' knowledge is traditional and rooted in past ancestral histories, a close look at CSIR's 2002 US Hoodia patent document reveals that its patented Hoodia knowledge is also rooted in ancestral histories— in this case, a past of antiobesity research manifested through its list of prior art sources. This list includes nineteen US patents from 1978 to 2000, ranging from new milkweed plant varieties to a chewing gum for treating obesity, and forty-six academic antiobesity studies in fields such as chemistry, botany, and medicine, ranging in topic from steroidal glycosides to the constituents of *Asclepiadaceae* plants. Patent officials at the USPTO examined these sources and the application's constructed histories of past obesity research to determine if knowledge of Hoodia as an appetite suppressant was previously known or anticipated. The materialities of patent documents thus reveal that CSIR scientific knowledge, like San knowledge, is generated from customs and practices emanating from its particular location and history.

Yet this examination also reveals not only that both CSIR knowledge and San knowledge are rooted in traditional pasts but that both are dynamic as well. CSIR scientists' knowledge of Hoodia at a molecular scale emanated from changing understandings of antiobesity research, and their knowledge of Hoodia's efficacy as an appetite suppressant was informed by past inventions. These past inventions include the use of chemical compounds such as phenylglycines and oxetanones to treat obesity and the invention of different processes for preparing chemical compounds and for extracting chemical properties from medicinal sources found in nature.[31] As CSIR documents and my interviews reveal, CSIR understandings of the plant's properties also changed over time, as researchers explored first its nutritional benefits for local laborers and then its potential to treat obesity. New understandings of Hoodia also developed through later collaborations between CSIR and Phytopharm, who together invented ways to use Hoodia properties to reduce gastric acid secretion in humans and animals.[32] A few months before Unilever terminated its Hoodia research in 2008, Phytopharm also filed Hoodia-based patents for new diabetes treatments in humans and new processes for making extracts with higher concentrations of steroidal glycosides and improving their flavor for use in food.[33] These patent applications, by situating CSIR's Hoodia knowledge within an ancestral past of obesity research and customary scientific practice and within a dynamic history that changes with every new Hoodia-related invention, thus render a vision of science as simultaneously modern and nonmodern.

San understandings of !Khoba are similarly rooted both in tradition and in change and flux. In conversation with me, ≠Khomani San individuals in Andriesville, South Africa (near the Namibian border), articulated multiple understandings of !Khoba as food, medicine, and appetite suppressant. Arrie Tities, for instance, reported having learned about !Khoba from ancestors who used it to "stay for many days in the veld."[34] Tommy Busakhwe said his plant knowledge had come from his mother, who "was the one who had the knowledge about medicinal plants."[35] Andries Steenkamp told me he had learned about Hoodia from his grandmother, who "told [him] many things about Hoodia."[36] As these responses indicate, certain San understandings have flowed from particular and gendered ancestral pasts. San mothers have depended on local plants to feed their small children while teaching them about the plants with which they coexist, making those plants an important facet of relations between mothers and their children and between members of the community. These conversations also revealed that San Hoodia knowledge has changed over time, becoming fused with CSIR Hoodia knowledge. Tities, for example, told me he had learned about Hoodia as a plant to treat obesity from "the technology people."[37] San ways of using the plant are also multiple, based on the changing historical conditions of San peoples. Tities and Busakhwe reported, for instance, that Hoodia has many uses—such as to "less[en] your hunger" when hunting, to satisfy "greedy children" who want food, and to provide "water" and "energy" while in the veld.[38]

Comparing ≠Khomani San uses of !Khoba and those proposed for various patented Hoodia-related inventions reveals that both San and scientists possess multiple ways of knowing and using the plant. Their ways of knowing Hoodia share attributes and participate in what Madhavi Sunder refers to as the "invention of traditional knowledge."[39] Both forms of knowledge production are thus also inventive, dynamic, and evolving, reflecting and sparking new understanding and uses of Hoodia/!Khoba that align with local interests.

Patent Ownership and the Different Materialities of Hoodia

These similarities between CSIR and San knowledge become less visible when examining the scientists' description of their invention in their patent applications. In both the United States and South Africa, temporary patents may be granted if the details of the invention are publicly disclosed and made available, as through Internet databases. The identical description of the same Hoodia-related invention in the 2002 US and 1999 South African patent applications demonstrate the divergence between CSIR and San ways of knowing Hoodia and its associated materiality, as isolated molecule in the former and as a "natural" plant in the latter.

To obtain patent rights under US law, an inventor must "isolate and purify" a product from nature and demonstrate that it is "markedly different" from its natural state.[40] Plant-related patent rights therefore extend only to the isolated and purified element of the plant, not to the plant itself. South African law implies a similar standard by specifying that mere discoveries cannot be patented.[41] According to this doctrine, inventors must isolate and purify Hoodia to its chemical compounds. Although the physical materiality of these chemical compounds is visible to scientists in the lab, in the domain of patent law, this materiality becomes an abstract chemical structural formula, as shown at the beginning of this chapter. Both the US and South African applications describe a "novel compound" of a "steroidal trisaccharide" that has appetite-suppressant properties; detail several other chemical compounds and their structural formulae; and explain how their "modifications to the molecule" enhance its properties for suppressing appetite.[42]

In both countries, patent ownership can attach not just to chemical compounds but also to extraction processes. Thus, the patent description explains that CSIR inventors "homogenized [plant material] in the presence of a suitable solvent, for example, a methanol/methylene chloride solvent, by means of a device such as a Waring blender."[43] It describes how they used filtration methods or centrifugation to separate the extraction solution from the plant material and used a rotary evaporator to remove the chloride solvent, in order to produce an extract that they then further purified through methanol/hexane extraction. According to this description, CSIR inventors also prepared an extract by "pressing collected plant material to separate sap from solid plant material" and then drying the extract to remove the moisture to form a "free-flowing powder."[44] This latter process appears similar to the methods of one ≠Khomani San woman, Sanna Witbooi, who explained to me that you "must clean [!Khoba] up and then you put it in the sun so you must dry it out and then you make powder with it."[45]

Hoodia patent ownership therefore depends on these technological modifications of Hoodia to reduce the plant to its chemical and molecular properties. What the law sanctions as inventive and novel is the way in which CSIR scientists manipulated the plant to isolate its productive chemical properties for suppressing appetite. This inventiveness, in other words, is based on what Nikolas Rose describes as new processes of "molecularization" within contemporary bioeconomies.[46] What the law certifies as modern, inventive, and novel are CSIR understandings of Hoodia molecules, in contrast to San knowledge of the plant's visible properties. These processes of molecularization therefore become epistemological boundary markers, valuing CSIR ways of knowing more highly that those of San. By codifying these normative epistemological practices, patent law thereby reinforces the binary of culture versus nature and Western views of whose knowledge matters most. As Thom van Dooren notes, such boundary making continues to classify indigenous peoples as closer to nature, relegated to "work *in* it, never *on* it."[47]

Although both South African and US Hoodia patent applications give similar descriptions of the invention that reveal different ways of knowing attached to distinct plant materialities, they differ in the drafting of claims, demonstrating how patent ownership is contingent. The precise drafting and wording of a claimed invention determines the parameters of patent ownership and its containment of nature. Each patent document specifies the scope of the Hoodia-related invention in precise but different ways in the process of laying claim to Hoodia's particular chemical compositions. Hoodia patent ownership is defined in the US application by 58 claims and in the South African one by 132 claims. This difference may be partially explained by a need to draft claims more concisely to satisfy patent examination in the United States. Claims in the South African patent provide more detail on the scientific processes of extraction, such as outlining a solvent extraction step involving methylene chloride or ethyl acetate, followed by chromatic separation.[48] In contrast, the US patent describes the same process in less technical language, as referring to an extract from which "all the non-active impurities have been removed" and in which the plant has been reduced to a "free-flowing powder."[49] The US patent contains fewer and less-detailed descriptions of technological processes and entirely excludes some of the extraction processes claimed in the South African patent. For instance, the South African patent specifies a process of preparing an extract from Hoodia by "pressing collected plant material to separate sap from solid plant material."[50] This process and the specific steps for preparing specific steroids, chemical compounds, and some carbohydrates are absent from the US patent claims.

Conclusion

Through the patenting of Hoodia, CSIR scientists asserted belonging and attachment to a changing nation-state aiming to establish itself as a producer of science and innovation within the global neoliberal economy. The patenting of Hoodia therefore can be understood not along neat lines of Global North/Global South or elites/nonelites, but rather within the contradictions, integral to the production of science projects in South Africa, that make for a different way of doing science. Even within the contradictions of Hoodia research, there are similarities, however. In this chapter, I engaged with the materialities of patent law through attention to different scales of nation-state jurisdictions, divergent ways of knowing, and biochemical states of plants to show how patent ownership rights are not so natural after all; rather, they are historical, sociocultural processes that have material facets and effects. Examining the materialities of patent law, I demonstrated how CSIR and San ways of knowing are in fact similar, as each is connected to past knowledge traditions and both are historically contingent. My analysis sought to challenge dichotomous assumptions of nature/culture, modern/nonmodern, Western/indigenous that have been historically used to subordinate indigenous peoples, women, and people of color, while demonstrating how those assumptions undergird patent law and serve to reinforce hierarchies of knowledge production. Studying different ways of knowing Hoodia further, the next chapter focuses on how scientists with Phytopharm, Pfizer, and Unilever produced new meanings and materialities for Hoodia as both solid drug and liquid food.

4

Botanical Drug Discovery of Hoodia, from Solid Drug to Liquid Food

> The healers had a song about a spider spinning his web, to catch
> a fly or other prey. The song was about how the healer hopes to
> see the illness and catch it, then throw it away, just like a spider
> catches prey in its web. As fast as the spider has to be to catch that
> prey, just as fast as the healer has to be to see the illness and catch
> it. Also, illness could be like a lizard that runs around a tree. If you
> want to catch it, it is there, already on the other side. You had to be
> very skillful because illness could run all around the tree. The people
> then had to clap loudly so the illness can stand still to be caught.
>
> —MENEPUTO (!XUN)

IN 2004, HOODIA APPEARED IN TWO DIFFERENT MODALITIES IN A single image on the Phytopharm website—half of it in pill form, representing its botanical drug promise, and the other half as a succulent plant, signifying its natural properties. Coalesced into a single image, these materialities of Hoodia stood as a fitting pictorial portrayal of the company's apt moniker and tag line: "Welcome to Phytopharm—Inspired by Nature." The image thus stood for the promise of Hoodia and provided a narrative of linear progress from Hoodia plants to an antiobesity botanical drug. The image would soon disappear from its site, though, following Pfizer's decision to terminate their partnership and its Hoodia research. When Phytopharm shortly thereafter announced its partnership with Unilever in 2004, it replaced the image with rows of growing Hoodia plants, marking its shift in focus from the scale of a botanical drug to a functional food as Unilever began producing large supplies of Hoodia plants and testing a Hoodia-infused yogurt drink that could be marketed as a weight-loss aid.[1]

This chapter employs three different modalities of Hoodia—as plant, drug, and food—as methodological starting points for a feminist decolonial technoscience analysis of the rise and fall of the expectations of the scientists who studied Hoodia and all the parties who hoped to benefit financially from it. It begins by examining how the research partners' understandings and representations of Hoodia reproduced nature/culture binaries in their attempt to possess Hoodia and make it belong to commercial scientific worlds. It then analyzes how the Hoodia plant resisted commercial desires to possess it—or, to use Meneputo's metaphor in the epigraph, how Hoodia refused to stand still and be caught. Examining Hoodia research along a temporal dimension, this analysis offers another demonstration of how notions of nature and culture continually shift and reflect mechanisms of power.

Hoodia Pronouncements:
From Botanical Drug to Functional Food

The previous chapter examined how CSIR scientists sought belonging as producers of science through the patenting of Hoodia, but this chapter tells the story of the research development that followed and considers the role of Phytopharm, Pfizer, and Unilever in the making of Hoodia. In June 1997, CSIR partnered with Phytopharm, a UK-based company engaged in pharmaceutical and functional food development, to commercially develop Hoodia into a botanical drug to treat obesity.[2] The Hoodia research collaboration was a major development for CSIR. Phytopharm's founder and CEO, Richard Dixey, a research scientist and self-described Buddhist, lauded the partnership as a testament to the value of traditional healing and plant medicines. In my conversations with Dixey, he explained that from its inception, Phytopharm was aimed at "short-circuiting the drug discovery process" by developing drugs not from synthetic or highly purified chemicals but from extracts of plant matter and their complex chemical compositions.[3] This goal required Phytopharm to work closely with the US Food and Drug Administration (FDA) to develop new regulatory guidelines for botanical drugs that would allow Phytopharm and others to develop plant-based drugs whose active ingredients were harder to isolate and thus more difficult to test clinically.[4]

According to Petro Terblanche, then director of CSIR's Bio/Chemtek unit, several pharmaceutical companies had approached CSIR about licensing the rights to use the patented Hoodia technology.[5] One, for instance, offered to pay CSIR $4,000 for the right to do the development work themselves and then pay a 3 percent royalty if they were successful, treating CSIR scientists solely as resource providers (in the form of their patented Hoodia invention) rather than as collaborative producers of science. Other companies, Terblanche reported, wanted to buy the patent rights outright and thus were even less interested in engaging with CSIR scientists.

According to Terblanche, CSIR had chosen instead to work with Phytopharm because Phytopharm proposed a collaboration that would ensure technology transfer and capacity building among CSIR scientists. In her words, Phytopharm was different from the other corporate suitors because they said, "No, we want to be your development partner"; that is, they agreed to collaborate with CSIR scientists as partners in the making of Hoodia-based products rather than merely extracting their patented technology. As Terblanche further noted, the agreements between Phytopharm and CSIR were joint development agreements, which she had signed "because firstly, they were my partner, [so] it will transfer knowledge and information to South Africa to do natural product development. That's why I went with Phytopharm. It was a much less lucrative deal than it could've been with the two or three other pharmaceutical companies." Reflecting on the partnership, Richard Dixey expressed a similar sentiment, praising CSIR for its Hoodia research and collaboration with Phytopharm researchers.[6]

The choice of Phytopharm as a development partner aligned with CSIR's desire for recognition as the inventors of Hoodia technology. A joint development agreement would give CSIR a greater opportunity to belong as a producer of science within both the international drug-making community and a South African politics increasingly focused on promoting innovation. But the ways in which Phytopharm represented its Hoodia research to the public and to potential partners and investors ultimately led to this promise being only partially fulfilled. The relationship between Phytopharm and CSIR becomes clearer through an understanding of how Phytopharm articulated its Hoodia research.

Hoodia as Pharmaceutical Drug

In June 1997, Phytopharm announced in a press release that they had entered into a joint agreement with CSIR to work together to transform a "naturally occurring appetite suppressant" into a "prescription medicine" that would be produced in South Africa and then marketed to consumers "world-wide."[7] In the early days of Hoodia research, CSIR scientists were both hopeful of its potential as a global botanical drug and eager to keep its production within South Africa. According to the press release, CSIR would retain exclusive marketing rights for an appetite-suppressant product in South Africa, while Phytopharm would pay CSIR licensing fees to sell it in other markets. Although this joint arrangement would bolster CSIR's participation in South African markets and was in line with its market model of research and development, it also limited CSIR from becoming a global leader in Hoodia and from realizing the full potential profits from selling Hoodia products to the estimated "70 million obese adults in the Western world" with a market share that Phytopharm announced was worth anywhere from "$4 billion up to $30 billion (which includes the over-the-counter market)."

In the same press release, Phytopharm also publicly announced that they had entered a more expansive agreement with CSIR in which they would "collaborate in the development of botanical medicines" beyond Hoodia-related products. CSIR had recently started an ethnobotanical screening program to examine various veld plants for medicinal properties and had agreed to give Phytopharm the right of first refusal to develop drugs from any promising plants they might discover. Phytopharm and CSIR therefore envisioned a more expansive and long-lasting partnership in the development of plant-based drug products that would further strengthen the position of both in the global botanical drug industry.

But because Phytopharm operated on a much smaller scale than many other biotechnology companies, and CSIR even more so, they would need a larger partner to help them develop and commercialize Hoodia into a drug. Thus, a year after Phytopharm and CSIR began working together, Phytopharm announced that a third party was joining their collaboration: Pfizer, a US-based pharmaceutical company best known for such highly profitable drugs as Lipitor (for lowering cholesterol) and

Viagra (for treating erectile dysfunction). According to their August 1998 press release, Phytopharm and CSIR would now work with Pfizer to develop and commercialize Hoodia's active compounds into an obesity drug they provisionally named P57, which meant Phytopharm Product #57, shifting the emphasis from plant to product.[8] Pfizer's entrance as a global development partner provided the capital necessary to manufacture and market the product globally, marking a significant turning point in the development of such a drug.

The partnership also represented a significant business opportunity for Phytopharm, which had begun trading on the London Stock Exchange only the year before. CEO Dixey, in the same press release, declared the partnership a "landmark in the development of Phytopharm." The announcement also noted that per their agreement, Pfizer would pay Phytopharm "up to $32 million in license fees and milestone payments" and $7 million to start an early stage development program for P57 and to grant Phytopharm rights to royalty payments on all future sales. The Phytopharm-Pfizer agreement also provided a further opportunity for CSIR, as Phytopharm, tasked with much of the initial work, would need to work closely with CSIR scientists to further study and test the plant. Pfizer's involvement therefore meant bigger opportunities for each party as they set their sights on developing P57 "globally as a prescription drug for obesity," though consumers in the United States offered "the largest opportunity for obesity drugs" given its estimated "35 to 65 million obese individuals" and potential market share for pharmaceutical drugs estimated "to be worth in excess of $3 billion."[9]

In their early announcements about these partnerships and efforts, Phytopharm represented Hoodia both as a drug product and as a South African plant, describing their goal as developing P57 into "an appetite suppressant derived from an extract of a South African plant."[10] These representations of Hoodia at the two materialities of potential drug and natural plant rhetorically supported the company's mission of producing botanical drugs inspired by nature while still presenting culture and nature as distinct. Whereas CSIR's *patenting* of Hoodia properties had required them to make claims to knowing Hoodia as isolated molecules and thereby distance their invention from Hoodia plants found in nature, the development of Hoodia into a marketable product was contingent on understanding Hoodia as both nature and culture.

As it continued its Hoodia drug research, however, Phytopharm began to place greater emphasis on Hoodia as P57 in its efforts to make it into an antiobesity drug. For instance, it announced on October 13, 1998, that it had started Phase I clinical trials related to the "anti-obesity drug candidate (P57)" without mentioning its connection to Hoodia plants.[11] This new emphasis served the rhetorical function of presenting P57 to the public and investors as an innovative drug candidate, stressing the precise scientific methods and objective research processes involved in transforming patented P57 into a commercial weight-loss drug and reinforcing the authority and expertise of the scientists who had invented it. This focus on P57 thus more closely resembled and reinforced the assumptions of patent ownership that had guided CSIR's patent applications.

As Phytopharm's Hoodia research continued and clinical tests yielded positive results, the focus of the company's communications about Hoodia again shifted to the plant in nature, emphasizing the company's mission of producing plant-based products. The focus also shifted in light of benefit-sharing negotiations between the South African San Council and CSIR, bringing attention to Hoodia as a plant from nature connected to San peoples. By April 2002, Phytopharm was no longer referring to the plant in general terms as a "South African plant" or as P57, instead referring to Hoodia gordonii by name, announcing plans to grow and cultivate Hoodia plants in South Africa, and including visual representations of Hoodia plants on its website.[12] With the success of Phase I clinical trials, Phytopharm's communications to the public and investors began to emphasize its goal of increasing the production of Hoodia "raw materials by 300 percent,"[13] thus again reconfiguring notions of nature and culture when Hoodia development shifted toward the need to cultivate supplies of Hoodia plants as a raw material.

As the South African San Council and CSIR agreed to benefit sharing, Phytopharm shifted the focus of its communications again to emphasize the relationship of Hoodia to San peoples. By 2004, Phytopharm began referring on its website to the "San Bushmen of the Kalahari desert" who had sometimes used Hoodia plants "as a food" in times of "hardship, or being away from familiar areas."[14] They also mentioned the San-CSIR agreement and noted that San "traditional knowledge first led to the investigation of the plant." Phytopharm thus reconfigured notions of nature and culture once more by connecting Hoodia plants to San cultures, albeit in a limited manner without elaborating on actual San histories, cultures, or heritage.

Hoodia as Functional Food

Only four months after the signing of the San-CSIR benefit-sharing agreement, and despite initial clinical findings that Hoodia was safe and generally well tolerated, Pfizer closed its Natureceuticals group and terminated its Hoodia research program, citing business reasons.[15] It would take Phytopharm and CSIR more than a year to find a new development partner; they signed an agreement with Unilever, a multinational consumer goods company based in the Netherlands and England, in December 2004.[16] Unilever sought to develop the plant as a functional food to expand its SlimFast brand of products.[17] Stressing that he was speaking individually and not on behalf of Unilever, Kevin Poovey, lead project manager for this Hoodia research, told me, "We saw the only chance of getting this approved for food use was to use a natural extract from the plant and argue it was a food 'ingredient' and not an 'additive.'"[18] Whereas Pfizer had focused on developing Hoodia active compounds into a drug, Unilever aimed to develop a natural extract from the plant that it could use as a food ingredient.

This shift from developing Hoodia as a drug to developing it as a food meant Unilever had to navigate multiple areas of law that constructed varied meanings for Hoodia. To sell a Hoodia-based functional food product, Unilever would have to meet legal requirements imposed by the FDA, which sets different rules for pharmaceuticals than for foods, and different rules for food additives than for food ingredients.[19] According to Poovey, Unilever was interested in developing Hoodia as a food ingredient rather than an additive in part because FDA regulates food additives more strictly than food ingredients. Unilever also continued to deploy patent law to secure support for the project from investors. Identifying CSIR's Hoodia patent as a key driver in Unilever's decision to take up the project, Poovey told me that "there's no one in their right mind going to spend that money on a project if they feel they can't get a return on it. And one way of getting a return, of course, is to be exclusive. You know, you're not going to spend a hundred million dollars and then find somebody who has only spent two million dollars could come to market tomorrow. . . . If you're not able to get intellectual property on the project, it simply won't happen."[20] By licensing the CSIR Hoodia patents, Phytopharm was able to also grant Unilever an exclusive license to develop Hoodia properties into a weight-loss product and protect Unilever from investing in a product that others might also have been working on, thus demonstrating that, as Dixey pointed out, "what drives all these relationships is the regulatory pathway."[21]

To navigate the project through these two different legal orders, Unilever was compelled to construct Hoodia as a food ingredient and as a patented object, reinforcing separate meanings of Hoodia as nature and culture. The FDA's less stringent requirements for food ingredients imply that they are more "natural" than food additives. Unilever therefore made strategic moves to characterize Hoodia as a food ingredient so as to construct Hoodia extracts as natural. Yet Unilever was also hoping to develop its own Hoodia-based patents, which would require instead reinforcing the notion of Hoodia as a cultural invention to satisfy patent law distinctions between what can be patented (culture) and what cannot (nature). Unilever scientists thus constructed Hoodia as both natural and innovative within these different areas of law, constructing Hoodia as nature and culture in distinct ways to successfully negotiate the requirements of different domains of the law, thereby continuing to maintain the binary of nature and culture.

While constructing Hoodia in different ways to meet different legal requirements, Unilever's business plans also began to emphasize Hoodia more as a cultivated plant and to develop supplier relationships with South African farmers. They formed some relationships with San in South Africa, but much of their focus was on building relationships with farmers.[22] During our conversation, Poovey told me that Unilever had focused on two primary goals: ensuring the "safety and efficacy" of the product and generating a "supply chain" of Hoodia plants.[23] To accomplish the latter, Unilever needed to secure large amounts of Hoodia for its development efforts, and it contracted with several large and small farms in South Africa to grow Hoodia plants. These relationships, according to Poovey, were also meant to "put money back into the region" and to "invest in South Africa."[24] Some of the farms, he explained, were "in very remote locations with quite high unemployment. So the mere project itself would have generated quite a lot of wealth, I think, for, you know, poor people in South Africa."[25] According to Poovey, Unilever had made sure that these farmers were "aware

that there was a possibility all along that we might have to stop" the research, given the uncertainties of product development, but also made a
commitment that "any farmers involved with us on the project would not
end up worse off than they were when we started the project."[26] Unilever
thereby provided agrotechnical jobs to various low-income communities
in South Africa, investing close to €5 million in Hoodia farming operations, including two farms managed by CSIR in the Pella and Onseepkans
districts along the Orange River near the Namibian border.[27]

The making of Hoodia into a functional food therefore depended on
the materiality of Hoodia as a cultivated plant. As Unilever began to emphasize its plans to cultivate Hoodia plants, it shifted notions of nature
and culture once again, keeping them dichotomous. As Unilever continued
to develop Hoodia as a functional food, scientists also became attached to
Hoodia as cultivated. The physical materialities of Hoodia as a functional
food and a cultivated plant were now entangled but remained unequal.
Although Unilever needed large amounts of Hoodia plants, its focus was
on developing a food product derived from Hoodia extracts containing
steroidal glycosides; thus, South Africans once again became merely sup-
pliers of a raw resource. By placing more value on the functional food than
on the plant, the market reinforced the distinction that viewed the process
of making the new product as more innovative and the growing of plants
as more natural.

Hoodia Refusals: From Solid Capsule Drug to Liquid Yogurt Drink

Yet, as this feminist decolonial technoscience analysis will show, Hoodia
plants refused these attachments and did not act according to these
commercial desires. To make these points, the analysis uses the model of
materiality discussed in chapter 2, which draws on Karen Barad's notion
of agency as an enactment or doing by analyzing how Hoodia's steroidal
glycosides affected the social worlds of botanical drug discovery.[28] By
studying how Hoodia's actions refused to align with commercial desires,
the analysis examines nonhumans as subjects that act rather than objects
to be acted upon, expanding on what Alaimo and Hekman refer to as the
"agentic force" of nonhumans by demonstrating that plants are not merely
reactive but organize and shape our worlds.[29] Without assigning liberal

notions of agency to nonhuman actors, this approach finds that Hoodia's steroidal glycoside molecules were both the focus and the undoing of Hoodia pharmaceutical research, as these active compositions refused to become the antiobesity product they were desired to be.

Hoodia in Solid Form as Pharmaceutical Antiobesity Drug

As I sat across from Vinesh Maharaj (now a professor at the University of Pretoria), he explained that the preferred route to production of a pharmaceutical "is synthesis, because of the risk associated with natural supply."[30] If scientists could synthetically produce the patented Hoodia molecules in the lab, they would not have to rely on obtaining large quantities of cultivated Hoodia, which are considered more unpredictable because plants continually change in response to such environmental conditions as floods, droughts, rains, and pests. Although plants must produce primary metabolites such as starch, glucose, and proteins to function, Maharaj explained, they also produce secondary metabolites in response to those outside stressors, such as an essential oil to ward off certain insects—or, in the case of *Hoodia gordonii*, active steroidal glycosides that combat stressors such as insects and droughts. This unpredictability of plants leads pharmaceutical companies to prefer a more stable supply of synthetically produced molecules for their development processes. Hoodia's complex chemical makeup was particularly difficult to reproduce synthetically. In the production of a pharmaceutical, medicinal chemists begin by trying to produce a plant's active molecules, such as Hoodia's steroidal glycosides, synthetically. Steroidal glycosides are molecules in which sugars are connected to other sugars or nonsugars through different glycosidic bonds, which form complex spatial arrangements of stereochemical configurations in which a molecule's atoms form different attachments that make up the precise structure of the molecule and its active chemicals. When exposed to an environmental stressor, a plant may produce an enzyme that activates some of these chemicals or leaves some inactive. In the case of Hoodia, scientists hoped that these activated chemicals in Hoodia could reduce weight in humans, but they would first need to synthesize its relevant steroidal glycoside molecules.

Although scientists were eventually able to synthesize and reproduce Hoodia's active chemicals in the lab, the plant's complex stereochemical centers made synthesis difficult, and therefore Phytopharm, as mentioned above, focused on botanical rather than synthetic drug discovery. Maharaj had first attempted to synthesize the active chemicals in *Trichocaulon piliferum,* a plant that, he explained, "was just about extinct . . . and I tried to synthesize it, and after thirty-seven steps and five grueling years, I managed to get 7 milligrams of the almost complete molecule in a little bottle." What makes the similar molecular arrangements in *Hoodia gordonii* so difficult to synthesize is that the plant's steroidal glycoside molecules "had many stereogenic centers on the molecule. Synthetic chemists can often synthesize complex molecules but often it is a challenge." The multiple spatial chemical arrangements of Hoodia's steroidal glycoside molecules and the agentic actions of those molecules made its synthetic reproduction particularly arduous.

Another way in which Hoodia chemical compositions thwarted commercial efforts to convert them into an antiobesity product was that they caused adverse effects when tested on human subjects in Phytopharm-sponsored clinical studies from 1999 to 2003. Although Phytopharm did not publish these findings, they provided CSIR with detailed clinical reports. According to Maharaj, the reports concluded that Hoodia was "generally safe and well tolerated, though in some subjects adverse events and tolerability issues were noted," and that the medication did not always reduce appetite, caloric intake, or body weight.[31]

In its early clinical studies, Phytopharm gave clinical subjects a single Hoodia weight-loss capsule daily at different dosage levels. In one study from October 1998 to February 1999, researchers gave clinical subjects a single Hoodia capsule with one of four possible doses (10, 30, 100, or 300 mg) and concluded that each dosage level was well tolerated and safe.[32] Although the Hoodia-based capsules caused a few subjects to experience flatulence, nausea, and headaches, they showed no serious adverse effects. Instead, the problem was that Hoodia failed to be quickly absorbed into the body and reduce body weight. Similar results were found in a second study, in which researchers gave subjects a single Hoodia capsule but considerably increased the doses (to 500, 1000, 2000, and 4000 mg),[33] which again produced no serious adverse effects but also had no clear effect on hunger, satiety, or mood. Hoodia produced similar results in a blind study a few months later, in which subjects were given either a placebo or 500 mg of Hoodia in a hard gelatin capsule.[34]

Maharaj's experience and these clinical reports reveal that Hoodia chemical compositions acted in ways that resisted the scientists' efforts. Whether because of the steroidal glycosides themselves, their forms as solid extracts, their delivery in single dosages, or even their interactions with other additives, Hoodia chemical compositions did not cause weight loss among study participants. As scientists acted on the plant in an attempt to make it do something, the plant acted in a different manner. The Hoodia chemical compositions tested in the single-dose studies caused some to experience flatulence, nausea, and headaches and caused scientists concern when it did not reduce weight.

Although Hoodia provoked these effects and concerns, Phytopharm scientists remained hopeful about its other potential effects and continued their Hoodia testing, this time by giving clinical subjects multiple doses of Hoodia over a several-day period. In this round of testing, scientists found that giving subjects a higher dose of Hoodia over a period of five days significantly reduced their calorie intake.[35] They were further encouraged by the results of giving subjects Hoodia capsules over a fifteen-day period, a regime that reduced calorie intake even more.[36] But even though Hoodia properties were now causing weight loss and thus complying with the scientists' commercial interests, they did not align with those interests entirely. They continued to cause side effects in some clinical subjects, such as paresthesia (tingling or burning of skin), taste perversion, and isolated reversible hyperbilirubinemia (high levels of bilirubin in blood). Despite these side effects, Pfizer continued to conduct clinical trials in March 2003 to determine the most appropriate dosage level.[37]

However, only four months later, in July 2003, Phytopharm announced that Pfizer was dropping the project and returning the exclusive licensing rights to Phytopharm.[38] Jasjit S. Bindra, head of Pfizer's Hoodia development team, detailed his concerns in the New York Times that Hoodia "could be a potent appetite suppressant. But there were indications of unwanted effects on the liver caused by other components, which could not be easily removed from the supplement. Clearly, hoodia has a long way to go before it can earn approval from the Food and Drug Administration."[39] According to Bindra, the safety concern was how the plant's active chemicals interacted with the other components used in making the extracts. Although the clinical studies discussed above did not suggest serious adverse effects, Pfizer communicated its concern over obtaining FDA approval for a Hoodia antiobesity drug. By having undesired effects on the human liver, Hoodia thus refused commercial promises by acting in relation to the other chemicals around it rather than in an autonomous fashion. Hoodia chemical compositions thus played a role in the undoing of its development.

In addition to the actions of the Pfizer scientists and the material qualities of the plant, economic and structural factors also played a role in the denouement of the corporation's Hoodia research program. Pfizer announced that although the clinical trials of Hoodia P57 were positive, the company had decided to close its Natureceuticals group, and the Hoodia development program therefore no longer fit its business objectives. Pfizer's decision to end its plans to develop a Hoodia-based pharmaceutical had significant material repercussions for its partners in South Africa. It meant the end of the large clinical supplies unit Pfizer had established at CSIR, which, according to Maharaj, was the "first FDA approvable herbal manufacturing center in the world" and had been expected to bring important benefits to South Africa in the form of jobs, manufacturing centers, and financial revenue.[40] It called into doubt the projected benefit sharing with San peoples, which were premised on the commercial success of Hoodia-based pharmaceuticals. The hopes of both thus shifted to Unilever's research into the materiality of Hoodia as a functional food in the form of a liquid yogurt drink.

Hoodia in Liquid Form as a Functional Food Yogurt Drink

More than a year after Pfizer terminated its Hoodia research, Unilever began to reinvent Hoodia once more, developing it into a functional food that could be marketed to curb appetite and reduce weight. In particular, Unilever scientists focused their energies on developing a Hoodia-based weight-loss yogurt drink. Unilever had previously held a significant share of the weight-loss supplement market through its SlimFast products, and it hoped that Hoodia would help the company reestablish that market position. In its licensing agreement with Phytopharm, Unilever promised Phytopharm an initial $12.5 million out of a potential $40 million in payments and an undisclosed amount of royalty payments on all sales of Hoodia-based products sold by Unilever, an arrangement that raised Phytopharm's stock price and prompted one Unilever executive to go work for Phytopharm.[41]

The promise of a Hoodia-based functional food would soon fade, however, as Unilever began its clinical testing of Hoodia. In a 2008 study, researchers gave inpatient participants a raspberry-flavored yogurt drink that contained 1110 mg of purified Hoodia extract one hour before breakfast and another one hour before lunch for fifteen days.[42] The Hoodia extract consisted of a mixture of steroid glycosides (79.3 percent of the extract's total weight), fatty acids, alkanes, plant sterols, and alcohols. To reconfigure the extract into a yogurt drink, researchers combined it with several other additives, including pectins, sugars, sweeteners, yogurt, colorants, and other flavors. The Unilever researchers reported that the Hoodia-based liquid drink caused some participants to experience disturbances in skin sensation, headache, dizziness, and nausea and significantly raised their heart rate, blood pressure, and bilirubin levels to above normal. Although the researchers did not consider these side effects severe or serious, they were testing Hoodia as a functional food, and unlike consumers of a pharmaceutical drug, who are informed of possible side effects and monitored by a physician, consumers of a weight-loss yogurt drink do not expect to suffer any undesirable side effects.

At least as disappointing was the finding that Hoodia as a yogurt drink did not have a more significant effect on the participant's energy intake or body weight than a placebo. Although Hoodia did act to reduce caloric intake and weight, so did the placebo. Clinicians found that the Hoodia-based yogurt drink and the placebo reduced energy intake by 24 percent and 18 percent, respectively, and reduced body weight by 1.2 ± 1.3 kg (2.6 lbs. ± 2.8 lbs.) and 1.2 ± 1.2 kg (2.6 lbs. ± 2.6 lbs.), respectively. Thus, the causal link between the Hoodia yogurt drink and weight loss was uncertain; researchers could not say for sure if the yogurt drink or some other factor had been responsible for the effect.

As evidenced by these clinical studies, Hoodia once again resisted scientists' efforts to transform it into a marketable object, this time hindering Unilever's efforts to reinvent it into a functional food. Although Hoodia in the form of a solid botanical drug appeared to have the slow-release properties necessary to reduce weight, the more quickly absorbed and metabolized Hoodia steroidal glycosides in a liquid formulation appeared to produce unwanted side effects and not have a significant effect on weight loss.

Again, Hoodia properties could not be contained or controlled for purposes of the market. The liveliness of the Hoodia steroid glycosides and their entangled interactions with pectins, sugars, and flavorings rendered its development questionable. By once again foiling plans for its commercialization, Hoodia also indirectly reduced the value of CSIR's patent ownership rights over it. Although CSIR's inventors maintained control over their patented invention, when Hoodia's chemical molecules did not cooperate with the scientists' claim that they suppressed human appetite, it became more difficult for CSIR and Phytopharm scientists to maintain or generate interest from commercial partners. Thus, on December 12, 2008, two months after the conclusion of the failed clinical trials, Phytopharm publicly announced that Unilever had terminated its Hoodia research.[43]

Conclusion

As this chapter has shown, the joint partnership between CSIR and Phytopharm and later with Pfizer and Unilever brought CSIR scientists into the global fold of Hoodia researchers, but their lack of decision-making control over the development of Hoodia meant that their belonging and recognition as producers of science remained contingent and unequal. Examining Hoodia research through the lens of the nature/culture binary also showed that even as scientists began to acknowledge Hoodia plants and San peoples on their websites, they continued to present both as mere sources of raw material. As such, this analysis provides yet another example of what Ruha Benjamin refers to as the "contradictory tendencies" of postcolonial technoscience, wherein those involved are simultaneously empowered and disempowered. Yet this feminist decolonial technoscience approach extends an analysis of these contradictory tendencies even further by examining how Hoodia chemical compositions acted in ways that refused and contradicted the commercial desires that sought to contain them. In doing so, it contests the patenting and naturalization of Hoodia as mere object by examining the natureculture worlds of Hoodia steroidal glycosides as they shape and are shaped here by science, law, the marketplace, and San peoples. By examining how nature informs law and science, it also demonstrates how these are historically contingent rather than natural processes, and thus that alternative ways of doing science and law are possible. Extending this analysis, the next chapter examines how the unpredictability of Hoodia plants complicated Hoodia growers' claims for belonging through knowing Hoodia as a cultivated plant.

5

Hoodia Growers and the Making of Hoodia as a Cultivated Plant

> If you went hunting and you could not find anything and you went to lie down somewhere to rest, thinking about your lack of luck, then there was a song for you to play. The song talked to our forefathers, telling them about your unhappiness. Then, if maybe the next day you went back hunting, you might find something and be happy about it. The other people would be happy with you and then you'd sing again!
>
> —LIKUA KABEMBE, SCHMIDTSDRIFT, SOUTH AFRICA [!XUN]

WHILE BEING SHOWN AROUND HIS SMALL FARM BY ROBBY GASS OF the South African Hoodia Growers Association (SAHGA), I came upon several tiny young Hoodia plants carefully planted in neat rows and shaded from the sun under a canopy of green netting.[1] Black rubber hoses gave the plants only small amounts of water to ensure that the soil stayed dry enough for them to produce optimal levels of steroid glycosides. Gass explained that he would soon pull up the young plants and replant them in a field close by. As we continued walking across the farm, I spotted long, straight rows of more mature Hoodia plants stretching across a field. Gass, describing these Hoodia plants as "rows of gold," pointed out that the slightly larger *Sutherlandia* plants growing beside them protected the Hoodia plants from the strong winds that whipped off the mountains. Brushing aside the dull pink flowers on one of the Hoodia plants, Gass carefully removed a few seeds and placed them in my hand. I cupped my hands together, trying hard to keep the brown flat seeds with their feathery soft white hairs from flying away in the wind. Standing there, the stark contrast between the rows of cultivated plants and the scattered growth patterns of Hoodia I had seen growing in the veld made me even more aware of the different materialities of the plant that would become central to Hoodia growers' claims to belonging.

This chapter tells the story of a second benefit-sharing agreement the South African San Council entered into, this one with an organization of South African Hoodia growers. With their ancestral connection to Afrikaner histories of farming, the Hoodia growers developed methods of growing and processing cultivated Hoodia plants for Hoodia herbal supplement markets. In contrast to the South African farmers who supplied Hoodia plants to Pfizer and Unilever, members of SAHGA transformed Hoodia into dried material that they then supplied to herbal supplement companies who sold Hoodia weight-loss powders and capsules to consumers via the Internet or their local pharmacies. This analysis of the San-SAHGA benefit-sharing agreement examines how Hoodia growers made claims to knowing Hoodia as a cultivated plant in ways that demonstrate a shift in postapartheid and neoliberal South Africa, where belonging is increasingly bestowed on those who claim attachment to ways of knowing. Emphasizing the need to address how certain modalities of plant materiality engage in moments of refusal even as they are commodified, it also examines how Hoodia plants acted in ways that created difficulties for their cultivation and hence for Afrikaner belonging.

Situating Hoodia: Afrikaner Histories of Indigeneity and Belonging

To understand the growers' motivations for entering the Hoodia market and forging a benefit-sharing agreement with San peoples requires first understanding the history of Afrikaner colonial settlers and their shifting relations to the nonhuman and to indigenous peoples.[2] As mentioned in chapter 1, Afrikaners are descended from Dutch, German, French, and Scottish colonialists who began arriving in the Cape region in the seventeenth century. Initially fearing the strange lands and peoples they encountered there, these white settlers committed acts of violence against Indigenous San and Khoi peoples that they justified as necessary to their survival as settlers.[3] Once they had established control over the region's land and peoples, these settlers began to develop a sense of belonging through a romanticized connection to the land. Having left their European past behind, they began to imagine an indigenous relationship to their newly conquered territory—to develop what Saul Dubow terms an "acquired indigeneity."[4]

This Afrikaner indigenized identity was built on a religious connection to the land and symbolic kinship with plants and animals—connections that worked to establish belonging. To assert their rights and control over the land, these Afrikaner colonial settlers characterized South African territories as having previously belonged to no one. Considering themselves chosen by God to rule South Africa, they worked the land and understood their bodies as molded into the landscape.[5] Their sense of belonging to the land did not include the indigenous peoples they encountered, whom they considered incapable of working the land and thus unable to fashion an attachment to it.[6] This indigenized Afrikaner identity arose in opposition not only to indigenous peoples, but also to later colonial settlers as they faced violence and imprisonment at the hands of British troops.

Afrikaner settlers' sense of belonging was thus based on viewing land, plants, and animals not as inert and passive entities but as central to their identity and humanness. In contrast to San and Khoi understanding of the nonhuman through notions of kinship—the nonhuman as familial relatives and ancestors, as expressed in the posters in the SASI offices described earlier—Afrikaner identity and belonging was contingent on their interdependent relationship to land, animals, and plants they viewed as natural, God-given gifts to be controlled by humans. Afrikaner identity thus developed out of a multispecies understanding of the world, but one that continued to deny agency to nonhumans and to the indigenous peoples they encountered.

This Afrikaner sense of belonging took on greater importance and unity with the 1948 establishment of apartheid, which formalized white supremacy in the name of Afrikaner identity and a historical connection to South African lands. Apartheid privileged whiteness by dissolving the distinctions between Afrikaner and British that had earlier fueled Afrikaner nationalism.[7] South Africans who identified as Afrikaner or English benefited from apartheid divisions of white and nonwhite that granted them political, economic, and legal advantages. The end of apartheid, however, brought an end to the political and legal control of white South

Africans, who also perceived this shift as a loss of economic control despite continued ownership of the majority of the nation's land and significantly higher levels of employment than nonwhites.[8]

Afrikaners' sense of place in the new South Africa is therefore increasingly tethered to maintaining economic control. Those who identify as Afrikaner may have more access to land and resources than nonwhites, but they do not hold more economic control than white South Africans more broadly. Although Afrikaner belonging remains sutured to the land and a multispecies understanding of the world, the end of apartheid has forced them to include the very humans they once considered nonhuman in that understanding. This was evident in debates leading up to the passage of the 2008 Regulations on Bio-prospecting, Access, and Benefit-Sharing, rules that would require those engaged in plant bioprospecting to share benefits with the indigenous peoples who first knew the plants. Although it was unclear at the time if the law would apply to small-scale farmers, the drafting of the legislation created an ethos that those who profit from medicinal plants should recognize and share benefits with the indigenous peoples who first knew about the plant and its useful properties. Hoodia growers were therefore under increasing pressure to reimagine their connections to plants and lands with an understanding of indigenous groups, but, as we shall see, in ways that simultaneously empowered and disempowered San peoples.

Incorporating Hoodia: SAHGA and San-SAHGA Benefit Sharing

To understand how this postapartheid Afrikaner identity may have been expressed in the SAHGA initiative to forge a benefit-sharing agreement with San peoples, I arranged to meet with the grower who first proposed the agreement, Steve Hurt. I met the then-owner of Afrigetics Botanicals, formerly known as Health Synergetics,[9] at a small café in Wilderness, South Africa. Hurt identified himself as African, a common response among whites in South Africa, where self-identification as Afrikaner (which literally means "African") has become less pronounced since the end of apartheid. Hurt explained that he had become interested in indigenous plants while studying geography as a student at the University of the Witwatersrand ("Wits") in Johannesburg. In 2003, while still at university, Hurt had started a small health-products business selling South African indigenous herbal products online and quickly went from "being a poor student to just having a booming business." He started Afrigetics about the same time as the San-CSIR benefit-sharing agreement was signed and the US media began publishing stories about Hoodia weight-loss products.[10]

In his late twenties and still a student, Hurt wanted to participate in the Hoodia herbal supplement market not just to generate personal income but to also help "save the world" and generate social good by signing benefit-sharing agreements with indigenous groups. Founding Afrigetics and initiating benefit sharing with the South African San Council enabled Hurt to contribute to their political efforts, but it also provided Hurt a pathway for establishing his own belonging in a South Africa in which whites were losing political power and being pressured to recognize formerly marginalized groups. As his business began to grow, Hurt recounted, he approached Roger Chennells about how to make sure that San peoples benefited from sales of Hoodia not only by Afrigetics but by all South African Hoodia growers. A benefit-sharing arrangement of this sort, however, would first require organizing Hoodia growers, so Hurt and Chennells devised a plan for incorporating Hoodia growers into a collective legal entity. Initially planning to register the group as a private company called South African Hoodia Growers (Pty) Limited (SAHG), they began holding meetings in 2005 to recruit members. According to Hurt, organizing Hoodia growers into a legal entity proved difficult: "The first meeting we called was pretty much like you had all these business competitors sitting together around a table having to agree to work together. There was completely not any interest in working together, so immediately after that meeting, there were all these factions."

Although many Hoodia growers declined to participate in benefit sharing, a small group of Hoodia growers did agree to unite under SAHG and to share benefits with San peoples. They included growers such as Robby Gass, owner of Zizamele Herbs (formerly Zizamele Indigenous Farming), and Adolf Joubert, owner of Afrinatural Phytomedicine CC, who were already organized under an entity called the Cape Ethnobotanical Growers Association (CEGA) but who also joined SAHG. Members of SAHG began to negotiate with the South Africa San Council, which was appointed by WIMSA to enter into talks. By February 2006 the parties signed a contractual benefit-sharing agreement in which SAHG agreed to allocate 6 percent of the gross value of Hoodia sold for the benefit of all San peoples. Of this 6 percent, 4 percent was allocated to a trust for all San peoples and 2 percent to WIMSA and the South African San Council. The agreement yielded royalties in the amount of R176,000 (US $22,000).[11] Maintaining SAHG as a for-profit entity, however, proved too difficult, in part because of its members' competing interests and the administrative demands of operating a private limited company, so the members dissolved SAHG as a legal entity.

Sustaining a market for Hoodia also became a challenge as consumer interest in Hoodia weight-loss products slowed down, prompting SAHG to rethink its benefit-sharing obligations. As Hoodia growers in South Africa eventually became aware, herbal supplement companies in the United States were selling and marketing Hoodia-based products that contained no actual Hoodia ingredients and had no effect on weight loss, increasing consumer distrust of Hoodia products.[12] This decline in the demand for Hoodia prompted growers to question whether the 6 percent benefit-sharing figure was too high. In response, members of SAHG, and this time also CEGA, reopened benefit-sharing negotiations with the South African San Council, seeking a more comprehensive agreement that included help from government agencies to monitor compliance and from San peoples to assist with marketing Hoodia products. Specifically, they began discussions with Cape Nature of the Western Cape Provincial Government and with the Department of Tourism, Environment, and Conservation (DETEC) of the Northern Cape Provincial Government, signing a memorandum of understanding in December 2006.[13] In this memorandum, SAHG and CEGA members agreed to negotiate the terms of a benefit-sharing agreement and to reorganize and recruit Hoodia growers into a new legal entity that would incur a smaller administrative burden. In turn, the South African San Council agreed to negotiate a benefit-sharing agreement with the new organization, to not enter into similar agreements with other growers without its permission, to support the new company as the sole provider of legitimate Hoodia products, and to assist it with the marketing of Hoodia products. For their part, Cape Nature and DETEC agreed to help the new company manage Hoodia conservation and trade by, for instance, monitoring permits, exports, international trade, and quality control.

Four months later, in March 2007, the SAHG and CEGA members re-incorporated themselves as a voluntary nonprofit association called the South African Hoodia Growers Association. According to its constitution, the new company's objectives were to promote the interests of Hoodia growers, to regulate the production and harvesting of Hoodia by its members, to promote a sustainable Hoodia industry, and to enter into benefit sharing with San peoples.[14] With these goals in mind, that same month SAHGA members signed a different benefit-sharing agreement than the one mentioned previously, promising to give San peoples across Southern Africa a levy of 24R per dry kg of Hoodia.[15] Cape Nature and DETEC agreed to monitor Hoodia exports flowing out of South Africa and to collect the levy prior to issuing a CITES export permit.

As the parties moved forward in implementing the San-SAHGA agreement, however, it produced limited gains for San peoples. If benefit sharing is understood as a form of politics that generates new publics and collectivities, as Cori Hayden argues, then the San-SAHGA agreement was successful, in that it forged relationships among San peoples, Hoodia growers, and government officials as it sought to ensure benefits for San peoples.[16] Yet the relationships, oversight, and benefits it sought to achieve were limited in several significant ways. Communications and relations between the parties were restricted to members of the South African San Council, for one, and did not extend to San peoples more broadly. And as the market for Hoodia weight-loss products continued to decline, a lack of resource capacity at Cape Nature and DETEC meant they were unable to adequately track the number of Hoodia plant exports and ensure that levy amounts were being paid.

Furthermore, as Hurt explained during our meeting, SAHGA found it difficult to recruit Hoodia growers to join and to comply with benefit sharing. Hurt expressed disappointment that "SAHGA never really took off. . . . I don't know why that happened. I mean, we clearly couldn't sell it to [growers], and also it was just a massive administrative thing. We had no real reason to put all of this effort into running an association when we had businesses to run." In addition to the time and resources required to ensure that benefits were being directed to San peoples, Hurt explained, SAHGA was "rife [with] opportunity for competitors to see what each company was doing and who they were trading with and everything. There was no trust." Although SAHGA offered Hoodia growers a chance to collectively organize to share benefits with indigenous groups, it had the potential to expose their propriety information and practices. As an alternative, according to Hurt, the members decided to make "SAHGA just a label, a stamp of approval with a tracking number to see the consignments, where you could log in and you could see." The project to organize Hoodia growers into an administrative agency thus dissolved into a more modest venture. In this new iteration, individual growers could negotiate agreements with the South African San Council to share benefits and then affix the SAHGA label to their products to publicize their commitment to benefit sharing, but the initial goal of organizing growers collectively to promote and institutionalize benefit sharing more widely never materialized, and as a result, benefits did not more broadly extend to San.

This inability to organize Hoodia growers through SAHGA and an increasing uncertainty over the new benefit-sharing regulations contributed to the end of the San-SAHGA agreement. "It all kind of collapsed after that," Hurt remarked, "although we did pay quite significant amounts of money over to the San."[17] As mentioned above, SAHGA members paid a portion of royalties, but in addition, in July 2008 Hurt's Afrigetics paid royalties to the San Hoodia Trust in the amount of R150,000 (US $20,329).[18] After the passage of the 2008 Regulations on Bio-prospecting, Access, and Benefit-Sharing, the San-SAHGA agreement was subject to government oversight. The parties submitted the agreement to the Department of Environmental Affairs and Tourism (DEAT) for approval, but it was never endorsed by DEAT. Although SAHGA and the South African San Council discussed the possibility of renegotiating the agreement, in the face of declining Hoodia markets, SAHGA had little incentive to renegotiate or to make the agreement comply with the new regulations. To this day, the agreement remains unenforceable.

San-SAHGA benefit sharing may have constituted new publics and collectives by "turning takings into promises of giving back," to use Hayden's words, but ultimately it did not rearrange relations of power or produce meaningful modes of belonging for San peoples.[19] When Hoodia markets and consequently San-SAHGA benefit sharing stalled, Hoodia growers lost revenue and were forced to cultivate fewer Hoodia plants, but they also had the resources and capital to maintain their businesses by shifting their focus to other, more profitable indigenous plants. Continuing their market participation and signing benefit-sharing agreements gave Hoodia growers the means to strengthen their belonging to South Africa through claims to Hoodia cultivation, and thus to satisfy postapartheid commitments to give back to indigenous peoples. However, the agreements did little to establish pathways of belonging for San peoples, as they failed to generate revenue and partnerships that would allow San to develop their own means of self-determination. In a neoliberal South Africa where, as Comaroff and Comaroff contend, the recognition of difference is mediated through market means, the mere act of entering into benefit sharing unfortunately seemed to be the most important factor for establishing Hoodia growers as committed to recognizing indigenous peoples, regardless of whether they actually transferred benefits.[20]

Signifying Hoodia: Cultivating Hoodia and Meanings of Afrikaner Belonging

During my visit to Gass's Zizamele Indigenous Farming operation in Barrydale, South Africa, it began to be clear to me that Hoodia growers' claims to belonging and negotiations over benefits were based not solely on their attachment to the land, but on a knowledge of growing Hoodia that was distinct from CSIR's knowledge of the plant at the molecular level and San knowledge of it as a plant occurring in nature.[21] After introducing himself, Gass described his ancestry as Scottish, although he chose to self-identify as South African rather than Afrikaner, thus representing himself as native to South Africa. As we spoke, Gass described his knowledge of Hoodia as a cultivated plant in terms of indigeneity, gender, the divine, and the nation-state, but emphasized its connections to San indigeneity and gender. He described Hoodia as a "high-energy plant" that historically had been used by "a Bushman running after or walking after an injured elephant" and needing "some sustenance." He was quick to inform me, however, that San peoples had used the plant not only while hunting but also as a "normal vegetable" and "a food." Aware that most Internet advertisements associated San "with the bow and arrow," he was insistent that "there are a million other pictures of the San" and that a more accurate image of the San relationship to Hoodia would be a "San woman with children [who] would certainly be eating Hoodia at home for the four or five days that they were waiting for Dad to come home with an eland."

Although Gass identified himself as South African, his response when asked to describe Zizamele's mission expressed his Afrikaner background and the historical constructions of Afrikaners as having been chosen by God to rule South Africa. According to Gass, "I prefer to lobby towards the idea of educating a nation. Teaching people really what's going on around them. So, my company exists from a dream to do two major things. One, learn as much as possible on how to cultivate wild material. In other words, what would normally be harvested in the veld, to actually turn it into agricultural product. Because I feel God made the indigenous crops of this country in the wild for the indigenous people of this country." Gass understood Hoodia as "wild material" and a gift from God that he and other growers had learned to cultivate. In this account, Hoodia growers had developed their own indigenous knowledge of how to transform Hoodia from mere wild veld plant to an agricultural product for the marketplace, thereby distinguishing the knowledge of Hoodia growers from that of San peoples.

In describing his distinct practice of cultivating Hoodia, Gass expressed a concern for wild Hoodia populations and a desire for passing benefits on to San peoples. During our discussion, he stressed that he cultivated Hoodia out of an environmental concern for wild Hoodia populations, which were being depleted and destroyed to the point of possible extinction because of the market for Hoodia plants. As Gass noted, "to provide America with a product from South Africa, you'd need to develop the agricultural possibility to cultivate that product and not take it from the wild. The wild will be depleted of it within a few months. Like Hoodia nearly did. So, cultivating the wild is the most important thing." Gass, in other words, cultivated Hoodia and other indigenous plant species not just to capitalize on market demand but also to curtail unsustainable harvesting of indigenous plants from the veld, a practice that related to understandings of Afrikaner identity as being charged with the caretaking of the land and its divine gifts. The second goal of his company, he explained, was to share the knowledge of how to cultivate Hoodia plants with local indigenous communities, to "pass on the knowledge to the indigenous communities that tend to live where there's barely any water and hardly any money for tractors and so on. And let them, with these hardy indigenous crops, produce an income. . . . So, teaching them how to do it is the other part of what we do. This is why the guys came for training."[22]

By *guys*, he was referring to local San and Khoi peoples he had invited to his farm to learn how to cultivate plants in order to produce their own income. As discussed earlier, the San-SAHGA agreement was meant not just to share financial benefits with San peoples but to create relationships through which growers could share their knowledge with San peoples about how to cultivate local indigenous plants and develop sustainable markets for them. These diverse goals for cultivating Hoodia—to capitalize on market demand, protect wild populations, and empower San peoples—depended, however, on distinguishing Hoodia growers' knowledge of how to cultivate the plant from San peoples' knowledge of how it grew in the veld, thus reinforcing social understandings of the former as more worthy for market purposes.

Those goals were also contingent on differentiating Hoodia growers' knowledge from scientists' knowledge emphasizing Hoodia as patented molecule. In setting the knowledge of Hoodia growers apart from that of CSIR, Gass again deployed narratives of the divine and a connection to nature. Dismissing Hoodia patents on chemical compositions as inventive, he said, "Composition. So. Congratulations. Well done. You've now somehow seemed to have been able to isolate certain . . . molecules. Great. Well done. You get a Nobel Prize for that. And the rest of the molecules in that plant, what do they do? Nothing. Try again. God makes plants. Scientists try to dissect them. Try. And they can't. . . . I don't know why you would try to patent something God made. I really don't understand why. It doesn't make sense to me or to any San Bushmen or to anybody else with a brain. I cannot understand how you consider patenting God's work." Through his remarks, Gass described CSIR knowledge of Hoodia as merely dissecting the plant and deployed an association of nature and the divine to repudiate Hoodia patents as not very inventive after all. In doing so, he characterized CSIR scientists' knowledge of how to isolate certain molecules in the plant as different from Hoodia growers' knowledge of how to cultivate it.

Gass was not the only Hoodia grower who sought to signify the plant in ways that linked Hoodia growers to the plant as cultivated. As Hurt explained to me, Hoodia growers focused on the dry version of the plant and not the molecule, "So Pfizer was saying to us, not directly, but through people like Roger, 'You may not trade in Hoodia. That's our plant. We own this. We have the rights to it. We have the benefit sharing agreement, or whatever it was, with CSIR. Leave that alone. Otherwise we're going to sue you.'"[23] Hurt explained that in response to Pfizer, he "said, no, that's not true. The plant is not the molecule. . . . So our angle on it was that there was Hoodia, the natural product, which was the plant and the dry version of the plant, and there was P57, which was a pharmaceutically derived raw material, active ingredient, which related specifically to a different kind of law." Hurt described Hoodia growers as linked to the materiality of the cultivated and dried plant, which differed from the plant as a molecule that mattered to CSIR and the legal regimes of patent law.

Through their remarks, both Gass and Hurt grounded the growers' Hoodia knowledge in two different scales or materialities of plant matter, which they recognized were valued differently by society, with molecules considered more worthy of patent protection and more useful for capital markets. By distinguishing these two materialities, Gass contested Hoodia patents that sought to own and control divine gifts of nature, which he implied were meant to be open and available to all peoples. By identifying his knowledge of and attachment to cultivated Hoodia as more natural and closer to God's plan, he characterized his Hoodia knowledge as distinct from CSIR's molecular knowledge and also as more refined than San knowledge of wild Hoodia.

As we continued our conversation, Gass also depicted Hoodia as a site of struggle over issues of gender as well as of indigeneity and belonging by contrasting the knowledge of Hoodia growers and that of San women. Describing the San-SAHGA negotiations, Gass recounted that when the growers were "negotiating with the San for their part of the benefit share, their little share, on the sale of Hoodia from South Africa, we took a flip chart and we drew—put a line through the middle. The top half we made a little pencil drawing . . . an outline drawing of a San-looking woman walking in the veld. Eating some Hoodia. On the same page below that line, we drew a field of what looked like rows of Hoodia and a tractor and a guy—a white farmer, you know, a bloke with this big head." Intrigued about their decision to use a woman rather than a man to represent San, I asked Gass what he thought San women knew about the plant. In response, he replied, "She got passed down from her inheritance, forebears, that she can eat that plant. The guy sitting on the tractor got the knowledge passed down from his forebears on how to plant them in a row and grow them and germinate them and bring them—collect them and turn them into farming. No San Bushman taught me what I know about farming. I'm teaching San Bushmen to learn about farming. So where's my intellectual property now? Where's my right?"[24] By associating white male farmers with Hoodia as a cultivated crop in neat rows awaiting a tractor and San women with Hoodia growing wild in the Kalahari, Gass constructed his "intellectual property" of how to cultivate the plant as a more sophisticated and advanced form of knowledge than the household knowledge and practices of San women feeding their children. In Gass's memory of the event, he had chosen to draw a woman to represent San peoples because he did not "want another guy with a bow and arrow and a big bum running after a buck," which he dismissed as "just one white scientist's example" and "not the only place in the San's culture where they eat Hoodia." Although his drawing sought to contest colonial images of San male hunters historically used to bolster whiteness and masculinity, the San woman ultimately functioned as a mere figure in opposition to which the Afrikaner Hoodia growers could claim belonging.

Hoodia Undoings: Hoodia Plant Properties and Their Unpredictability

Although Hoodia growers constructed their sense of belonging within South Africa and the global economy through their attachments to Hoodia as a cultivated plant, such modes of alignment are unstable because, as discussed in earlier chapters, biological matter itself is unpredictable and cannot be entirely contained. The materiality of Hoodia plants acted in ways that also interrupted and hindered Hoodia growers' claims to knowing and cultivating Hoodia plants. Plant properties can develop quickly, slowly, or not at all, and plant species can move, change, wither, or alter their environments, and accordingly can also support, challenge, and re-configure the very relations in which they become entangled. In this case, as we shall see, Hoodia's actions and inactions continually interrupted Hoodia growers' efforts to cultivate the plant for the overseas herbal supplement market and contributed to the undoing not only of the Hoodia industry but of the growers' claims for belonging through their attachment to Hoodia.

That Hoodia is a slow-growing plant made it difficult for the growers to keep up at times of high demand and create a sustainable market for

Hoodia products. Although Hoodia plants in the veld commonly take three to six years to produce their first flowers, the growers' goal was to cultivate Hoodia so it matured more quickly. As Gass explained, "Two and a half years is the youngest you can consider harvesting and—because by then they should have gone through at least one cycle, if not two, of flowering and seed forming. Which is layman's proof that they're grown up. They're mature. An immature plant can't make seed." Hoodia growers, however, disagreed among themselves about how long it took to cultivate Hoodia. Adolf Joubert, owner of the renamed Afrinatural Holdings, lamented that Hoodia took five to six years to cultivate and harvest, whereas Hurt reported that the plant grew a little faster, claiming that if "you don't give it too much water, and then in 3–4 years, it's got a really nice P-57 content."[25] But however long it takes, Hoodia grows much more slowly than the more customary eighteen months it takes for other native plants, such as rooibos, to be harvestable.[26]

The manner in which Hoodia seeds propagate also complicated the growers' efforts to produce enough of the plant for market purposes. According to Joubert, when "you're trying to put a hundred thousand seeds out and hoping you will get eighty thousand plants out of it, that's not natural. That is definitely not natural. . . . Nature, you get a hundred thousand seeds going, you might have ten thousand plants growing, so the ratio is—you're pushing the limits. You're pushing the productivity. You're getting more seedlings growing [based on] your knowledge of flowers or about maize or about anything else where you've been taught why and how you get a better yield and better production." Cultivating Hoodia plants on farms does not follow the same process as how Hoodia "naturally" grows in the Kalahari Desert. Cultivation practices involve getting large numbers of seeds going, which is not easy and requires a lot of upfront labor. As Joubert remarked, growing Hoodia is "incredibly labor intensive": "You have to put up the shade net, you have to clear the land, you have to harvest the seeds, you have to do these seedling beds, you have to pick them out." Hoodia plants were particularly known for dispersing their seeds widely and suddenly, so Hoodia growers had to devise strategies for containing those seeds to ensure adequate yields. Joubert stressed the need to prevent ripe Hoodia seedpods from "bursting" and "shooting seeds all over" (punctuating his description with a loud popping sound) and explained that to do so, he needed to "put bags around [the seeds], and stockings and wires" to keep the seeds contained and available to plant.

Hoodia's sensitivity to moisture levels and susceptibility to external threats also made extra work for Hoodia growers. Growers not only had to find ways to produce large yields but also to optimize the steroidal glycoside content within the plants. Gass said that he needed to keep his Hoodia fields "clean, weed free . . . because you don't want little moisture—the weeds hold back moisture." At the same time, too much moisture would cause germinating Hoodia seeds to rot, so growers had to develop specific techniques for irrigating the plants at precise schedules to carefully control the amounts of water the plants received. Insects help pollinate Hoodia plants but can also threaten them, so growers also worked hard to protect the plants from these risks. Joubert, for example, reported having to take precautions against the plant's susceptibility to fungus and "a certain wasp that lays its egg in the pod, and by the time you harvest it, there are no more seeds left."

Hoodia's complex stereochemistry also means that its levels of steroidal glycosides are sensitive to the drying process, requiring Hoodia growers to develop precise drying techniques to ensure optimal levels of active ingredients. According to Joubert, the process of drying begins by slicing Hoodia "like a salad, and you've got buckets full of these salads, and you dump it onto nets with heat blowing from the bottom, trying to get through all of this. And as it starts drying, it starts drying faster . . . but at the beginning you start with so much salad lying on a box with heat, air trying to get through from the bottom . . . and you would start turning the stuff around, so that the bottom stuff can come to the top, and the top stuff can come to the bottom. So slowly, they would get drier and drier." The drying of Hoodia plant material required continual labor but also precise temperature standards and technologies such as a vortex mill, heating canisters, and liquid petroleum gas. When the plants were thoroughly dried and, in Joubert's words, "reasonably heading towards crispy," one would then have to "put it into bag, and when you need to— totally separate exercise—you put it through a mill. You mill it—pulverize it to a powder."[27] The steroidal glycosides in Hoodia plants thus actively responded to the drying process in various ways, meaning that growers had to make sure not to dry the plants too much or too little in order to optimize their active properties.

The materiality of cultivated Hoodia plants therefore did not always neatly align with growers' desire to cultivate them and make claims for belonging to the nation and the marketplace. Hoodia was a slow-growing plant, so growers had trouble keeping up when the demand for Hoodia spiked. If plants were harvested prematurely, they did not have the right levels of steroidal glycosides to suppress appetite. When demand slowed, growers were forced to scale back their operations. Attempting to take advantage of the new interest in Hoodia, growers were, according to Joubert, "anticipating that within three years the plant might be mature. We found after three years it wasn't. After five or six years it was. But after we passed the three-year point, the market fell apart." Growers began to question whether cultivating Hoodia was worth it. Some dramatically curtailed their Hoodia operations, and many gave up growing Hoodia entirely.

Marketing Hoodia: Connectivities of San Peoples, White Women, and Hoodia Growers

Another shared interest between the Afrikaner growers and San peoples was marketing Hoodia as an indigenous South African plant, of which its traditional use by San had become the symbol. As Gass put it, they wanted Hoodia to "be seen as a Southern African plant. Foodstuff. Good. Strong plant. A really good indigenous food. And a great medicine for the stomach. For the body." And to that end, he added, "the San should be seen on the marketing." The SAHGA and San accordingly agreed to brand the SAHGA products with a logo specifying that their product was the only legitimate Hoodia weight-loss supplement endorsed by the South African San Council and was being sold for the benefit of San peoples. To avoid reinscribing stereotypical images of San peoples to market their products, SAHGA Hoodia growers marked their advertising and products with just the words "Endorsed by the South African San Council" rather than incorporating San images or symbols.

This decision was an attempt on the part of SAHGA and the South African San Council to counter the images of San other companies used to sell their Hoodia products, such as in those online advertisements that first sparked my interest in Hoodia. Those herbal supplement companies marketed Hoodia products by describing the plant as having historically been used by San hunters and by deploying masculine and colonial images of San as traditional peoples.[28] Although the websites avoided gender-specific references to San, their gender-neutral text was accompanied by images of San males that, while recognizing the long history of San hunting Likua Kabembe alluded to in this chapter's epigraph, also characterized the history as strictly gendered male and masculine.

For example, a website for TraZic Hoodia Gordonii, a US company, claimed that "San Bushmen" chewed on the plant "when they were deprived of food on long hunting expeditions in the desert."[29] Alongside images of the Hoodia plant, the site presented photos of San men standing next to a dirt road dressed in loincloths and shooting bows and arrows. Under the tagline "A Gift From Mother Nature," a website for Bushmen Hoodia, a South African company, similarly described San as using Hoodia on "long hunting trips." A scrolling ticker at the top of the site flashed images of San men in loincloths bearing bows and arrows alongside pictures of seemingly white women posing in bikini bathing suits and two supposed San women with their breasts exposed. On a third website, a US company named Desert Burn used both sound and images to entice consumers to purchase Hoodia products.[30] As consumers opened the site's home page, they were greeted by the loud music of tribal drums as a large arrow shot across the page above an image of San men, each covered with only a piece of cloth around his hips, walking across a vast desert in search of Hoodia.

By employing the figure of the San hunter in gendered and racialized ways, these websites fashioned complicated transnational relations between the plant, San peoples, and consumers. Establishing what Inderpal Grewal refers to as "transnational connectivities," the sites reinforced unequal modes of belonging by casting San peoples as nonmodern subjects.[31] Whereas SAHGA members attempted to attract customers through their partnership with the South African San Council, who had certified their products, these websites deployed images of San male hunters with bows and arrows to certify Hoodia as pure and authentic, implying that San were traditional peoples untouched by modernity, and therefore that their knowledge of Hoodia should be considered natural and unchanged. By constructing San as fixed in time and unchanging, the websites also obscured the history of colonial and apartheid violence against San peoples and San efforts to survive and resist. By focusing on images of San hunters as male, they also obscured the role of San women as hunters,[32] a silence that ≠Khomani San educational programs have attempted to correct.[33] The websites' images also obscured the ways in which San have historically used the plant in other gendered ways, such as (in Arrie Tities's words) how the "moms they use it for the baby."

Unlike SAHGA members, who declined to use stereotypical images of women, the other websites' use of contrasting images of indigenous peoples and white women to sell their products reflected colonial practices of what Anne McClintock calls "commodity racism," describing advertisements that bolstered Victorian notions of domesticity by contrasting images of black male bodies as less pure and in need of civilizing with portrayals of white woman as pure and virtuous.[34] These Hoodia advertisements similarly reduced both San peoples and women's bodies to mere spectacle to entice consumers to purchase Hoodia weight-loss products, albeit in different and complicated ways.[35] Their images of women in bikinis reinforced social norms of femininity and the gendered, racialized, classed, and heteronormative privileging of the slender body that also contributes to fatphobia.[36] By affixing San to the realm of the traditional, however, the advertisements also constructed white women as modern figures of self-control in contrast to primitive and rootless San men. These marketing strategies therefore both reinforced and subordinated the image of white women as modern agents. Both sets of advertisements, we must also recognize, continued to obscure the role of San women in San culture and the impact of colonialism on San gender relations, as discussed in chapter 1.

Preliminary market research conducted by Unilever can offer additional insight into how potential consumers may have perceived these raced and gendered images and whether those images enticed consumers to purchase Hoodia products. Although the company never actually marketed a Hoodia-based weight-loss product to consumers, it tested potential marketing campaigns with consumer focus groups. Kevin Poovey, Unilever's lead project manager for Hoodia products, explained that the company had decided against marketing Hoodia with images of San peoples because their test marketing found that stereotypical San images "didn't really connect with a lot of people" and because—as the benefit-sharing struggles had proven—the company recognized that those depictions were "not really how . . . those populations are really living these days."[37] Instead, Poovey recalled, their market research found that the most effective way to market the product was to recognize that if "targeting a product at women, you use different language than you use with men: if you say it controls your appetite . . . that's not very well liked by women. Whereas men actually think it's okay. If you say this helps you to control your appetite, that's much more acceptable to women. So, one is you're in control, and the other, it's controlling you." From this research, they concluded that the best way to market weight-loss products would be through testimonials and images of people who had experienced weight loss and through specific language targeting male and female consumers rather than through images of San men or of women in bikinis.

Although some SAHGA members who used the South African San Council endorsement mark did deploy images of San peoples, they did so in very different ways from the other websites discussed. The 2007 website of Hurt's Health Synergetics, for instance, displayed members of the South African San Council attending a professional meeting to sign a benefit-sharing agreement with Hurt's company. Publicizing Health Synergetics' commitment to giving back to San peoples by using images of San peoples helped bolster its image as an ethical company as part of its appeal to consumers. The images of San on their website showed San in modern dress, unlike the more stereotypical images on other sites, thus characterizing San both as traditional knowers of Hoodia and as modern political subjects engaged in negotiating with their SAHGA counterparts.

Members of SAHGA may have deployed less-stereotypical images of San peoples than other websites, but their use of San images and logo benefited the interests of Hoodia growers more than San peoples, thus reinforcing relations of power. The images SAHGA used fit easily within neoliberal South Africa's increasing focus on indigenous plants and knowledge as key sources of economic growth for the country without attention to the indigenous peoples who may have developed such knowledge. The images allowed Health Synergetics to establish modes of belonging by capitalizing on two scales or modalities of Hoodia: in the form of San peoples' knowledge of Hoodia as a plant from nature, and in the form of growers' knowledge of Hoodia as a cultivated plant. However, despite the benefit-sharing agreement and value attributed to both ways of knowing, as Hurt would likely acknowledge, San peoples continued to lack decision-making authority over Hoodia cultivation, struggled to develop plans to create their own indigenous plant industries, and continued to wait for royalties from benefit sharing; thus, inequality remained intact in ways that advantaged Hoodia growers more.

The continued circulation of images of San as traditional peoples thus remains a deep concern for San peoples as they struggle to navigate and develop their own modes of belonging in South Africa. In speaking with ≠Khomani San about these Internet images in 2009, I learned that some took issue not with the images per se, but with non-San peoples using them without consent. As Tities remarked, "I don't have a problem with the traditional image. For me it is very, very important because the San is a unique people"; the more pressing issue, he claimed, was "how you explain this image" and "how you do it."[38] The issue of consent, as Tities implies here, is important because it enables San to control how their images can be used. Tommy Busakhwe (≠Khomani San Bushman) also acknowledged that these images are useful because they can sell the product "very quickly, then people see what kind of traditional people it is using that product," but he, too, took issue with how "images are being used without permission and without buying the copyrights from the ≠Khomani San."[39] Having attended meetings at the United Nations on indigenous peoples and intellectual property rights, Busakhwe was aware of copyright law and offered an alternative indigenous intellectual property framework of rights to prevent the misuse of San images; as indigenous peoples work to establish their own set of customary intellectual property rights, such a framework is not outside of the realm of possibility. Regardless, even as the advertisers technically held the copyright to the images, San could choose to file a defamation claim against the advertisers for harming their reputation as modern political subjects.

When I discussed the issue of Hoodia advertisements with San a few years later in 2015, some expressed a continued sense of their legal rights and a frustration over the misuse of their images without their consent. I met with Collin Louw (≠Khomani San Bushman) and Tities at a restaurant in Upington, South Africa, and we looked at and discussed some of these websites on my computer. As we examined the website of Desert Burn, the two men pointed to an image of a man referred to as "Sean—A South African Bushman and Our Friend" holding a bottle of Desert Burn and said that they knew him. Tities was taken aback by seeing that Desert Burn was selling Hoodia products for $60, or almost R600,[40] while Louw declared the use of the images to be "daylight robbery, because you can't use the images of the San when you don't have benefit sharing. You see, that's my problem."[41] In his remarks here, Louw implied an obligation for companies to recognize San rights to both their knowledge and their images. When I spoke to a ≠Khomani San woman who wanted to be referred to as Tasha about the same image, she declared: "Who gave them the right to put it on the websites? Huh? Do you understand what I mean? Because nowadays for everything that you use, you should really get an agreement or get permission."[42] Tasha placed much of the blame squarely on academic and commercial researchers who "come here. They do research. They pay [San like Sean] a small piece of money, and because they don't have an income, they say it's fine to take his photo. They don't know—I don't even know if [Sean] knows he's on this website. I don't think he knows that." For Tasha, the websites demonstrate how research can lead not only to financial opportunities for San but also to their continued exploitation.

During my same conversation with Louw and Tities at the restaurant, Louw went further, declaring that even if Desert Burn had signed a benefit-sharing agreement with the South African San Council, he would still not be okay with their use of images of San peoples "because we [would] negotiate for a logo. Not for that. Yeah, the logo was chosen: This is a product of the San. The San is part of this. But not pictures." He saw the use of San individuals' images as problematic because of the unauthorized uses to which they might be put: "They can make postcards. They can do other stuff with it. You see? The logo is a stamp that says we are in negotiation." Given South Africa's colonial history and historic treatment of San, Louw was concerned that images of San peoples might be used to depict them as nonmodern, whereas he saw the use of the South African San Council endorsement mark as portraying San peoples as modern political subjects capable of negotiating their own right to self-determination.

Louw also objected to the website's juxtaposing images of San individuals and white women, declaring "that it's not right to compare [San] people with this lady in a bikini" because it misrepresented San knowledge: "San people did not say Hoodia make people thin." During my later conversation with Tasha, she similarly complained about this comparison's reconfiguration of the histories of Hoodia and San people, asking, "Why do they compare the Bushman against the white person? Or . . . ?

I mean, how does she fit in the history of the Hoodia? I know she fits in when it comes to the using, but how does she fit into the history? Because this tells the history. But she doesn't have a history with the Hoodia."

These Hoodia advertisements' images of San peoples and white women produced and expanded a new set of transnational connectivities that brought San peoples, Hoodia plants, and potential US consumers into relation in unequal ways, as mentioned above. Despite the circulation of these images, Tities concluded in the end, though, that "We still believe that the Hoodia is a good thing and that came good out of it. If the people are using it in the right way, using the right material, the right plant, [and] they're not putting other stuff using other plants [in the product]."[43]

Conclusion

This examination of Hoodia growers' knowledge of Hoodia at the scale of cultivated plant provides further support to the book's argument that in neoliberal, postcolonial South Africa, national belonging is being crafted through difference attached to the governing of knowledge production in new ways. San-SAHGA benefit sharing, though envisioned as a way of bringing San into fold of belonging in South Africa, also marked the Afrikaner growers as subjects willing to embrace the new scripts of South Africa as the Rainbow Nation even as it served their economic and political interests. SAHGA growers could secure their economic power and control over cultivating Hoodia by demonstrating themselves as active participants in giving back and recognizing San peoples as native to South African lands, yet Hoodia plant materialities made cultivation difficult and complicated their claims for belonging through growing Hoodia. Their efforts also did not assuage the fact that San peoples had no control over Hoodia cultivation or marketing, received few financial benefits in comparison to those of growers, and struggled to develop their own indigenous plant industries and to oppose the circulation of images of them as nonmodern peoples.

In making claims to Hoodia, growers also put forth an alternative understanding of indigeneity through belonging not as rooted in place but as attached to a particular nonhuman materiality of Hoodia as cultivated. Belonging in South Africa is increasingly bestowed, as Comaroff and Comaroff note, upon those claiming indigeneity, origin, and a "'native' rootedness."[44] Scholars such as Sarah Ives have found that Afrikaner rooibos farmers, for example, secured their belonging to and rootedness in South Africa by using geographic indicators to assert rooibos as indigenous to a particular region.[45] In contrast, Hoodia growers made claims for belonging by locating their sense of native rootedness not in place, but in the materialities of nonhuman plants. In other words, their acquired indigeneity became linked to knowledge and attached to a particular scale of nonhuman matter that was valued more than San knowledge of Hoodia as a plant in nature, but less than CSIR knowledge of Hoodia as a molecule. Their indigeneity is affixed less to place and more to specific materialities of Hoodia as cultivated in tidy rows. Hoodia growers claim not to be the first to know the plant, but the first to know how to cultivate it for commercial purposes. Faced with the uncertainty of San and CSIR claims to Hoodia and of South African legislation requiring benefit sharing with indigenous peoples, Hoodia growers were forced to shift and narrow their historical relationship of farmer to plant and replace it with farmer to cultivated plant. As the growers perceived a loss of control over land and resources, they developed new ways to assert belonging and control through attachment to certain scales of plant matter and knowledge. In the South African postcolony, as modes of belonging continue to shift and climate change alters the terms of place itself, such human claims to particular materialities of the nonhuman offer an emerging site of struggle over who does and does not belong.

Epilogue

Implications of a Feminist Decolonial Technoscience

> It is a whole process. . . . We expect a good future, but there is a lot
> of work. There will be difficulties, but if you tackle something with
> a vision, you can win. We have something to strive for.
>
> —PETRUS VAALBOOI [≠KHOMANI SAN BUSHMAN]

THE SIGNING OF THE HOODIA BENEFIT-SHARING AGREEMENT AT
the Molopo Lodge ceremony described earlier in this book marked a significant moment in the politics of both San peoples and South Africa. It
was a result of San peoples coming together through their own council to
protest patents, demand benefits, change science, and alter San futures.
Petrus Vaalbooi's signing of the agreement as a representative of the South
African San Council demonstrated possibilities for belonging in a new
South Africa recently founded on principles of dignity, equality, and freedom enshrined in its constitution. By agreeing to share benefits, CSIR
scientists demonstrated that not just South African society but the practice of science was changing. Through the process of negotiating benefits,
the South African San Council had compelled CSIR scientists, and science
more broadly, to begin to confront colonial and apartheid pasts and find
new ways of working with indigenous peoples. Despite its limitations, it
served as an important step in what Vaalbooi refers to in the epigraph as
the "whole process" of working toward indigenous self-determination.

Lessons learned from San political organizing around Hoodia provided
a foundation for continued San mobilization and further establishment
of best practices around benefit sharing. San peoples have built on the
success of the San-CSIR benefit-sharing agreement to demand further
rights based on San ways of knowing, being, and becoming. In particular,

the South African San Council has mobilized and negotiated additional benefit-sharing agreements, including a 2007 landmark agreement with the South African company HGH Pharmaceuticals regarding the *Sceletium tortuosum* plant, which had long been used by San and Khoi peoples for its mood-enhancing properties.[1] In 2013, the South African San Council and the National Khoisan Council signed a benefit-sharing agreement with Cape Kingdom Nutraceuticals in South Africa, this one regarding the *Buchu* plant.[2] These agreements suggest the possibilities of benefit sharing as a standard practice in collaborations between scientists and indigenous peoples. The two councils are currently making similar demands for benefit sharing from the South African rooibos industry.[3]

Indigenous San and Khoi leaders continue to mobilize in order to secure benefit sharing not only to improve the financial futures of their peoples but as a part of a broader movement toward self-determination. By positioning San and Khoi peoples as modern political subjects, these agreements have also bolstered efforts to gain representation within South Africa's National House of Traditional Leaders, which has become a possibility given recent debates over the 2015 Draft Traditional and Khoi-San Leadership Bill.

Indigenous and local communities in South Africa are devising their own customary laws, decision-making processes, priorities for development, and conditions for engaging with outside actors through a formal and community-led process of establishing biocultural community protocols.[4] Although the idea of such protocols is nothing new, a nongovernmental organization in Cape Town called Natural Justice, organized through a coalition of lawyers, researchers, and indigenous peoples, is helping develop protocols backed by benefit-sharing obligations under the 2010 Nagoya Protocol and under South Africa's 2015 amendments to the Regulations on Bio-prospecting, Access, and Benefit-Sharing.[5] Since then, indigenous and local groups in Latin America, Asia, and Africa have begun asserting their rights to self-determination through such biocultural community protocols. In Bushbuckridge, South Africa, for instance, a group of female traditional healers developed protocols that guided their negotiations with government officials, enabling them to gain access to plants on previously restricted lands. There is much more work to be done, but in establishing their own guidelines for engagement, indigenous peoples and local communities in South Africa are reimagining their relationships with the technoscience world.

Although I originally embarked on this examination of contestations over Hoodia to better understand patent ownership and benefit sharing in South Africa, what I found was a story of struggle over scientific knowledge production that revealed a previously unexamined shift in modes of belonging in South Africa. In our increasingly technology- and science-driven world, what is considered most worthy are those ways of knowing and forms of matter that have greater value for our knowledge economy. Building on others' observation that belonging in postapartheid South Africa has been bestowed on those who claim to be first in place or to have a native rootedness to South Africa,[6] this analysis reveals that the struggle for belonging has expanded in new yet familiar ways to include distinctions based on the first to know particular modalities of materiality (e.g., Hoodia as a molecule, as cultivated, or as from nature). While the claims of San peoples, Hoodia growers, and CSIR scientists implied their own rootedness in place to land and lab, the story of their interactions demonstrate that their claims to belonging were also rooted in their attachments to certain ways of knowing and nonhuman plant matter that remain unequally valued by society.

In postapartheid South Africa, where new laws promoting intellectual property rights and indigenous knowledge are reinforcing the primacy of the knowledge economy, new questions arise as to how the originating principles of liberation that promoted freedom are increasingly being replaced by a narrow notion of freedom to participate in the marketplace. That pathways to belonging are shifting in South Africa is also suggested by the movement of support away from the African National Congress party in the 2016 elections and recent student demands that higher education become more inclusive, affordable, and open to knowledge traditions other than the normative European canon. This analysis of San struggles over Hoodia reveals that efforts to decolonize knowledge must also address how relations of power are constituted through the governing of matter and knowledge in new ways. The mere recognition or inclusion of indigenous knowledge will not be sufficient to unsettle those relations in today's market-based hierarchies that differentially value certain ways of knowing and being over others, nor is a truly just and prosperous nonracial future likely to be forged within scientific and legal practices that remain tied more to market than to social justice principles.

Nonetheless, this analysis has made visible the contributions of indigenous peoples dismissed as Oompa-Loompas in the conventional narrative of patent law presented in the law school classroom described earlier. As it has shown, a more just answer to the question of who the law should consider the inventor when granting a patent would require scholars and policy makers to view patent ownership as itself an invention, to take account of colonial pasts, to address gendered and racialized hierarchies of knowledge production, and to acknowledge the contributions of indigenous peoples as well as scientists. As a historical and sociocultural process, patent ownership is not merely a set of objective legal rules but an expression of society's judgment that forms of knowledge and matter that have market potential are more valuable than other forms. The even more urgent question this investigation raises, therefore, is how we might develop ways of doing science and law that place less emphasis on securing property rights and more on building meaningful collaborations that truly strengthen modes of belonging for indigenous peoples.

Modes of belonging and their attendant relations of power are being forged at the nexus of difference, materiality, property, and knowledge. Struggles over Hoodia demonstrate how notions of difference are themselves being reconfigured within our increasingly technoscientific world as San peoples, CSIR scientists, and Hoodia growers made claims for belonging that were informed by race and indigeneity, but also by attachments to different forms of knowledge and materiality of Hoodia that were valued in unequal ways. The South African San Council asserted San as indigenous peoples and as first to know Hoodia as a plant from nature, but their claims were subsumed by CSIR scientists and Hoodia growers who made claims for belonging not based on their identity as racialized subjects per se but as knowers of particular materialities of Hoodia. CSIR scientists sought recognition as producers of science located in the Global South by asserting themselves as the first to know Hoodia molecules, while Hoodia growers attempted to secure white Afrikaner belonging by asserting themselves as the first to know Hoodia as a cultivated plant. Their strategies for belonging remain fastened to identity but also to distinctions based on ways of knowing and forms of matter. These understandings have profound implications for social justice projects and the field of gender studies, which aim to address the continued subordination of nonhumans as mere objects and of those individuals and groups who have been historically excluded from the production of knowledge and control over its making. As the global knowledge economy elevates the importance of technoscientific worlds, a feminist decolonial technoscience approach capable of illuminating both the possibilities and drawbacks of these changing modes of belonging and notions of difference becomes increasingly urgent.

As this examination of the struggles over Hoodia makes clear, the feminist technoscience project of decolonizing the production and ownership of scientific knowledge will require robust interdisciplinary and intersectional analyses that deploy multiple models for understanding materiality. This requires an understanding of materialities as polyvalent with many material-discursive forms that are valued differently in society. The way Hoodia plants grew slowly in the ground, spread their seeds widely, evolved in patchy spatial distributions, and interacted with the human body all shaped the very relations of law, science, and market that tried to contain them. By revealing how Hoodia plants are constituted through political, scientific, and socio-legal arrangements of power and, in turn, how Hoodia plants act or fail to act in ways that reconfigure such arrangements, this study offers a deeper understanding of how human culture and nonhuman nature can affect one another and how those interactions are also historical rather than natural processes thus open to change. In doing so, it demonstrates that there are moments of possibility and rupture even as these arrangements delimit what forms of materiality are deemed to matter most.

More meaningful strategies for engendering belonging are likely to be found in considering the connections across disparate ways of knowing and forms of matter. Although San peoples, Hoodia growers, and CSIR scientists recognized the need to distinguish their knowledge from one another's in order to claim recognition, their ways of knowing shared some attributes. The materiality of patent documents revealed that both San and CSIR Hoodia knowledge were rooted in the past and similarly dynamic and changing, while Hoodia materialities showed how all three actors actually shared relationships to Hoodia as a plant from nature, as a molecule, and as cultivated. Thinking back to Elizabeth "Bettie" Tieties in her garden, Robby Gass on his farm, and Unilever's growing of Hoodia plants in South Africa, they all shared an interest, albeit for different reasons, in growing Hoodia and harnessing its active chemical properties. Examining these connections through an understanding of multiple modalities of materiality, this book argues, can offer a pathway toward building more meaningful and alternative modernities that can enable diverse ways of knowing, being, and belonging to flourish. Although developing such rich analyses may be difficult liberation work, as Petrus Vaalbooi reminds us in the epigraph, it is a process and a vision worth striving for.

Appendix 1

Community Protocols and Research Guidelines for Working with Indigenous Peoples

Aboriginal and Torres Strait Islander Research Engagement Protocol
www.nintione.com.au/resource/Aboriginal-Research-Engagement
-Protocol_template-for-use.pdf

Alaska Federation of Natives Guidelines for Research
www.ankn.uaf.edu/IKS/afnguide.html

Bio-cultural Community Protocol of the Traditional Healers of the
Malayali Tribes
www.community-protocols.org/wp-content/uploads/documents
/India-Malayali_Vaidyas_BCP.pdf

Biocultural Protocol of Gunis and Medicinal Plants Conservation
Farmers of Mewar
www.community-protocols.org/wp-content/uploads/documents
/India-Gunis_and_Medicinal_Plant_Conservation_Farmers
_BCP.pdf

Biocultural Protocol of the Traditional Health Practitioners of
Bushbuckridge
http://community-protocols.org/wp-content/uploads/documents
/South_Africa-Bushbuckridge_Biocultural_Protocol.pdf

Deh Cho First Nation Traditional Knowledge Research Protocol
www.reviewboard.ca/upload/ref_library/DCFN%20TK%20
research%20protocol.pdf

Hopi Cultural Preservation Office: Protocol for Research, Publication, and Recordings: Motion, Visual, Sound, Multimedia, and Other Mechanical Devices

www8.nau.edu/hcpo-p/ResProto.pdf

Kahniakehaka Nation Akwesasne Good Mind Research Protocol

https://reo.mcmaster.ca/download/akwesasne.pdf

Lingayat Bio-Cultural Protocol

www.community-protocols.org/wp-content/uploads/documents/
India-Lingayat_Biocultural_Protocol.pdf

Model Tribal Research Code

https://ccph.memberclicks.net/assets/Documents/
CBPRCurriculum/AppendixF/mdl-code.pdf

Pashtoon Biocultural Community Protocol

www.pastoralpeoples.org/docs/pashtoon_biocultural_protocol.pdf

Protocols and Principles for Conducting Research in a Nuu-Chah-Nulth Context

www.cahr.uvic.ca/nearbc/documents/2009/NTC-Protocols-and-
Principles.pdf

Raika Bio-Cultural Protocol

www.community-protocols.org/wp-content/uploads/documents/
India-Raika_Community_Protocol.pdf

The Samburu Community Protocol

http://community-protocols.org/wp-content/uploads/documents/
Kenya-Samburu_Community_Protocol.pdf

Six Nations Council Research Ethics Committee Protocol

www.sixnations.ca/admResearchEthicsProtocol.pdf

Tl'azt'en Nation Guidelines for Research in Tl'azt'en Territory

http://cura.unbc.ca/governance/CEM-Tlazten%20Guidelines.pdf

Working with Gwich'in Traditional Knowledge in the Gwich'in Settlement Region (Gwich'in Traditional Knowledge Research Policy)

www.grrb.nt.ca/pdf/GTCTKPolicy.pdf

Appendix 2

Strategies for Patent Litigation

ALTHOUGH THE MATERIALITIES OF PATENT RULES AND DOCUMENTS offer resources for theorizing the sameness and difference of CSIR and San ways of knowing and patent ownership as a historical, sociocultural process, they also reveal specific strategies that South African San, and indigenous peoples more broadly, can take to formally challenge a patent in a court of law and render the patent invalid. They suggest, for instance, that indigenous peoples may find that challenging a US-issued patent on the grounds of nonobviousness (arguing that the claimed invention was obvious to an ordinary person skilled in the art) would be a more effective strategy than some others. The Leahy-Smith America Invents Act changed the date for determining nonobviousness to the date the patent was filed rather than when the invention was made, which means that now, under 35 U.S.C. §103, a patent is invalid if it is deemed obvious to a person with ordinary skill in the pertinent art. Prior art for the purposes of §103 is determined by what is prior art according to the §102 novelty provisions. Challenging a patent based on nonobviousness thus differs from challenging it on novelty, the latter of which determines anticipation by comparing the claimed invention and a single source of prior art. In contrast, during a court challenge San could demonstrate nonobviousness under §103 by combining two or more prior art references.[1] Hypothetically, for instance, the South African San Council could argue that a person with ordinary skill in the pertinent art would have found the claimed invention obvious when they read a printed publication describing the properties of the plant and when San peoples told them about how they used it. These two prior art references (printed publication and oral disclosure) in combination could potentially demonstrate that the patent on the invention is invalid because it should have been obvious to a person skilled in the art.

But as discussed, it is unclear whether an oral disclosure by indigenous peoples would be considered prior art due to the geographical distinctions under the previous law. Such an argument would be difficult given that in a claim of nonobviousness, the prior art must be "pertinent" or "analogous." Prior art is analogous if it is *reasonably related* to the same field of endeavor as the invention, or if not, then to the particular problem to which the inventor is involved.[2] This means that US scientists could argue against indigenous peoples' claims of nonobviousness by saying that the printed publication and oral disclosure by indigenous peoples were not reasonably related to the particular problem of isolating the plant-based chemical compositions to suppress appetite.

What arises, then, is a "reasonable person" standard within patent law, which feminist legal scholars have interrogated as based in masculine norms.[3] In the case of Hoodia, this means an ordinary or reasonable scientist skilled in chemistry. San may find more legal room to challenge a patent based on nonobviousness, but they still need to show that a scientist skilled in chemistry would ordinarily engage with and consult the oral disclosures and publications made by or referencing the knowledge of indigenous peoples. So placing critical attention on changing practices of science to encourage more meaningful engagement between scientists and indigenous peoples not only makes for better science, but can also change the meaning of what an "ordinary person skilled in the art" means under the law, thus providing more possibilities for indigenous peoples to challenge patented inventions.

Notes

Introduction

This book's epigraphs are taken from a San community–led publication in which San peoples have theorized and produced their own histories. Willemien le Roux and Alison White, eds., *Voices of the San: Living in Southern Africa Today* (Cape Town: Kwela Books, 2004).

1   For more on San histories, see chapter 1. See also John Parkington, David Morris, and Neil Rusch, *Karoo Rock Engravings* (Cape Town: Creda Communications, 2008); le Roux and White, *Voices of the San*; Andy Smith et al., *The Bushmen of Southern Africa: A Foraging Society in Transition* (Cape Town: David Philip, 2000); Nigel Penn, *The Forgotten Frontier: Colonist and Khoisan on the Cape's Northern Frontier in the Eighteenth Century* (Athens: Ohio University Press, 2005); Richard B. Lee, *The Dobe Ju/'hoansi*, 3rd ed. (Belmont, CA: Wadsworth Thomson Learning, 2003).

2   *Hoodia gordonii* is one of several species within the genus *Hoodia*, which also includes *Hoodia corrorii, Hoodia flava, Hoodia piliferum*, and *Hoodia officinale*, that are known for their appetite-suppressing properties. Unless otherwise noted, I generally refer to *Hoodia gordonii* simply as Hoodia or by its San name, !Khoba. For more information on the plant, see Peter V. Bruyns, *Stapeliads of Southern Africa and Madagascar* (Hatfield, South Africa: Umdaus Press, 2005).

3   Members of the World Conservation Union drafted a resolution in 1963 to begin negotiations for implementing a convention for the protection of trade in wild animals and plants across nation-state borders. The convention, which was agreed to in March 1973 and went into force in July 1975, now has 175 parties (including South Africa, the United States, and the United Kingdom). Appendix 1 lists species threatened with extinction, and appendix 2 "includes species not necessarily threatened with extinction, but in which trade must be controlled in order to avoid utilization incompatible with their survival." In 2009, the CITES species listed *Hoodia gordonii*

in appendix 2. The Convention on International Trade in Endangered Species, Art. IV, § 2, mandates that the export of any listed Hoodia species requires an export permit from the state, which are granted only if the trade in the species is "not . . . detrimental" to its survival, not obtained illegally, and shipped "as to minimize the risk of injury" to the species. United Nations Environmental Programme, "Convention on International Trade in Endangered Species," July 1, 1975, www.cites.org/eng/disc/text.php.

4   Rachel P. Wynberg, Doris Schroeder, and Roger Chennells, *Indigenous Peoples, Consent, and Benefit Sharing: Lessons from the San-Hoodia Case* (New York: Springer, 2009).

5   Nick Shepard, "Disciplining Archaeology: The Invention of South African Prehistory, 1923-1953," *Kronos* 28, no. 1 (2002): 129.

6   This work includes Rachel P. Wynberg, "Rhetoric, Realism, and Benefit Sharing: Use of Traditional Knowledge of Hoodia Species in the Development of Appetite Suppressant," *Journal of World Intellectual Property* 7, no. 6 (2004): 851–76; Rachel P. Wynberg and Sarah A. Laird, "Bioprospecting: Tracking the Policy Debate," *Environment: Science and Policy for Sustainable Development* 49, no. 10 (2007): 20–32; Rachel P. Wynberg, "Navigating a Way through Regulatory Frameworks for *Hoodia* Use, Conservation, Trade, and Benefit Sharing," in *Wild Product Governance: Finding Policies That Work for Non–Timber Forest Products*, ed. Sarah A. Laird, Rebecca McLain, and Rachel P. Wynberg (London, UK: Earthscan, 2010), 309–26; and Rachel P. Wynberg et al., "Formalization of the Natural Product Trade in Southern Africa: Unintended Consequences and Policy Blurring in Biotrade and Bioprospecting," *Society and Natural Resources* 28 (2015): 559–74. See also the following works by Roger Chennells: "Ethics and Practice in Ethnobiology: The Experience of the San Peoples of Southern Africa," in *Biodiversity and the Law: Intellectual Property, Biotechnology and Traditional Knowledge*, ed. Charles R. McManis (London: Earthscan, 2007), 413–27; "The ≠Khomani San of South Africa," in *Indigenous Peoples Protected Areas in Africa: From Principles to Practice*, ed. John Nelson and Lindsay Hossack (Moreton-in-Marsh, UK: Forest Peoples Programme, 2003), 269-93; "Vulnerability and Indigenous Communities: Are the San of South Africa a Vulnerable People?," *Cambridge Quarterly of Healthcare Ethics* 18, no. 2 (2009): 147–54; "Toward Global Justice through Benefit Sharing," *Hastings Center Report* 40, no. 1 (2010): 3; "Traditional Knowledge and Benefit Sharing after the Nagoya Protocol: Three Cases from South Africa," *Law, Environment, and Development Journal* 9, no. 2 (2013): 165–84. Other works on this topic include Saskia Vermeylen, "Contextualizing 'Fair' and 'Equitable': The San's Reflections on the Hoodia Benefit-Sharing Agreement," *Local Environment* 12, no. 4 (2007): 423–36, and "From Life Force to Slimming Aid: Exploring Views on the Commodification of Traditional Medicinal Knowledge," *Applied Geography* 28, no. 3 (2008): 224–35; Doris Schroeder, "Informed

Consent: From Medical Research to Traditional Knowledge," in *Indigenous Peoples, Consent, and Benefit Sharing*, ed. Rachel P. Wynberg, Doris Schroeder, and Roger Chennells (New York: Springer, 2009), 27–52; and George Sombe Mukuka, *Reap What You Have Not Sown: Indigenous Knowledge Systems and Intellectual Property Laws in South Africa* (Pretoria: Pretoria University Law Press, 2010).

7   Carrie Friese, *Cloning Wild Life: Zoos, Captivity, and the Future of Endangered Animals* (New York: New York University Press, 2013), 2.

8   James Boyle, *The Public Domain: Enclosing the Commons of the Mind* (New Haven, CT: Yale University Press, 2008); Arti K. Rai and Rebecca S. Eisenberg, "Bayh-Dole Reform and the Progress of Biomedicine," *Law and Contemporary Problems* 66, nos. 1-2 (2003): 289–314; Rochelle Dreyfuss, "Protecting the Public Domain of Science: Has the Time for an Experimental Use Defense Arrived?," *Arizona Law Review* 46, no. 3 (2004): 457–72; Lawrence Lessig, *The Future of Ideas: The Fate of the Commons in a Connected World* (New York: Random House, 2001); Jonathan Kahn, "Race-ing Patents / Patenting Race: An Emerging Political Geography of Intellectual Property in Biotechnology," *Iowa Law Review* 92, no. 1 (2007): 353–402; and Jonathan Kahn, "Exploiting Race in Drug Development: BiDil's Interim Model of Pharmacogenomics," *Social Studies of Science* 38, no. 5 (2008): 737–58.

9   James Boyle, *Shamans, Software, and Spleens: Law and the Construction of the Information Society* (Cambridge, MA: Harvard University Press, 1996); Peter Drahos and Ruth Mayne, eds., *Global Intellectual Property Rights: Knowledge, Access, and Development* (New York: Palgrave Macmillan, 2002); J. M. Finger and Philip Schuler, eds., *Poor People's Knowledge: Promoting Intellectual Property in Developing Countries* (Washington, DC: World Bank and Oxford University Press, 2004).

10 Michael F. Brown, "Can Culture Be Copyrighted?" *Current Anthropology* 39, no. 2 (1998): 193–222, and *Who Owns Native Culture?* (Cambridge, MA: Harvard University Press, 2003); Jane E. Anderson, *Law, Knowledge, Culture: The Production of Indigenous Knowledge in Intellectual Property Law* (Cheltenham, UK: Edward Elgar, 2009); and Boatema Boateng, *The Copyright Thing Doesn't Work Here: Adinkra and Kente Cloth and Intellectual Property in Ghana* (Minneapolis: University of Minnesota Press, 2011).

11 Joshua Rosenthal, "Integrating Drug Discovery, Biodiversity Conservation, and Economic Development: Early Lessons from the International Cooperative Biodiversity Groups," in *Biodiversity and Human Health*, ed. Grifo Francesca and Joshua Rosenthal (Washington, DC: Island Press, 1997), 281–301.

12 Shane Greene, "Indigenous People Incorporated? Culture as Politics, Culture as Property in Pharmaceutical Bioprospecting," *Current Anthropology* 45, no. 2 (2004); 211–37.

13 Cori Hayden, *When Nature Goes Public: The Making and Unmaking of Bioprospecting in Mexico* (Princeton, NJ: Princeton University Press, 2003), and

"Taking as Giving: Bioscience, Exchange, and the Politics of Benefit-Sharing," *Social Studies of Science* 37, no. 5 (2007): 729–58.

14 Vermeylen, "Contextualizing 'Fair' and 'Equitable'"; Chennells, "Toward Global Justice through Benefit Sharing"; Debra Harry and Le`a Malia Kanehe, "The BS in Access and Benefit Sharing (ABS): Critical Questions for Indigenous Peoples," in *The Catch: Perspectives in Benefit Sharing*, ed. Beth Burrows (Edmonds, WA: Edmonds Institute, 2005) 81–120; and Wynberg, "Rhetoric, Realism and Benefit Sharing."

15 Elan Abrell et al., *Imagining a Traditional Knowledge Commons: A Community Approach to Ensuring the Local Integrity of Environmental Law and Policy* (Rome: Natural Justice, 2009); Adam Haupt, *Stealing Empire: P2P, Intellectual Property, and Hip-Hop Subversion* (Cape Town: Human Sciences Research Council, 2008); Caroline B. Ncube and Tobias Schonwetter, "New Hope for Africa? Copyright and Access to Knowledge in the Digital Age," *Info* 13, no. 3 (2011): 64–74; and Caroline B. Ncube, "The Development of Intellectual Property Policies in Africa: Some Key Considerations and a Research Agenda," *Intellectual Property Rights* 1, no. 1 (2013): 1–5.

16 Sandra Harding, *Sciences from Below: Feminisms, Postcolonialities, and Modernities* (Durham, NC: Duke University Press, 2008).

17 Scholars who have produced valuable insights into gender and patents using this approach include Kjersten Bunker Whittington and Laurel Smith-Doerr, "Gender and Commercial Science: Women's Patenting in the Life Sciences," *Journal of Technology Transfer* 30, no. 4 (2005): 355–70; and Jerry G. Thursby and Marie C. Thursby, "Gender Patterns of Research and Licensing Activity of Science and Engineering Faculty," ibid.: 343–53. Attention to patent ownership incites a broader inquiry into the systemic discrimination and inequality historically faced by women in society and the sciences—a major focus of research into women and STEM. Historians of science who have documented that men have historically held a higher number of patents than females include Deborah J. Merritt, "Hypatia in the Patent Office: Women Inventors and the Law, 1865-1900," *American Journal of Legal History* 35, no. 3 (1991); 235–306; and B. Zorina Khan, "'Not for Ornament': Patenting Activity by Nineteenth-Century Women Inventors," *Journal of Interdisciplinary History* 31, no. 2 (2000): 159–95. Laws of coverture designating married women as the property of their husbands are partially to blame, B. Zorina Khan suggests in "Married Women's Property Laws and Female Commercial Activity: Evidence from United States Patent Records, 1790-1895," *Journal of Economic History* 56, no. 2 (1996): 356–88. Unable to own property for themselves, married women were often prevented from establishing themselves as inventors. As laws of coverture began to dissolve, women became patent owners in greater numbers. Middle-class white women made up the majority of these new patent owners, but according to Merritt ("Hypatia in the Patent Office"), at least four Black women became early patent owners between 1865 and

1900. This included furniture by Miriam E. Benjamin, a writing desk by Sarah E. Goode, and an ironing board by Sarah Boone. One of the four was an anonymous Black woman, inventor of a new clothes wringer, who in an 1891 issue of *The Woman Inventor* explained that she sold her patent rights because "if it was known that a negro woman patented the invention, white ladies would not buy the wringer" (ibid.: 305). Given histories of slavery, it is not surprising that Black women held fewer patents than white women. Becoming a patent owner is onerous when one has historically been deemed property.

Feminist scholars of science have recently called attention to how female scientists in both university and commercial sectors continue to hold fewer patents than their male colleagues; see Whittington and Smith-Doerr, "Gender and Commercial Science." Their lower rate of patenting has a negative impact on the professional advancement of female scientists, Sue Rosser argues in "The Gender Gap in Patents," in *Women, Science, and Technology: A Reader in Feminist Science Studies*, ed. Mary Wyer et al. (New York: Routledge, 2014); 111–32. Scholars attribute the smaller number of female patent owners to gender bias in the sciences (Annette I. Kahler, "Examining Exclusion in Woman-Inventor Patenting: A Comparison of Educational Trends and Patent Trends and Patent Data in the Era of Computer Engineer Barbie®," *Journal of Gender, Social Policy, and the Law* 19, no. 3 [2011]: 773–98), lack of connections to industry (Waverly W. Ding, Fiona Murray, and Toby E. Stuart, "Gender Differences in Patenting in the Academic Life Sciences," *Science* 313, no. 5787 [2006]: 665–67), hierarchical work settings (Kjersten Bunker Whittington and Laurel Smith-Doerr, "Women Inventors in Context: Disparities in Patenting across Academia and Industry," *Gender and Society* 22, no. 2 [2008]: 194–218), a gender gap in higher education (Rainer Frietsch et al., "Gender-Specific Patterns in Patenting and Publishing," *Research Policy* 38, no. 4 [2009]: 590–99), and motherhood (Kjersten Bunker Whittington, "Mothers of Invention? Gender, Motherhood, and New Dimensions of Productivity in the Science Profession," *Work and Occupations* 38, no. 3 [2011]: 417–56). Although women tend to hold fewer patents, in "Gender and Commercial Science," Whittington and Smith-Doerr point out that women's patents tend to be cited more often than men's, perhaps indicating quality over quantity, but women's patents tend to have lower technological impact than men's, argue Cassidy R. Sugimoto, Chaoqun Ni, Jevin D. West, and Vincent Larivière in "The Academic Advantage: Gender Disparities in Patenting," *PLOS One* 10, no. 5 [2015]: 1–10. Alarmed by these trends, the World Intellectual Property Organization has stressed the need for women to become intellectual property owners as a "tool of economic and social empowerment." www.wipo.int/about-ip/en/women_ip.html (last visited March 14, 2014).

Feminist scholars of science have also examined how patents prevent scientific innovation and curtail women's health care by restricting access to important scientific materials and processes. See Eileen Kane, "Molecules and Conflict: Cancer, Patents, and Women's Health," *Journal of Gender, Social Policy, and the Law* 15, no. 2 (2007): 305–35. The ACLU Women's Rights Project successfully argued in a 2013 US Supreme Court case that Myriad's gene sequence patents were invalid; Sandra S. Park, "Gene Patents and the Public Interest: Litigating *Association for Molecular Pathology v. Myriad Genetics* and Lessons Moving Forward," *North Carolina Journal of Law and Technology* 15, no. 4 (2014): 519–36.

Although the court left open the possibility that patents could be filed on synthetic DNA sequences, the case was lauded as a victory for women's health care and for medical research more broadly by ensuring open access to genetic sequences.

18 Winona LaDuke, *Recovering the Sacred: The Power of Naming and Claiming* (Cambridge, MA: South End Press, 2005); and Linda Tuhiwai Smith, *Decolonizing Methodologies: Research and Indigenous Peoples* (London: Zed Books, 1999).

19 Harry and Kanehe, "The BS in Access and Benefit Sharing (ABS)"; and Victoria Tauli-Corpuz, "Is Biopiracy an Issue for Feminists in the Philippines?," *Signs: Journal of Women in Culture and Society* 32, no. 2 (2007): 332–37.

20 Vandana Shiva and Ingunn Moser, *Biopolitics: A Feminist and Ecological Reader on Biotechnology* (London: Zed Books, 1995); and Vandana Shiva, *Biopiracy: The Plunder of Nature and Knowledge* (Boston: South End Press, 1997).

21 NGO Forum, Beijing Declaration of Indigenous Women, UN Fourth World Conference on Women, Huairou, Beijing, China, Sept. 4-15, 1995, available at www.ipcb.org/resolutions/htmls/dec_ beijing.html; Indigenous Women's Biodiversity Network, Mankun, Sabah, Malaysia, Feb. 4-5, 2004, Manukan Declaration, available at www.ipcb.org/resolutions/htmls/manukan.html; and *Permanent Forum on Indigenous Issues,* 3rd Sess., Supp. No. 23, at 12-14, U.N. Doc. E/C.19/2004/23.

22 The analysis here also benefits from scholarship by Donna Haraway in *Modest_Witness@Second_Millennium.FemaleMan_Meets_OncoMouse: Feminism and Technoscience* (New York: Routledge, 1997) that examines how struggles over patent ownership involve "who gets to count as nature's author," and by Shobita Parthasarathy in "Whose Knowledge? Whose Values? The Comparative Politics of Patenting Life Forms in the United States and Europe," *Policy Sciences* 44, no. 3 (2011): 267–88, that shows how patent domains have different "expertise barriers" that make it difficult to recognize alternative forms of knowledge. For more on feminist science studies' attention to patent ownership, see Laura A. Foster, "Situating Feminisms, Patent Law, and the Public Domain," *Columbia Journal of Gender and Law* 20, no. 2 (2011): 261–347, "Patents, Biopolitics, and Feminisms: Locating Patent Law Struggles over Breast Cancer Genes and the *Hoodia* Plant," *International Journal of Cultural Property* 19, no. 3 (2012): 371–400, "The Making and

Unmaking of Patent Ownership: Technicalities, Materialities, and Subjectivities," *PoLAR: Political and Legal Anthropology Review* 39, no. 1 (2016): 127–43, and "Decolonizing Patent Law: Postcolonial Technoscience and Indigenous Knowledge in South Africa," *Feminist Formations* 28, no. 3 (2016): 148–73. See also Kara W. Swanson, "Getting a Grip on the Corset: Gender, Sexuality, and Patent Law," *Yale Journal of Law and Feminism* 23, no. 1 (2011): 57–115, and "Intellectual Property and Gender: Reflections on Accomplishments and Methodology," *Journal of Gender, Social Policy, and the Law* 43, no. 1 (2015): 175–98.

23   Lucile Brockway, *Science and Colonial Expansion: The Role of the British Royal Botanic Gardens* (New York: Academic Press, 1979); Donna J. Haraway, *Primate Visions: Gender, Race, and Nature in the World of Modern Science* (New York: Routledge, 1989); Sharon Traweek, *Beamtimes and Lifetimes: The World of High Energy Physicists* (Cambridge, MA: Harvard University Press, 1988); and Shiva, *Biopiracy*.

24   Rosi Braidotti, *Women, the Environment, and Sustainable Development: Towards a Theoretical Synthesis* (London: Zed Books, 1994); Catherine V. Scott, *Gender and Development: Rethinking Modernization and Dependency Theory* (Boulder, CO: Lynne Rienner, 1995); and Nalini Visvanathan et al., eds., *The Women, Gender, and Development Reader* (London: Zed Books, 1997).

25   Sandra Harding, *Sciences from Below*, and *Is Science Multicultural? Postcolonialisms, Feminisms, and Epistemologies* (Bloomington: Indiana University Press, 1998); Judith Ann Carney, *Black Rice: The African Origins of Rice Cultivation in the Americas* (Cambridge, MA: Harvard University Press, 2001); Hayden, *When Nature Goes Public*; Kavita Philip, *Civilizing Natures: Race, Resources, and Modernity in Colonial South India* (New Brunswick, NJ: Rutgers University Press, 2004); Reardon, *Race to the Finish*; Ruha Benjamin, "A Lab of Their Own: Genomic Sovereignty as Postcolonial Science Policy," *Policy and Society* 28, no. 4 (2009): 341–55; Carole R. McCann, "Malthusian Men and Demographic Transitions: A Case Study of Hegemonic Masculinity in Mid-Twentieth-Century Population Theory," *Frontiers: A Journal of Women's Studies* 30, no. 1 (2009): 142–71; Sandra Harding, *The Postcolonial Science and Technology Studies Reader* (Durham, NC: Duke University Press, 2011); Gabrielle Hecht, *Being Nuclear: Africans and the Global Uranium Trade* (Cambridge, MA: MIT Press, 2012); Chikako Takeshita, *The Global Biopolitics of the IUD: How Science Constructs Contraceptive Users and Women's Bodies* (Cambridge, MA: MIT Press, 2012); Clare Ching Jen, "How to Survive Contagion, Disease, and Disaster: The 'Masked Asian/American Woman' as Low-Tech Specter of Emergency Preparedness," *Feminist Formations* 25, no. 2 (2013): 107–28; Kim TallBear, *Native American DNA: Tribal Belonging and the False Promise of Genetic Science* (Minneapolis: University of Minnesota Press, 2013); Anne Pollock, "Places of Pharmaceutical Knowledge-Making: Global Health, Postcolonial Science, and Hope in South African Drug Discovery," *Social Studies of Science* 44, no. 6 (2014): 848–73; and Deboleena Roy and

Banu Subramaniam, "Matter in the Shadows: Feminist New Materialism and the Practices of Colonialism," in *Mattering: Feminism, Science, and Materialism*, ed. Victoria Pitts-Taylor (New York: New York University Press, 2016), 23–42. Also see the following discussions in *Science, Technology, and Human Values* 41, no. 6 (2016): Angela Willey, "A World of Materialisms: Postcolonial Feminist Science Studies and the New Natural," 991–1014; Lindsay Adams Smith, "Identifying Democracy: Citizenship, DNA, and Identity in Postdictatorship Argentina," 1037–62; Ruha Benjamin, "Informed Refusal: Toward a Justice-Based Bioethics," 967–90; Sandra Harding, "Latin American Decolonial Social Studies of Scientific Knowledge: Alliances and Tensions," 1063–87; and Laura A. Foster, "A Postapartheid Genome: Genetic Ancestry Testing and Belonging in South Africa," 1015–36.

26 See Elaine Salo and Benita Moolman, "Introduction: Biology, Bodies, and Human Rights," *Agenda: Empowering Women for Gender Equity* 27, no. 4 (2013): 3–9.

27 For reviews of this literature, see Sandra Harding, "Postcolonial and Feminist Philosophies of Science and Technology: Convergences and Dissonances," *Postcolonial Studies* 12, no. 4 (2009): 401–21; and Anne Pollock and Banu Subramaniam, "Resisting Power, Retooling Justice: Promises of Feminist Postcolonial Technosciences," *Science, Technology, and Human Values* 41, no. 6 (2016): 951–66.

28 As Harding notes, even though work within this field deploys the term *postcolonial*, it retains a critical stance toward this language and associated terms such as *non-Western, Global South,* and *Third World* (*Postcolonial Science and Technology Studies Reader*, 23). Harding explains that the use of these terms remains highly problematic as they continue to center Western notions of modernity while precluding the political concerns of those who have developed their own forms of modernity. Any contrast between such binaries as West and non-West results in homogenizing both groups and obscures the complex social relations and inequalities among various groupings within each. Furthermore, even alternatives such as *globalization* and *transnationalism* are not politically neutral; therefore, in light of any good alternatives, feminist postcolonial science studies scholars must contend with the fact that even the terms in which they develop their critiques remain partial and problematic.

29 Eden Medina, Ivan da Costa Marques, and Christina Holmes, *Beyond Imported Magic: Essays on Science, Technology, and Society in Latin America* (Cambridge, MA: MIT Press, 2014); Harding, "Latin American Decolonial Social Studies of Scientific Knowledge"; Subramaniam et al., "Feminism, Postcolonialism, and Technoscience."

30 Banu Subramaniam et al., "Feminism, Postcolonialism, and Technoscience," in *Handbook of Science and Technology Studies*, ed. Clark Miller et al. (Cambridge, MA: MIT Press, 2016).

31 Frantz Fanon, *The Wretched of the Earth*, trans. Richard Philcox (New York: Grove Press, 2004); Achille Mbembe, *On the Postcolony* (Berkeley: University of California Press, 2001); and Ngũgĩ wa Thiong'o, *Decolonising the Mind: The Politics of Language in African Literature* (London: James Currey, 1986).

32 Linda Tuhiwai Smith, *Decolonizing Methodologies*.

33 For other calls for attention to scale in science studies, see Michel Callon, "Some Elements of a Sociology of Translation: Domestication of the Scallops and the Fishermen of St. Brieuc Bay," in *Power, Action, and Belief: A New Sociology of Knowledge?*, ed. John Law (London: Routledge, 1986), 196–223; Bruno Latour and Steve Woolgar, *Laboratory Life: The Construction of Scientific Facts* (Princeton, NJ: Princeton University Press, 1986). In sociolegal studies, see Boaventura de Sousa Santos, "A Map of Misreading: Toward a Postmodern Conception of Law," *Journal of Law and Society* 14, no. 3 (1987): 279–302; and Sally Engle Merry, "Legal Pluralism," *Law and Society Review* 22, no. 5 (1988): 869–96; in feminist science studies, see Michelle Murphy, *Seizing the Means of Reproduction: Entanglements of Feminism, Health, and Technoscience* (Durham, NC: Duke University Press, 2012); and Alondra Nelson, "Bio Science: Genetic Genealogy Testing and the Pursuit of African Ancestry," *Social Studies of Science* 38, no. 5 (2008): 759–83.

34 Abena Dove Osseo-Asare, *Bitter Roots: The Search for Healing Plants in Africa* (Chicago: University of Chicago Press, 2014); and Murphy, *Seizing the Means of Reproduction*.

35 For more on scale and intersectional analysis, see Vivian M. May, *Pursuing Intersectionality, Unsettling Dominant Imaginaries* (New York: Routledge, 2015); and Patricia Hill Collins and Sirma Bilge, *Intersectionality* (Malden, MA: Polity Press, 2016).

36 For an excellent example of storytelling as methodological technique in critical race legal theory, see Patricia A. Williams, *The Alchemy of Race and Rights* (Cambridge, MA: Harvard University Press, 1991).

37 The students were also not aware that the first British edition of *Willy Wonka and the Chocolate Factory* was criticized for its portrayal of Oompa-Loompas as black African pygmies used to replace white workers; see Emma Robertson, *Chocolate, Women, and Empire: A Social and Cultural History* (Manchester: Manchester University Press, 2013).

38 For early work on representations of indigenous peoples, see Vine Deloria Jr., *Custer Died for Your Sins: An Indian Manifesto* (New York: Macmillan, 1969); on representations of Africa, see V. Y. Mudimbe, *The Invention of Africa: Gnosis, Philosophy, and the Order of Knowledge* (Bloomington: Indiana University Press, 1988).

39 For more on gendered metaphors related to intellectual property rights, see Malla Pollack, "Towards a Feminist Theory of the Public Domain, or Rejecting the Gendered Scope of United States Copyrightable and Patentable Subject Matter," *Journal of Women and Law* 12 (2006): 603–26; Dan L. Burk,

"Feminism and Dualism in Intellectual Property," *Journal of Gender, Social Policy, and the Law* 15, no. 2 (2007): 183–206, and "Do Patents Have Gender?," *Journal of Gender, Social Policy, and the Law* 19, no. 3 (2011): 881–919; and Debora J. Halbert, "Feminist Interpretations of Intellectual Property," *Journal of Gender, Social Policy, and the Law* 14, no. 3 (2006): 431–60.

40 For instance, Karen Barad investigates Bohr's philosophy-physics to shift feminist understandings of the material and discursive by investigating their intra-actions in her *Meeting the Universe Halfway: Quantum Physics and the Entanglement of Matter and Meaning* (Durham, NC: Duke University Press, 2007). Vicki Kirby interrogates the fields of biology, mathematics, and physics through theories of deconstruction to challenge feminist theorizing of nature and culture in *Quantum Anthropologies: Life at Large* (Durham, NC: Duke University Press, 2011). Elizabeth Wilson explores how scientific theories of depression might challenge feminist theory to attend to biological data and its own aggression in *Gut Feminism* (Durham, NC: Duke University Press, 2015). Stacy Alaimo and Susan Hekman address theories that restore the material in feminist theory in their edited volume *Material Feminisms* (Bloomington: Indiana University Press, 2008). Yet Sarah Ahmed also warns that positioning this engagement with matter as "new" as opposed to an "old" antibiological feminism risks eliding important genealogies of feminist thought that have engaged with biology and matter from their inception; "Open Forum Imaginary Prohibitions: Some Preliminary Remarks on the Founding Gestures of the 'New Materialism,'" *European Journal of Women's Studies* 15, no. 1 (2008): 23–39.

41 Angela Willey, *Undoing Monogamy: The Politics of Science and the Possibilities of Biology* (Durham, NC: Duke University Press, 2016).

42 This model of materiality has been theorized by actor-network scholars who have examined how nonhumans participate as "actants" within social networks. See, for instance, Bruno Latour, *Science in Action: How to Follow Scientists and Engineers through Society* (Cambridge, MA: Harvard University Press, 1987); and Callon, "Some Elements of a Sociology of Translation." Feminist science studies scholarship that has addressed nonhumans in similar ways but with much more attention to dynamics of power and conflict include Adele Clarke and Theresa Montini, "The Many Faces of RU486: Tales of Situated Knowledges and Technological Contestations," *Science, Technology, and Human Values* 18, no. 1 (1993): 42–78; and Adele E. Clarke and Susan Leigh Star, "The Social Worlds Framework: A Theory/Methods Framework," in *The Handbook of Science and Technology Studies*, ed. Edward J. Hackett et al. (Cambridge, MA: MIT Press, 2008), 113–38. Early feminist critiques of science also examined the complex interplay of nature and culture by asking how science constructs nature and, in turn, how nature and biology shape people's lives. See, for instance, Sandra Harding, *The Science Question in Feminism* (Ithaca, NY: Cornell University Press,

1986) and *Whose Science? Whose Knowledge? Thinking from Women's Lives* (Ithaca, NY: Cornell University Press, 1991); Anne Fausto-Sterling, *Myths of Gender: Biological Theories about Women and Men* (New York: Basic Books, 1985); Ruth Hubbard, Mary Sue Henifin, and Barbara Fried, eds., *Biological Woman—the Convenient Myth: A Collection of Feminist Essays and a Comprehensive Bibliography* (Cambridge, MA: Schenkman, 1982) and *Women Look at Biology Looking at Women: A Collection of Feminist Critiques* (Boston: G. K. Hall, 1979); Ruth Bleier, *Science and Gender: A Critique of Biology and Its Theories on Women* (New York: Pergamon Press, 1984) and *Feminist Approaches to Science* (New York: Pergamon Press, 1986); Evelyn Reed, *Is Biology Woman's Destiny?* 2nd ed. (New York: Pathfinder Press, 1985) and *Sexism and Science* (New York: Pathfinder Press, 1978); Helen E. Longino, *Science as Social Knowledge: Values and Objectivity in Scientific Inquiry* (Princeton, NJ: Princeton University Press, 1990); Evelyn Fox Keller, "Feminism and Science," *Signs: Journal of Women in Culture and Society* 7, no. 3 (1982): 598–602; Nancy Tuana, ed., *Feminism and Science* (Bloomington: Indiana University Press, 1989); Brighton Women and Science Group and Lynda I. A. Birke, eds., *Alice through the Microscope: The Power of Science over Women's Lives* (London: Virago, 1980); Carolyn Merchant, *The Death of Nature: Women, Ecology, and the Scientific Revolution* (San Francisco: Harper and Row, 1980); and Susan Griffin, *Woman and Nature: The Roaring inside Her* (New York: Harper and Row, 1978).

43   For more information, see Alaimo and Hekman, *Material Feminisms*; and Barad, *Meeting the Universe Halfway*.

44   Jacques Derrida, "Force of Law: The 'Mystical Foundation of Authority,'" *Cardozo Law Review* 11, nos. 5-6 (1990): 919–1046.

45   For examinations of law that deploy science studies to suggest the materiality of legal documents, see Mariana Valverde, "Jurisdiction and Scale: Legal 'Technicalities' as Resources for Theory," *Social and Legal Studies* 18, no. 2 (2009): 139-57; and Annelise Riles, "A New Agenda for the Cultural Study of Law: Taking on the Technicalities," *Buffalo Law Review* 53, no. 3 (2005): 979–1033, and *Collateral Knowledge: Legal Reasoning in the Global Financial Markets*, Chicago Series in Law and Society (Chicago: University of Chicago Press, 2011).

46   For instance, Adriana Petryna's study of the emergence of "biological citizenship" in the Ukraine after the Chernobyl nuclear disaster finds that individuals made claims through new regulatory regimes for inclusion into the post-Soviet welfare state based on their bodily injury and that the Ukrainian nation-state began to recognize a new group of subjects, granting them rights based on their biology. Petryna, *Life Exposed: Biological Citizens after Chernobyl* (Princeton, NJ: Princeton University Press, 2002). For more on biological citizenship, see Nikolas Rose, *The Politics of Life Itself: Biomedicine, Power, and Subjectivity in the Twenty-First Century* (Princeton, NJ: Princeton University Press, 2006).

47 An analysis that begins to theorize these connections through a discussion of knowledge workers is Aihwa Ong, *Neoliberalism as Exception: Mutations in Citizenship and Sovereignty* (Durham, NC: Duke University Press, 2006).

48 Catherine MacKinnon argues that the very terms of law itself were determined by masculine norms and thus excluded women from the protections of the state, and Kimberlé Crenshaw similarly argues that the law denied Black women protection from sexual violence at the structural, political, and representational level because their intersectional lives were unintelligible to the law. See Catharine A. MacKinnon, "Feminism, Marxism, Method, and the State: An Agenda for Theory," *Signs: Journal of Women in Culture and Society* 7, no. 3 (1982): 515–44; and Kimberlé Crenshaw, "Mapping the Margins: Intersectionality, Identity Politics, and Violence against Women of Color," *Stanford Law Review* 43, no. 6 (1991): 1241–99. Sandra Harding argues that science fails to account for women's lives because it is produced from the understandings of dominant groups, which is supported by Evelynn Hammonds's demonstration that science and society construct understandings of disease in ways that exclude certain people of color. See Harding, *Whose Science?*; and Evelynn Hammonds, "Race, Sex, AIDS: The Construction of 'Other,'" in *Race, Class, and Gender: An Anthology*, ed. Margaret Anderson and Patricia Hill Collins (Belmont, CA: Wadsworth Publishing Company, 1995 [1987]), 402–13.

49 Sarah Nuttall argues that the end of apartheid meant that whites could not assume their belonging to the nation-state but had to become citizens through processes of mutual recognition from others, whereas nonwhites were assumed to belong but had to be actively bound to the nation-state after apartheid. Nuttall, "Subjectivities of Whiteness," *African Studies Review* 44, no. 2 (2001): 115–40.

50 Andrea Smith, "Native Studies at the Horizon of Death: Theorizing Ethnographic Entrapment and Settler Self-Reflexivity," in *Theorizing Native Studies*, ed. Andrea Smith and Audra Simpson (Durham, NC: Duke University Press, 2014), 207–34.

51 Ibid.

52 Although Chennells identifies as white and speaks Afrikaans, he has an extensive history working with indigenous peoples in South Africa and was actively involved in antiapartheid movements. During our conversations, he reminded me that even though the South African San Council asserted agency in hiring him as their lawyer, it remains important to critically question who represents San peoples.

53 Collin Louw, in discussion with author in South Africa, March 9, 2009 (on file with author).

54 Benjamin, "Informed Refusal."

55 Amanda Lock Swarr and Richa Nagar, *Critical Transnational Feminist Praxis* (Albany: SUNY Press, 2010), 7.

56 For more on giving back and reciprocity, see the following articles in *Journal of Research Practice* 10, no. 2 (2014): Jeffrey M. Romm, "The Researcher's Personal Pursuit of Balance between Academic and Practical Contributions," N10; Jade Sasser, "The Limits to Giving Back," M7; Megan Ybarra, "Don't Just Pay It Back, Pay It Forward: From Accountability to Reciprocity in Research Relationships," N5; Sarah Cahill Sawyer, "Failing to Give Enough: When Researcher Ideas about Giving Back Fall Short," N12; and Kathryn Joan Fiorella, "The Researcher's Personal Pursuit of Balance between Academic and Practical Contributions," N11.

57 Kim TallBear, "Standing with and Speaking as Faith: A Feminist-Indigenous Approach to Inquiry," ibid.: N17.

58 Stephen B. Brush and Doreen Stabinsky, *Valuing Local Knowledge: Indigenous People and Intellectual Property Rights* (Washington, DC: Island Press, 1996).

59 I thank DeAnna Rivera, former director of the Tribal Learning and Community and Educational Exchange (TLCEE) at the University of California–Los Angeles, for bringing this to my attention.

60 See Secretariat of the United Nations Permanent Forum on Indigenous Issues, Resource Kit on Indigenous Peoples' Issues, (2008), available at www.un.org/esa/socdev/unpfii/documents/resource_kit_indigenous_2008.pdf (last accessed November 30, 2015).

61 Subramaniam et al., "Feminism, Postcolonialism, and Technoscience."

62 TallBear, *Native American DNA*.

63 Andrew Le Fleur and Lesle Jansen, "Country Report: The Khoisan in Contemporary South Africa: Challenges of Recognition as an Indigenous Peoples" (Cape Town: Konrad-Adenauer-Stiftung, 2013).

64 Osseo-Asare, *Bitter Roots*.

65 Audra Simpson, "On Ethnographic Refusal: Indigeneity, 'Voice,' and Colonial Citizenship," *Junctures* 9 (2007): 72.

Chapter 1. Colonial Science and Hoodia as a Scientific Object

Stapelia Gordoni drawing from Francis Masson's *Stapeliae Novae*

1 Francis Masson, *Stapeliae Novae: Or, a Collection of Several New Species of That Genus; Discovered in the Interior Parts of Africa* (London: W. Bulmer and Co., 1796); and Mia C. Karsten, "Francis Masson, a Gardener-Botanist Who Collected at the Cape," in *Francis Masson's Account of Three Journeys at the Cape of Good Hope, 1772-1775*, ed. Frank R. Bradlow (Cape Town: Tablecloth Press, 1994), 203–14.

2 Even so, Paula Gunn Allen (Laguna Pueblo) reminds us that to establish a beginning and an end is itself a Western notion of progress; Allen, *Grandmothers of the Light: A Medicine Woman's Sourcebook* (Boston: Beacon Press, 1991). Shannon Jackson and Steve Robins warn that to engage in cultural critique through telling counternarratives similarly risks reinscribing colonial

violence because "in South Africa the colonial past rests too heavily on its present"; Jackson and Robins, "Miscast: The Place of the Museum in Negotiating the Bushman Past and Present," *Critical Arts* 13, no. 1 (1999): 70.

3   For more on histories of San and classification, see Andy Smith et al., *The Bushmen of Southern Africa*, 40.

4   For more on the Harvard Kalahari Research Group and debates in anthropology over traditionalist and revisionist understandings of San peoples, see Alan Barnard, "Laurens Van Der Post and the Kalahari Debate," in *Miscast: Negotiating the Presence of the Bushmen*, ed. Pippa Skotnes (Cape Town: University of Cape Town Press, 1996), 239–47.

5   For more information on histories of San peoples, see Leonard Thompson, *A History of South Africa*, 4th ed. (New Haven, CT: Yale University Press, 2014); William Beinart, *Twentieth-Century South Africa*, 2nd ed. (Oxford: Oxford University Press, 2001); Heike Becker, "The Least Sexist Society? Perspectives on Gender, Change, and Violence among Southern African San," *Journal of Southern African Studies* 29, no. 1 (2003): 5–23; Chennells, "The ≠Khomani San of South Africa"; Silke Felton and Heike Becker, *A Gender Perspective on the Status of the San in Southern Africa* (Windhoek, Namibia: Legal Assistance Centre, 2001); le Roux and White, *Voices of the San*; Andy Smith et al., *The Bushmen of Southern Africa*; and Nigel Penn, *The Forgotten Frontier*, and "'Fated to Perish': The Destruction of the Cape San," in *Miscast: Negotiating the Presence of the Bushmen*, ed. Pippa Skotnes (Cape Town: University of Cape Town Press, 1996), 81–92.

6   Thompson, *A History of South Africa*.

7   Ibid.

8   Penn, *The Forgotten Frontier*.

9   Ibid.

10 Thompson, *A History of South Africa*.

11 Ibid.

12 Ibid.

13 Ibid.

14 Ibid.

15 LaDuke, *Recovering the Sacred*.

16 Penn, *The Forgotten Frontier*.

17 Ibid.; Thompson, *A History of South Africa*.

18 Thompson, *A History of South Africa*.

19 Ibid.

20 Premesh Lalu, "When Was South African History Ever Postcolonial?," *Kronos* 34, no. 1 (2008): 267–81.

21 For more on the history of patent law and intellectual property law, see Peter Drahos, *A Philosophy of Intellectual Property* (Dartmouth, MA: Dartmouth Publishing Group, 1996); Christopher May and Susan K. Sell, *Intellectual Property Rights: A Critical History* (Boulder, CO: Lynne Rienner, 2006); Ikechi Mgbeoji, *Global Biopiracy: Patents, Plants, and Indigenous*

Knowledge (Vancouver: UBC Press, 2006); and Rosemary J. Coombe, *The Cultural Life of Intellectual Properties: Authorship, Appropriation, and the Law* (Durham, NC: Duke University Press, 1998).

22   May and Sell, *Intellectual Property Rights*.

23   Drahos, *A Philosophy of Intellectual Property*.

24   For a feminist analysis of invention and male norms, see Clare Pettitt, *Patent Inventions: Intellectual Property and the Victorian Novel* (Oxford: Oxford University Press, 2004); and Shelley and Hunter, *Frankenstein*.

25   Mgbeoji, *Global Biopiracy*.

26   For more information on South African law, see François du Bois, ed., *Wille's Principles of South African Law* (Cape Town: Juta and Co., 2007); and Timothy Donald Burrell, *Burrell's South African Patent and Design Law*, 3rd ed. (Durban: Butterworths, 1999).

27   Burrell, *Burrell's South African Patent and Design Law*.

28   Harding, *Is Science Multicultural?*; Londa L. Schiebinger, *Plants and Empire: Colonial Bioprospecting in the Atlantic World* (Cambridge, MA: Harvard University Press, 2004); and Philip, *Civilizing Natures*.

29   Helen Tilley, *Africa as a Living Laboratory: Empire, Development, and the Problem of Scientific Knowledge, 1870-1950* (Chicago: University of Chicago Press, 2011).

30   For more on Francis Masson, see Bruyns, *Stapeliads of Southern Africa and Madagascar*; Frank R. Bradlow, *Francis Masson's Account of Three Journeys at the Cape of Good Hope, 1772-1775* (Cape Town: Tablecloth Press, 1994); Karsten, "Francis Masson"; Alain White and Boyd L. Sloane, *The Stapelieae: An Introduction to the Study of This Tribe of Asclepiadaceae* (Pasadena, CA: Abbey San Encino Press, 1933).

31   Bradlow, *Francis Masson's Account*.

32   Karsten, "Francis Masson."

33   Alain White and Boyd L. Sloane, *The Stapelieae*, vol. 3, 2nd ed. (Pasadena, CA: Abbey San Encino Press, 1937), 1051.

34   According to White and Sloan, Masson could draw, but "it is not known who executed the figures in Masson's work," and some suggest that D. Oldenburg, a soldier employed by the Dutch East India Company who served as Masson's guide in 1772, might have drawn the image; *The Stapelieae: An Introduction*, 18. Bruyns, however, states that Colonel Robert Jacob Gordon is believed to be the author behind the figure of *Stapeliae Gordoni* in Masson's book; Bruyns, *Stapeliads of Southern Africa and Madagascar*.

35   In a notation by the drawing in *Stapeliae Novae*, Masson attributes the discovery of the plant to a Mr. Gordon: "This unique species of Stapelia I have neither seen nor examined. For the copy from which the picture has been made, I have to thank the favour of Mr. Gordon." Gordon was a Dutch officer of Scottish descent who explored the territory around the Orange River in South Africa. According to White and Sloane, he was in command of the Dutch military forces when the colony was surrendered to England around

1795, and is said to have committed suicide out of indignation over the English occupation. White and Sloane, *The Stapelieae: An Introduction*, 19.

36 Changes in technology, such as photography and the microscope, later gave rise to new conceptions of what Daston and Galison refer to as a "mechanical objectivity"; Lorraine Daston and Peter Galison, "The Image of Objectivity," *Representations*, no. 40 (1992): 96. As a result, scientists increasingly came to distrust drawn illustrations of plants as reflecting the bias and subjective temptations of the artist.

37 For Masson's travel journal, see Francis Masson, *An Account of Three Journeys from the Cape Town into the Southern Parts of Africa; Undertaken for the Discovery of New Plants, Towards the Improvement of the Royal Botanical Gardens at Kew* (London: Royal Society of London, 1776). Masson uses the terms *Hottentot* and *Bosjesman* interchangeably, making it difficult to determine if San and Khoi were depicted differently in the text—a conflation that, as Saul Dubow notes, was common in colonial writings until the mid-nineteenth century; Saul Dubow, *Scientific Racism in Modern South Africa* (Cambridge: Cambridge University Press, 1995).

38 Mary Terrall, "Heroic Narratives of Quest and Discovery," in *The Postcolonial Science and Technology Studies Reader*, ed. Sandra G. Harding (Durham, NC: Duke University Press, 2011), 84–102.

39 The following is an illustrative passage from one of his travel journals: "The ancient inhabitants of this country, called the Dutch Boschmenschen, are a savage people and very thievish; often carrying off 700 sheep at a time, and killing their shepherds. They use bows and arrows, and poison the arrows with venom of serpents mixed with the juice of a species of *euphorbia*, which we had no opportunity of seeing. These Hottentots have neither flocks or herds; nor any fixed habitation, nor even skins to cover them; but live in the cavities of rocks, like baboons." Masson, *An Account of Three Journeys*, 314.

40 Premesh Lalu, *The Deaths of Hintsa: Postapartheid South Africa and the Shape of Recurring Pasts* (Cape Town: HSRC Press, 2009).

41 Michel Foucault, *The Order of Things: An Archaeology of the Human Sciences* (New York: Vintage Books, 1973), 131.

42 Anne McClintock, *Imperial Leather: Race, Gender, and Sexuality in the Colonial Contest* (New York: Routledge, 1995), 30.

43 Sweet uses accent marks in his spelling of *Stapèlia Gordòni*. Robert Sweet, *Hortus Britannicus: Or, a Catalogue of Plants, Indigenous, or Cultivated in the Gardens of Great Britain; Arranged According to Their Natural Orders*. (London: James Ridgway, 1830).

44 Londa Schiebinger, "The Loves of the Plants," *Scientific American*, February 1996: 110–15.

45 Sweet spelled the Asclepiadaceae family differently, as Asclepiadeae, demonstrating how botanical classifications are always in flux. According to Bruyns, prior to Sweet's classification of Hoodia, a botanist named Robert

Brown created the Asclepiadaceae family (which he also spelled Asclepiadeae) in 1810 when he removed plants whose pollen was attached to "translators" from the Apocynaceae family and put them in the new Asclepiadaceae family. Prior to that, Linnaeus's 1753 *Species Plantarum* classified the plants from each family together under a large grouping called the Pentandria Digynia, which included all plants where each flower had five anthers and two ovaries, meaning that species within the Apocynaceae and Asclepiadaceae families had been separated since 1810. Thus, when Sweet devised his own classification scheme for *Stapèlia Gordòni*, he placed it within his new *Hoodia* genus within the Asclepiadaceae family. Bruyns, *Stapeliads of Southern Africa and Madagascar*.

46 White and Sloan describe Hood as a "shadowy figure of whom no other mention has come to our attention," but a little archival digging finds a reference by Curtis and Sims to a Mr. Hood from Surgeon, South Lambeth, who possessed and successfully cultivated rare succulent plants. White and Sloane, *The Stapelieae*, 1051; William Curtis and John Sims, *Curtis's Botanical Magazine or Flower-Garden Displayed*, vol. 51 (London: T. Curtis, 1824), 2518.

47 For more about these debates, see Stephen Jay Gould, "American Polygeny and Craniometry before Darwin: Blacks and Indians as Separate, Inferior Species," in *The "Racial" Economy of Science: Toward a Democratic Future*, ed. Sandra G. Harding (Bloomington: Indiana University Press, 1993), 84–115.

48 Carl Linnaeus, *Systema Naturae*, vol. 1, 10th ed. (Stockholm: Laurentii Salvii, 1758).

49 For more on colonial science in South Africa and construction of San and Khoi peoples as colonial scientific objects, see Dubow, *Scientific Racism in Modern South Africa*; Clifton C. Crais and Pamela Scully, *Sara Baartman and the Hottentot Venus: A Ghost Story and a Biography* (Princeton, NJ: Princeton University Press, 2009); and Yvette Abrahams, "Gender and Locating Sarah Baartman in the Present," in *Democracy X: Marking the Present, Re-Presenting the Past*, ed. Andries Walter Oliphant, Peter Delius, and Lalou Meltzer (Pretoria: University of South Africa, 2004), 151–62.

50 For more on how science and society are co-constituted or coproduced, see Steven Shapin and Simon Schaffer, *Leviathan and the Air-Pump: Hobbes, Boyle, and the Experimental Life* (Princeton, NJ: Princeton University Press, 1985); Sheila Jasanoff, "The Idiom of Co-Production," in *States of Knowledge: The Co-Production of Science and Social Order*, ed. Sheila Jasanoff (London: Routledge, 2004); and Reardon, *Race to the Finish*.

51 For more information on cultural representations of San peoples, see Andy Smith et al., *The Bushmen of Southern Africa*, 40; Shane Moran, *Representing Bushmen: South Africa and the Origin of Language* (Rochester, NY: University of Rochester Press, 2009).

52 Moran, *Representing Bushmen*, 48–66.

53 David Chidester, "Bushmen Religion: Open, Closed, and New Frontiers," in

Miscast: Negotiating the Presence of the Bushmen, ed. Pippa Skotnes (Cape Town: University of Cape Town Press, 1996), 54.

54 Nicholas Edward Brown claims to have amassed large quantities of Stapeliads from the governor of the Cape Colony, Henry Barkly. N. E. Brown, "Asclepiadeae," in *Flora Capensis: Being a Systematic Description of the Cape Colony, Caffrara, and Port Natal*, ed. Sir William T. Thiselton-Dyer (London: Lovell Reeve and Co., 1909), viii. Brown provided a more detailed description of *Hoodia gordoni* (spelled with one *i*) than Sweet, noting its height, shape, and coloring in relation to its seven new kin members. He also expressed relief that the striking features of South Africa's flora would not be "doomed to gradual and irremediable extinction" because European gardeners were cross-fertilizing and featuring Stapeliads in their home gardens.

55 White and Sloane, *The Stapelieae*, 3, and *The Stapelieae: An Introduction.*

56 Bruyns, *Stapeliads of Southern Africa and Madagascar.*

57 Chidester, "Bushmen Religion."

58 Le Roux and White, *Voices of the San*, 7.

59 White and Sloane, *The Stapelieae: An Introduction*, 3.

60 Ibid.; *The Stapelieae*, 3.

61 White and Sloane, *The Stapelieae: An Introduction.*

62 Ibid.

63 Ibid.

64 Ibid.

65 Ibid.

66 Ibid.

67 For more, see Population Registration Act of 1950, Sections 5(1), 1(3), and 1(10). The Prohibition Act of Mixed Marriages of 1949 and the Immorality Act of 1950 also punished interracial marriage and sexual relations.

68 Thompson, *A History of South Africa*, 191.

69 Fiona McLachlan, "The Apartheid Laws in Brief," in *The Anti-Apartheid Reader: The Struggle against White Racist Rule in South Africa*, ed. David Mermelstein (New York: Grove Press, 1987), 76–98.

70 Ernest F. Dube, "Racism and Education in South Africa," in ibid., 177–84.

71 Deborah Posel, "Race as Common Sense: Racial Classification in Twentieth-Century South Africa," *African Studies Review* 44, no. 2 (2001): 87–113.

72 For more on the history of San and land dispossession, see Chennells, "The ≠Khomani San of South Africa"; and Phillipa Holden, "Conservation and Human Rights: The Case of the Khomani San (Bushmen) and the Kgalgadi Transfrontier Park, South Africa," *Policy Matters* 15 (2007): 57–68.

73 Le Roux and White, *Voices of the San*, 7.

74 John Sharp and Stuart Douglas, "Prisoners of Their Reputation? The Veterans of the 'Bushman' Battalions in South Africa," in *Miscast: Negotiating the Presence of the Bushmen*, ed. Pippa Skotnes (Cape Town: University of Cape Town Press, 1996), 323–29.

75 For more information on South African San and the war with South West Africa, see Barnard, "Laurens Van Der Post and the Kalahari Debate."

76 Sharp and Douglas, "Prisoners of Their Reputation?"

77 *Constitution of the Republic of South Africa*, Bill of Rights, Ch. 2, Sec. 9-10 (1996).

78 For more on South African property law, see P. J. Badenhorst, Juanita M. Pienaar, and Hanri Mostert, eds., *Silberberg and Schoeman's The Law of Property* (Durban: LexisNexis Butterworths, 2006), 593.

79 !Ae!Hai Kalahari Heritage Park Agreement, signed by Magrieta Eiman, Mavuso Msimang, Wallace Amos Mgoqi, Sigcau Stella, Sophia Katrina Coetzee, Angela Thokozile Didiza, P. B. Yako, and David Raimund Dosch, May 29, 2002 (copy on file with author). This victory was only partial, however, as it also created new tensions among ≠Khomani San over who could access the land and how it should be developed. For more on San land claims, see Steven Robins, "NGOs, 'Bushmen,' and Double Vision: The p khomani San Land Claim and the Cultural Politics of 'Community' in the Kalahari," *Journal of Southern African Studies* 27, no. 4 (2001): 833–53; and Steven Robins, Elias Madzudzo, and Matthias Brenzinger, *An Assessment of the Status of the San in South Africa, Angola, Zambia and Zimbabwe* (Windhoek: Legal Assistance Centre, 2001).

80 The Community Properties Association Act of 1996 was intended to provide a new form of juristic person to acquire, hold, and control property on behalf of certain communities. To make claims for land, San must register as a community properties association and meet the statutory provisions under the act, which requires drafting a constitution that defines the members of the ≠Khomani San community. Badenhorst, Pienaar, and Mostert also note that the act was meant to broaden landownership to members in the community, such as females, whose access to land had historically been limited. Badenhorst, Pienaar, and Mostert, *Silberberg and Schoeman's The Law of Property*, 593. The ≠Khomani San CPA enabled San to negotiate for the !Ae!Hai Kalahari Heritage Park Agreement, but San governance also has its limitations. The ≠Khomani San are defined as a community according to their CPA constitution, which designates that membership is approved by ≠Khomani San elders and is based on parental descent or identification with and acceptance into the community by its members. In terms of the law, ≠Khomani San identity is therefore defined through legal requirements of the Community Properties Association Act and the CPA Constitution. Although this benefits San in giving them a voice with which to negotiate with the state and outside parties, it forces them to organize and define who is considered to be San through governing structures that may not align with their own customary law.

81 For more information on WIMSA, see www.wimsanet.org (last accessed March 1, 2009).

82 Andrea Smith, "Native American Feminism, Sovereignty, and Social Change,"

in *Making Space for Indigenous Feminism*, ed. Joyce Green (Black Point, NS: Fernwood, 2007); Joyce Green, "Taking Account of Aboriginal Feminism," in ibid., 20–31; M. A. Jaimes, "Savage Hegemony: From 'Endangered Species' to Feminist Indiginism," in *Talking Visions: Multicultural Feminism in Transnational Age*, ed. Ella Shohat (New York: New Museum of Contemporary Art, 1998), 413–39.

83   Becker, "The Least Sexist Society?"

84   Ibid. For more on gendered relations among San peoples, see also Renée Sylvain, "San Women Today: Inequality and Dependency in a Post-Foraging World," *Indigenous Affairs* 1-2, no. 4 (2004): 89–110, and "At the Intersections: San Women and the Rights of Indigenous Peoples in Africa," *International Journal of Human Rights* 15, no. 1 (2011): 89–110.

85   Felton and Becker, *A Gender Perspective on the Status of the San in Southern Africa*.

86   Ibid.

87   Ibid.

Chapter 2. San Demands for Benefits by Knowing !Khoba as a Plant from Nature

!Khoba plant in Kalahari Desert, South Africa (Photo courtesy of Steve Hurt)

1   Andries Steenkamp, in discussion with author in South Africa, March 4, 2009 (on file with author).

2   Kim TallBear, "Native-American DNA.Com: In Search of Native American Race and Tribe," in *Revisiting Race in a Genomic Age*, ed. Barbara A. Koenig, Sandra Soo-Jin Lee, and Sarah S. Richardson (New Brunswick, NJ: Rutgers University Press, 2008), 235–52.

3   For a more detailed account of San-CSIR negotiations, see Wynberg, Schroeder, and Chennells, *Indigenous Peoples, Consent and Benefit Sharing*.

4   Banu Subramaniam, *Ghost Stories for Darwin: The Science of Variation and the Politics of Diversity* (Urbana: University of Illinois Press, 2014). For more on the notion of naturecultures, see Donna J. Haraway, *The Companion Species Manifesto: Dogs, People, and Significant Otherness* (Chicago: Prickly Paradigm Press, 2003), and *When Species Meet* (Minneapolis: University of Minnesota Press, 2008).

5   Tommy Busakhwe, in discussion with author in South Africa, March 4, 2009 (on file with author).

6   Katriena Rooi, in discussion with author in South Africa, March 4, 2009 (on file with author).

7   LaDuke, *Recovering the Sacred*, 153.

8   Andries Steenkamp, in discussion with author in South Africa, March 4, 2009 (on file with author).

9   Elizabeth "Bettie" Tieties, in discussion with author in South Africa, March 4, 2009 (on file with author).

10　Oom Jan van der Westruishen, in discussion with author in South Africa, March 4, 2009 (on file with author).

11　Collin Louw, in discussion with author in South Africa, March 9, 2009 (on file with author).

12　Sanna Witbooi, in discussion with author in South Africa, March 4, 2009 (on file with author).

13　Driven by concerns over the exploitation of biodiverse resources, 193 nation-states, not including the United States, ratified the Convention on Biological Diversity (CBD) in 1992 at a meeting in Rio de Janeiro, Brazil. The CBD aimed to achieve the conservation of biological diversity, sustainable use of its components, and the fair and equitable sharing of the benefits arising out of the utilization of genetic resources. Convention on Biological Diversity, Rio de Janeiro, 5 June 1992, 1760 UNTS 79; 31 ILM 818 (1992), Article 1, available at www.cbd.int/convention/text/. Much to the dismay of indigenous peoples involved in CBD discussions, the CBD granted nation-states sovereignty over natural resources and in doing so reinforced colonial histories. For an indigenous critique of the CBD, see Debra Harry and Le`a Malia Kanehe, "The Right of Indigenous Peoples to Permanent Sovereignty over Genetic Resources and Associated Indigenous Knowledge," *Journal of Indigenous Policy*, no. 6 (2007): 28–43. Although the CBD calls on nation-states to respect indigenous communities and encourages the equitable sharing of benefits with them, the governments of nation-states are given control over the terms of engagement. Although fraught in its privileging of the nation-state, the CBD provides binding international law for indigenous peoples to rely on even as its language pressures indigenous peoples to make demands for benefit sharing by representing themselves as traditional peoples and closer to nature.

　　The issue of Hoodia benefit sharing thus arose in a context of intense international debates over access and benefit sharing. The debates eventually led South Africa to implement the principles of the CBD and its benefit-sharing requirements by passing the 2004 Biodiversity Act and the 2008 *Regulations on Bio-prospecting, Access, and Benefit-Sharing* while also signing the Nagoya Protocol on Access and Benefit Sharing (ABS) in 2010. *Biodiversity Act of 2004*, Government Gazette No. 25436; 2008 *Regulations on Bio-prospecting, Access, and Benefit-Sharing Regulations*, Government Gazette No. 30739. The Nagoya Protocol further specified such measures as requiring researchers to obtain prior informed consent from indigenous and local peoples and to offer benefit sharing to them for the use of their knowledge and resources. These provisions sought to align ABS more closely with indigenous peoples' rights by including the UN Declaration on the Rights of Indigenous Peoples in its preamble. Nagoya Protocol on Access to Genetic Resources and the Fair and Equitable Sharing of Benefits Arising from their Utilization to the Convention on Biological Diversity, U.N. Doc. UNEP/CBD/COP/DEC/X/1, 2010. For more on the Nagoya Protocol and the CBD, see Pamela Andanda et al., "Legal Frameworks for Benefit Sharing: From Biodiversity to Human Genomics," in *Benefit Sharing: From Biodiversity to Human Genetics*, ed. Doris Schroeder and Julie Cook Lucas (New York: Springer, 2013): 33–64.

14 For a discussion of biopiracy, see Shiva, *Biopiracy*. For critiques of biopiracy as rhetoric, see Alain Pottage, "The Inscription of Life in Law: Genes, Patents, and Bio-Politics," *Modern Law Review* 61, no. 5 (1998): 740–65.

15 David Firn, "African Cactus Could Help Fight Obesity," *London Financial Times*, April 11, 2001, 2.

16 For more on colonial narratives of extinction, see Dubow, *Scientific Racism in Modern South Africa*.

17 Chennells explained to me that international nongovernmental organizations had encouraged the South African San Council to challenge the validity of the Hoodia patent, but "we said no, we are actually going to make a lot of money out of this patent if it works. So why on earth should we oppose our own patent? Because we now had a 6% share of the patent actually. It became the San patent." According to Chennells, a Switzerland-based nongovernmental organization called the Berne Declaration eventually sought to challenge the recognition of Hoodia patents by the Swiss government. Roger Chennells, in discussion with author in South Africa, February 4, 2009 (on file with author).

18 Petro Terblanche, in discussion with author in South Africa, July 29, 2014 (on file with author).

19 Roger Chennells, in discussion with author in South Africa, February 4, 2009 (on file with author).

20 Andries Steenkamp, in discussion with author in South Africa, March 4, 2009 (on file with author).

21 Greene, "Indigenous People Incorporated?"

22 Roger Chennells, in discussion with author in South Africa, February 4, 2009 (on file with author).

23 Petro Terblanche, in discussion with author in South Africa, July 29, 2014 (on file with author).

24 Wynberg, Schroeder, and Chennells, *Indigenous Peoples, Consent and Benefit Sharing*.

25 Robins makes a similar point in his essay on the ≠Khomani San land claim in "NGOs, 'Bushmen,' and Double Vision."

26 Jennifer A. Hamilton, *Indigeneity in the Courtroom: Law, Culture, and the Production of Difference in North American Courts* (New York: Routledge, 2009).

27 Hyo Yoon Kang, "An Exploration into Law and Narratives: The Case of Intellectual Property Law of Biotechnology," *Law Critique* 17, no. 1 (2006): 245.

28 Benefit Sharing Agreement between the CSIR and the South African San Council, South Africa, signed by Dr. Sibusiso Sibisi and Mr. Petrus Vaalbooi, March 24, 2003, Section (a) (hereinafter BSA 2003).

29   The Department of Arts, Culture, Science, and Technology was divided into the Department of Arts and Culture and the Department of Science and Technology in 2002.

30   The full text of Moses's speech is as follows: "As hunter-gatherers the San have survived directly from the land for centuries already. In the past, however, we had control over land and natural resources, so our ancestors had what they needed to survive despite a dry climate and any other difficult conditions they might have faced. They learnt to be attentive to what was happening with the weather, the land and the animals; they became keenly aware of rainfall patterns, game movements and veld-food availability. These skills enabled us to survive. When other groups in the region also became aware of the land's richness in resources, they occupied much of the richest land. Our ancestors were dispossessed of their land. Not being regarded as equals of the new 'landowners,' they were killed, forced into slavery on their own land or otherwise driven into marginal areas. Though nearly all San groups around the region lost their land base and some almost lost their language too, the elderly San continued passing on to the younger generations the traditional knowledge of fauna and flora. The Hoodia is a good example of a plant that all generations of San have learnt about from their forebears. We San of Angola, Namibia, Botswana and South Africa know that Hoodia sap can be used to treat eye infections; that the brew of boiled Hoodia pieces can be used to treat severe stomach pain; and of course, that Hoodia suppresses hunger and helps to maintain a high energy level. Indeed Hoodia is one of the important traditional medicinal plants that San have collected and utilised for centuries past. We are delighted that a part of our traditional knowledge is being honoured on this historic occasion. For us it is an occasion to celebrate. It is of critical importance to us that the Council for Scientific and Industrial Research (CSIR) has acknowledged our traditional knowledge of the Hoodia as the source of information that started the process leading to the granting of the patent in 1995. From the start the WIMSA General Assembly has closely observed the South African San Council and CSIR negotiations around the Hoodia. I am happy to say that the South African San Council took its mandate seriously and deserves praise for a job well done. My dear fellow San, I wish to thank you for your hard work, in which you were supported by our remarkable lawyer, Roger Chennells, to whom I also extend a hearty thanks. After the first round of negotiations we rejoiced in the signing of a memorandum of understanding between the San and the CSIR. Today we rejoice in the signing of a benefit-sharing agreement as the outcome of the second round. The San culture—including our traditional knowledge—has been put to use by external parties for multiple purposes, with little or no benefit accruing to the San. Recently the CSIR and several media workers and academics have set a positive example by signing agreements with the San and thus not exploiting us as has been the norm. The international interest

that the agreement between the San and the CSIR has aroused has helped the San umbrella body, WIMSA, to raise awareness of the need to protect and control San intellectual property. We hope that commercial concerns will soon follow the CSIR example and stop using images of San in their adverts without our prior consent and without ensuring that we also benefit, financially or otherwise. It must be noted that all benefits accruing to us from our sharing of our intellectual property are put to use by WIMSA through its many San member organisations in implementing sound and sustainable development projects, in providing skills training and education to San, and in building institutional capacity among San groups across the region. Again I thank the members of the South African San Council and our lawyer Roger Chennells, as well as the CSIR representatives and the organisers of this splendid celebration for their respective contributions. May we all enjoy the day in harmony and peace!" www .culturalsurvival.org/images/media/WIMSA_Hoodia_Speech.pdf (on file with author).

31 The full text of Ngubane's speech is as follows: "The significance of today's event and signing ceremony is enormous. To appreciate it fully, allow me to remind you of the complexity of some of the issues involved. The concept of traditional knowledge has only in recent years acquired the recognition it deserves, as the broader society increasingly started to recognise that there could be no life without roots. Science and society began to reconnect and the seeds of mainstreaming Indigenous Knowledge Systems [IKS] were sown. As part of this process, the Department of Science and Technology will release in June this year, a policy on indigenous knowledge, resulting in a [bill] and a range of practical measures to protect indigenous knowledge that will represent the country's first national policy and legislation on IKS. The role of indigenous knowledge in our national system of innovation is also clearly spelled out in the National Research and Development Strategy I released last year after being approved by Cabinet. But for this case for once, IKS in practice demanded to be dealt with before the policies and legislation on IKS were in place. The CSIR and the San—in formulating this agreement—carried the responsibility of drafting an agreement that anticipates future government policies in this area, would withstand scrutiny from many quarters as well as serving as an acceptable basis for the development of similar agreements in future. Part of the challenge in this domain presents itself in the contrasting nature of traditional knowledge, handed down from generation to generation and being community-owned, and Intellectual Property Rights, which views knowledge as being owned by an individual or company. South Africa's new draft bill addresses this issue and makes provision for providing legal protection of the intellectual property rights of communities, not just individuals. The agreement signed today is a landmark case in terms of an indigenous community staking its claim and it symbolises the restoration of the dignity of indigenous societies.

This agreement in particular illustrates the benefit that can be unleashed when owners of traditional knowledge and local scientists join forces to add value to the biodiversity and IKS of our region. The responsibility that comes from playing in the field of biodiversity, arguably Africa's richest asset, is not slight either. I am pleased to note the two parties' commitment to the conservation of biodiversity by applying 'best practices' with the collection of any plant species for scientific investigation, and by ensuring that no negative environmental impacts flow from the proposed bioprospecting collaboration. In this respect too, a draft [bill], the National Environmental Management: Biodiversity Bill has been published by the Department of Environmental Affairs and Tourism. It sets out an enabling regulatory framework for the integrated management of South Africa's biodiversity. Other complexities impacting in this arena include dealing with man-made borders that do no[t] apply to cultural groups and biodiversity; deciding and agreeing on what constitutes equitable benefit-sharing: how to proportionally distribute benefits and reward knowledge; how to contract when the revenue or benefits to the parties are uncertain, contingent, and linked to the outcome of future clinical trials; balancing 'trade secret'/ knowledge protection with transparency; and how to administer the potential future benefits. To the CSIR, San and government teams who have consulted, talked, learned, laboured, travelled, debated, and debated some more to come to an agreement on a complex matter: well done. However, as much as the matter is complex, it is simple. The agreement signed today is simply about doing the 'right thing'. The right thing in terms of benefit-sharing with the holders of traditional knowledge, of delivering on the promise that bioprospecting can create social and economic benefit to a nation, including its poorest communities. The right thing in terms of engaging in bioprospecting and not biopiracy; and in terms of fulfilling a responsibility of recognising indigenous knowledge and not merely acting charitable. If the road to getting it right—to arriving at a responsible, mutually-acceptable agreement that will withstand local and international scrutiny—has been bumpy, it had been a small price to pay in the interest of advancement in a field which has been crying for it for so long. You will agree that few things feel as good as 'doing the right thing.' And, while it will be many years before the benefits from P57/Hoodia will be realised, 'doing the right thing' will give our celebrations meaning, when the time for celebrating comes. I thank you." www.info.gov.za/speeches/2003/03032410461009.htm (on file with author)

32   Haupt, *Stealing Empire*.
33   Anderson, *Law, Knowledge, Culture*; and Elizabeth A. Povinelli, *The Cunning of Recognition: Indigenous Alterities and the Making of Australian Multiculturalism* (Durham, NC: Duke University Press, 2002).
34   Harry and Kanehe, "The BS in Access and Benefit Sharing (ABS)," 8.
35   Andries Steenkamp, in discussion with author in South Africa, March 4,

2009 (on file with author); Sanna Witbooi, in discussion with author in South Africa, March 4, 2009 (on file with author).

36 Sanna Witbooi, in discussion with author in South Africa, March 4, 2009 (on file with author).

37 Arrie Tities, in discussion with author in South Africa, March 3, 2009 (on file with author).

38 Tommy Busakhwe, in discussion with author in South Africa, March 4, 2009 (on file with author).

39 Jean Comaroff and John L. Comaroff, "Naturing the Nation: Aliens, Apocalypse, and the Postcolonial State," *Journal of Southern African Studies* 27, no. 3 (2001): 627–51, and *Theory from the South, or How Euro-America Is Evolving toward Africa* (Boulder, CO: Paradigm, 2012).

40 Barad, *Meeting the Universe Halfway*, 21.

41 Alaimo and Hekman, *Material Feminisms*, 7.

42 Elsabe Swart, "Hoodia Gordonii in Southern Africa," Department of Tourism, Environment and Conservation, 2008.

43 Wynberg, Schroeder, and Chennells, *Indigenous Peoples, Consent and Benefit Sharing*.

44 Agreement between the Association of Nama Traditional Leaders and the San Council of Namibia, South Africa, signed by the Association of Nama Traditional Leaders and the San Council of Namibia, July 16, 2009.

Chapter 3. South African Scientists and the Patenting of Hoodia as a Molecule

Illustration of the chemical structure of a patented *Hoodia gordonii* chemical composition from South African patent application filed in 1998

1 When CSIR was created by an Act of Parliament in 1945, its mandate was to engage in "multi-disciplinary research and technological innovation . . . for the improvement of the quality of life of the people" of South Africa. CSIR's mandate is further articulated in Section 3 of the Scientific Research Council Act (Act 46 of 1988, as amended by Act 71 of 1990). According to CSIR's website in 2011, 40 percent of its research funding came from the South African Parliament by way of the Department of Science and Technology (DST), while its remaining income was generated from public and private research contracts, IP royalties, and commercial dividends.

2 Andrew Bailey, in discussion with author in South Africa, February 29, 2009 (on file with author).

3 Wynberg, "Rhetoric, Realism, and Benefit Sharing."

4 Osseo-Asare, *Bitter Roots*.

5 D. Walwyn and P. Steyn, *A Short History of Natural Product Research in the CSIR* (Pretoria, South Africa: CSIR, 2006). www.csir.co.za/csir_conference _2006/LinkedDocuments/K4570_CSIR_Poster72_DevV4.indd.pdf. Copy on file with the author.

6   Vinesh Maharaj, in discussion with author in South Africa, February 12, 2015 (on file with author).

7   Rudolf Marloth, *The Flora of South Africa with Synopsis of the South African Genera of Phanerogamous Plants*, vol. 3 (London: Wheldon and Wesley, 1932).

8   Mary E. Endress and Peter V. Bruyns, "A Revised Classification of the Apocynaceae S.L.," *Botanical Review* 66, no. 1 (2000): 1–56; and Bruyns, *Stapeliads of Southern Africa and Madagascar.*

9   CSIR filed a provisional patent on its Hoodia-based invention in 1994. According to South African Patent Regulations of 1978, Section 27 (amended 2006), a provisional application is good for twelve months and allows an inventor to work on his invention and/or test the market to find out if the invention is viable, but after twelve months a "complete patent application" should be filed. A formal examination is performed six months after a complete application is filed. Unlike the USPTO, however, South Africa Companies and Intellectual Property Commission (CIPC) is a "non-examining" patent office, so applications are reviewed only for form and not on the merits. According to Sections 40 and 41 of the same regulations, if all proper documentation has been submitted and "prescribed formalities" are met, patent ownership is awarded. A patent attorney or patent agent is the only one who can file a complete application, whereas any individual can file a provisional patent application. The filing of a complete patent application allows the inventor to claim priority from the date of the provisional application. CSIR also filed a patent application on their Hoodia-based invention in the United Kingdom, which the European Patent Office initially denied but later approved.

10   For more on neoliberalism in South Africa, see Patrick Bond, *Elite Transition: From Apartheid to Neoliberalism in South Africa* (Pietermaritzburg, South Africa: University of Natal Press, 2000); Graham Harrison, "Post-Neoliberalism?," *Review of African Political Economy* 37, no. 123 (2010): 1–5; Paul Williams and Ian Taylor, "Neoliberalism and the Political Economy of the 'New' South Africa," *New Political Economy* 5, no. 1 (2010): 21–40; James Ferguson, *Global Shadows: Africa in the Neoliberal World Order* (Durham, NC: Duke University Press, 2006); and Stephen Gelb, "Macroeconomic Policy in South Africa: From RDP through GEAR to ASGISA," in *At the End of the Rainbow? Social Welfare in the New South Africa*, ed. Gorm Gunnarsen, Patrick Mac Manus, Morten Nielsen, and Hans Erik Stolten (Copenhagen: Southern Africa Contact, 2007), 17–28. For discussions of neoliberalism in general, see David Harvey, *A Brief History of Neoliberalism* (Oxford: Oxford University Press, 2005); Jamie Peck and Adam Tickell, "Neoliberalizing Space," *Antipode* 34, no. 3 (2002): 380–404; and Philip Mirowski and Dieter Plehwe, *The Road from Mont Pèlerin: The Making of the Neoliberal Thought Collective* (Cambridge, MA: Harvard University Press, 2009). For feminist analyses of neoliberalism, see Wendy Larner, "Neo-Liberalism: Policy, Ideology,

Governmentality," *Studies in Political Economy* 63 (2000): 5–25; Amy Bhatt, Madhavi Murty, and Priti Ramamurthy, "Hegemonic Developments: The New Indian Middle Class, Gendered Subalterns, and Diasporic Returnees in the Event of Neoliberalism," *Signs: Journal of Women in Culture and Society* 36, no. 1 (2010): 127–52; and Lisa Rofel, *Desiring China: Experiments in Neoliberalism, Sexuality, and Public Culture* (Durham, NC: Duke University Press, 2007).

11   Many scholars attribute this shift to the ANC's 1996 decision to move away from its more redistributive Reconstruction and Development Program (RDP) toward a set of privatization initiatives within the Growth, Equity, and Reconstruction Programme (GEAR), but it was also shaped by legacies of apartheid and pressures to repay structural adjustment loans. See Bond, *Elite Transition*; and Steven L. Robins, *Limits to Liberation after Apartheid: Citizenship, Governance, and Culture* (Athens: Ohio University Press, 2005). Identifying GEAR as a key moment of a South African neoliberal turn should not, as Hein Marais argues, obscure the impact of complex external economic pressures, internal political struggles, and the legacy of the apartheid regime on the ANC; Hein Marais, *South Africa Pushed to the Limit: The Political Economy of Change* (London: Zed Books, 2011).

12   In general, patents have been touted as key drivers of economic growth, but according to Christopher May and Susan K. Sell, debates after 1945, in the post–World War II era, deemphasized patent ownership and questioned the importance of patents within a renewed welfare state; May and Sell, *Intellectual Property Rights*. Patent ownership would become prominent again in the 1980s; Susan K. Sell, *Private Power, Public Law: The Globalization of Intellectual Property Rights* (Cambridge: Cambridge University Press, 2003).

13   The timing of the Hoodia patents correlated with increasing opposition to patent law and neoliberal globalization by social movements in South Africa and internationally. The social movements in South Africa were particularly focused on the patenting of HIV/AIDS drugs. The signing of the World Trade Organization's Agreement on Trade-Related Aspects of Intellectual Property Rights (TRIPs) in 1994 had further yoked patent ownership to neoliberalism by harmonizing patent law rules across WTO nation-state members and charging them with enforcing the patent rights of other nations or risking trade sanctions. As a result, South Africa would have to enforce US patents on HIV/AIDS drugs and forgo using cheaper generic medications, with severe consequences for the large number of people infected with HIV/AIDS in South Africa. When the South African government revised its laws in 1997 to make it easier to import generic HIV/AIDS drugs, the Pharmaceutical Manufacturers Association of South Africa, joined by thirty-nine international pharmaceutical companies (many located in the United States), quickly filed a lawsuit in South Africa's High Court alleging patent infringement and trade violations under TRIPs.

(They withdrew the lawsuit in 2001.) A South Africa–based nongovernmental organization called the Treatment Action Campaign swiftly mobilized against this lawsuit by framing patent rights not as drivers of economic growth, but as tools of injustice that intensified inequalities between the Global North and South. The South African Parliament's Committee on Women also voiced opposition, condemning HIV/AIDS patents as a women's health issue because women were the fastest-growing portion of the population suffering from the disease. For more on South African struggles against HIV/AIDS patents, see David Barnard, "In the High Court of South Africa, Case No. 4138/98: The Global Politics of Access to Low-Cost AIDS Drugs in Poor Countries," *Kennedy Institute of Ethics Journal* 12, no. 2 (2002): 159–74; and Melinda Cooper, *Life as Surplus: Biotechnology and Capitalism in the Neoliberal Era* (Seattle: University of Washington Press, 2008). For a discussion of patents, women, and HIV/AIDS in South Africa, see Pregs Govender, *Love and Courage: A Story of Insubordination* (Auckland Park, South Africa: Jacana Media, 2007).

14 Pollock, "Places of Pharmaceutical Knowledge-Making," 855.

15 Itty Abraham, "The Contradictory Spaces of Postcolonial Techno-Science," *Economic and Political Weekly* 41, no. 3 (2006): 210–17.

16 Marilyn Strathern, "Cutting the Network," *Journal of the Royal Anthropological Institute* 2, no. 3 (1996): 517–35.

17 Tommy Busakhwe, in discussion with author in South Africa, March 3, 2009 (on file with author).

18 Andries Steenkamp, in discussion with author in South Africa, March 4, 2009 (on file with author).

19 Adele E. Clarke, *Disciplining Reproduction: Modernity, American Life Sciences, and "the Problems of Sex"* (Berkeley: University of California Press, 1998), 267.

20 Pratt, *Imperial Eyes*.

21 Riles, *Collateral Knowledge* and "A New Agenda for the Cultural Study of Law"; Derrida, "Force of Law."

22 Valverde, "Jurisdiction and Scale."

23 Fanie Retief Van Heerden, Robert Vleggaar, Roelof Marthinus Horak, Robert Alec Learmonth, Vinesh Maharaj, and Rory Desmond Whittal, Pharmaceutical Compositions Having Appetite Suppressant Activity, Republic of South Africa Patent 97/3170, filed April 15, 1998, and issued Dec. 29, 1999.

24 Fanie Retief Van Heerden, Robert Vleggaar, Roelof Marthinus Horak, Robert Alec Learmonth, Vinesh Maharaj, and Rory Desmond Whittal, Pharmaceutical Compositions Having Appetite Suppressant Activity, United States Patent 6,376,657, filed October 13, 1999, and issued April 23, 2002.

25 United States Patent Act [hereafter as USPA] Section 102(a) uses the language of a single "prior art" reference, whereas South African Patent Act [herein as SAPA] specifies a "state of art" reference.

26 This requirement of novelty applies to both US and South African law. For more on novelty claims and anticipation in both countries, see *Verdegaal Bros. v. Union Oil Co. of California*, 814 F.2d 628 [Fed. Cir. 1987] and *Gentiruco AG v. Firestone (South Africa) (Pty) Ltd*, 1971 BP 58 (A) at 138F–139A.

27 SAPA, Section 25(6).

28 USPA, Section 102(a).

29 USPA, Section 102(a).

30 Andrew Rens, personal communication in United States, March 21, 2014.

31 Pierre Barbier, Fernand Schneider, and Ulrich Widmer, Oxetanones, United States Patent 4,931,463, filed December 17, 1987, and issued June 5, 1990; Ian T. Barnish, Peter E. Cross, John C. Danilewicz, and Malcolm Morville, L- and DL-Phenylglycines to Treat Diseases or Conditions Attributable to Reduced Carbohydrate Metabolism, United States Patent 4,185,116, filed August 30, 1978, and issued January 22, 1980; Laura Chiodini, Mauro Gobbini, Sergio Mantegani, Daniel Ruggieri, Aldemio Temperilli, Gabriella Traguandi, and Patrizia Ferrari, Aminoglycoside Steroids, a Process for Their Preparation, Their Use and Pharmaceutical Compositions Containing Them, United States Patent 4,882,315, filed October 29, 1987, and issued November 21, 1989; Bruce D. Cherksey, Method of Preparing *Muira puama* Extract and Its Use for Decreasing Body Fat Percentage and Increasing Lean Muscle Mass, United States Patent 5,516,516, filed May 23, 1994, and issued May 14, 1996; Shinobu Mori, Yuji Ichii, Norihiro Tanaka, Hidenori Yorozu, Satoshi Kanazawa, and Yoshinori Nishizawa, Lipolysis Acceleration Method, United States Patent 5,698,199, filed March 5, 1996, and issued December 16, 1997. United States Patent 4,185,116 on Phenylglycines to Treat Diseases Or Conditions Attributable to Reduced Carbohydrate Metabolism was assigned to Pfizer, Inc.

32 John Hakkinen, Roelof Marthinus Horak, and Vinesh Maharaj, Gastric Acid Secretion, United States Patent 6,488,967, filed October 18, 2000, and issued December 3, 2002; John Hakkinen, Roelof Marthinus Horak, and Vinesh Maharaj, Gastric Acid Secretion, United States Patent 6,808,723, filed June 17, 2002, and issued October 26, 2004.

33 Ian Duncan Rubin, Jasjit Singh Bindra, and Michael Anthony Cawthorne, Extracts, Compounds and Pharmaceutical Compositions Having Anti-Diabetic Activity and Their Use, United States Patent 7,033,616, filed June 27, 2001, and issued April 25, 2006; Smail Alaoui Ismaili, Sybille Buchwald-Werner, Frederik Michiel Meeuse, and Kevin John Poovey, Processes for Production of Hoodia Plant Extracts Containing Steroidal Glycosides, United States Patent 7,807,204, filed August 14, 2007, and issued October 5, 2010; Amir Maximiliaan Batenburg, Mohamed Said Chaara, Egge Aart Eddy Rosing, Frederik Michiel Meeuse, Salomon Leendert Abrahamse, Hoodia Plant Extract with Improved Flavor, United States Patent 7,923,435, filed April 21, 2008, and issued April 12, 2011.

34   Arrie Tities, in discussion with author in South Africa, March 3, 2009 (on file with author).

35   Tommy Busakhwe, in discussion with author in South Africa, March 3, 2009 (on file with author).

36   Andries Steenkamp, in discussion with author in South Africa, March 4, 2009 (on file with author).

37   Arrie Tities, in discussion with author in South Africa, March 3, 2009 (on file with author).

38   Ibid.; Tommy Busakhwe, in discussion with author in South Africa, March 3, 2009 (on file with author).

39   Madhavi Sunder, "The Invention of Traditional Knowledge," *Law and Contemporary Problems* 70, no. 2 (2007): 97–124.

40   *Ass'n for Molecular Pathology v. Myriad Genetics, Inc.*, 133 S. Ct. 2107 (2013).

41   SAPA, Section (1)(26)(2).

42   South Africa Patent 97/3170 (1999), 4-6; United States Patent 6,376,657 (2002), 11.

43   United States Patent 6,376,657 (2002), 10.

44   Ibid., 10.

45   Sanna Witbooi, in discussion with author in South Africa, March 4, 2009 (on file with author).

46   Rose, *The Politics of Life Itself*, 5–6.

47   Thom van Dooren, "Inventing Seed: The Nature(s) of Intellectual Property in Plants," *Environment and Planning D: Society and Space* 26, no. 4 (2008): 682.

48   South Africa Patent 97/3170 (1999), 118.

49   United States Patent 6,376,657 (2002), 4.

50   South Africa Patent 97/3170 (1999), 120.

Chapter 4. Botanical Drug Discovery of Hoodia, from Solid Drug to Liquid Food

Hoodia/pill amalgamation (Image courtesy of Alamy and design by Scott Pitkin)

1   Phytopharm's website (www.phytopharm.com) replaced its Hoodia plant/pill image and language regarding Hoodia P57 with pictures of Hoodia plants and brief references to the plant and San peoples later that year. The site's Factfile described *Hoodia gordonii* as "a succulent plant found in the Kalahari desert of South Africa" and noted that it was clearly different from a cactus. It also specified that "only Phytopharm's patented *Hoodia* product is botanically verified to contain pure *Hoodia*" and "has had extensive safety studies performed and been clinically proven to reduce calorie intake." This claim grew stronger in subsequent years as the Factfile began warning that many Hoodia products sold over the Internet as herbal

supplements "contain little or no Hoodia" and that Phytopharm and Unilever had urged "relevant authorities" to regulate these fraudulent acts. The Hoodia Factfile also assured the public that *Hoodia gordonii* was protected under Appendix II of the Convention on International Trade in Endangered Species (CITES), and therefore its harvesting and trade were "controlled at an international level in order to conserve indigenous plant populations within the range states (South Africa, Namibia, Botswana)."

2 "Phytopharm plc to Develop Natural Anti-obesity Treatment" [press release, Phytopharm, London, June 23, 1997]. Phytopharm began trading on the London Stock Exchange on April 25, 1996, and by June 1997, when the partnership with CSIR was announced, the company was trading at a share price around 2.57P. In September 2013, Phytopharm merged with a medical technology and diagnostics company, IXICO, and its shareholders saw a 49 percent increase in the stock price, up to 50.1P. For more on the merger, see Steve McGrath, "Phytopharm Shares Leap as Trading Resumes after Merger Deal," *Alliance News,* September 24, 2013; www.lse.co.uk/AllNews .asp?code=t5lq3wdy (last accessed October 27, 2015).

3 Richard Dixey, in discussion with author via Skype, September 13, 2016 (on file with author).

4 For more on legal regulation of botanical drugs, see "Guidance for Industry: Botanical Drug Products" by the US Department of Health and Human Services, Food and Drug Administration, and Center for Drug Evaluation and Research (June 2004) at www.fda.gov/downloads/drugs/guidance complianceregulatoryinformation/guidances/ucm070491.pdf (last accessed October 25, 2016).

5 Petro Terblanche, in discussion with author in South Africa, July 29, 2014 (on file with author).

6 Richard Dixey, in discussion with author via Skype, September 13, 2016 (on file with author).

7 "Phytopharm plc to Develop Natural Anti-obesity Treatment."

8 "Phytopharm plc Collaboration with Pfizer to Develop and Commercialise Obesity Drug (P57)" [press release, Phytopharm, London, August 24, 1998].

9 Ibid.

10 Ibid.

11 "Phytopharm plc Anti-Obesity Drug Candidate (P57) Enters Phase I Clinical Trial" [press release, Phytopharm, October 13, 1998]. According to the press release, "P57 is derived from an extract of *Hoodia gordonii,* a South African succulent plant."

12 "Phytopharm plc Opens New Manufacturing Unit in South Africa" [press release, Phytopharm, London, April 11, 2002].

13 In reporting this announcement, however, the *Financial Times* failed to name the plant, stating that Phytopharm had "completed a fourfold increase in production capacity for its P57 obesity treatment at a factory in

Pretoria, South Africa." Patrick Jenkins, "Pfizer Set to Bolster Phytopharm Programme," *Financial Times,* April 12, 2002.

14 The website, at www.phytopharm.com, contained new content titled the "Hoodia Factfile," which explained, for example, that "for many centuries the San Bushmen of the Kalahari desert have used Hoodia plants as a food. The species *Hoodia gordonii* was less often used because of its lingering bitter taste being considered unpleasant. However, in times of hardship, or being away from familiar areas, it was sometimes eaten." The website also informed the public that "the CSIR have entered a benefit sharing agreement with an organization representing the San people, to ensure that any financial benefit flowing from the commercialization of the patented *Hoodia* extract is shared with people whose traditional knowledge first led to the investigation of the plant."

15 V. J. Maharaj, *Summary Reports for Key Hoodia Clinical Studies,* research space.csir.co.za/dspace/bitstream/10204/5375/1/Maharaj_2011_Hoodia%20 summary%20reports.pdf (last accessed October 27, 2015); "Pfizer Returns Rights of P57" [press release, Phytopharm, London, July 30, 2003].

16 "Phytopharm and Unilever Enter into a License and Joint Development Agreement for *Hoodia gordonii* Extract" [press release, Phytopharm, London, December 15, 2004].

17 Kevin Poovey, in discussion with author in South Africa via Skype, March 9, 2009 (on file with author).

18 Kevin Poovey, e-mail correspondence with author, June 30, 2016.

19 Under sections 201(s) and 409 of the US Federal Food, Drug, and Cosmetic Act, any substance that becomes a component of food is considered an additive, unless it is generally recognized as safe according to qualified scientific studies or a substantial history of common use, in which case it can be considered a food ingredient. By these rules, if a component is classified as a food additive, it is subject to premarket review and approval by the FDA, whereas a food ingredient is not.

20 Kevin Poovey, in discussion with author in South Africa via Skype, March 9, 2009 (on file with author).

21 Richard Dixey, in discussion with author via Skype, September 13, 2016 (on file with author).

22 Unilever also met with CSIR and San peoples. For instance, Poovey reported that he had gone with "the Phytopharm team on several occasions to update and review the project with the CSIR management team, but day-to-day contact was carried out by the Phytopharm team." He also noted that his team had "a number of contacts with the San people," including a colleague who visited with San Council members and joined them on a hunting trip in South Africa. Poovey also invited Roger Chennells to the United Kingdom to "see what we were doing with our safety and efficacy studies and explain the process of getting FDA approval." Kevin Poovey, e-mail correspondence with author, June 30, 2016.

23 Kevin Poovey, in discussion with author in South Africa via Skype, March 9, 2009 (on file with author).

24 Ibid.

25 Ibid.

26 Ibid.

27 "Technology for Sustainable Livelihoods: Essential Oils Sites" [undated report, Department of Science and Technology, Pretoria, South Africa]. According to this report, the goal of the Pella and Onseepkans farms was not only to provide raw plants for Unilever, but also to provide local jobs and facilitate the growing partnership between CSIR and the South African San Council. CSIR was growing approximately 2.5 hectares (6 acres) of *Hoodia gordonii* (60,000 plants per hectare) under "scientifically controlled conditions" in both Pella and Onseepkans. The South African Department of Science and Technology (DST) supported the two farms as a part of its Ten-Year Innovation Plan to promote a "Farmer to Pharma (F2Ph)" drug-discovery process and to "combine biotechnology with South Africa's indigenous knowledge systems (IKS) and rich biodiversity to strengthen the emerging bio economy in the country." The Hoodia farms at Pella and Onseepkans were also intended to strengthen "community production of indigenous medicinal herbs, scientifically proven to possess medicinal and or healing properties" and to provide locals with agrotechnical business and labor relations training. According to the report, twenty-three individuals worked full-time at Pella and there were seventeen full-time and five casual laborers at Onseepkans, but given that several indigenous plants were grown at both locations, it is unclear how many of those employees worked with Hoodia plants. DST also sponsored other farms growing medicinal plant projects, which generally employed roughly equal numbers of men and women, but CSIR did not report the exact ratios of men to women working at Pella and Onseepkans.

28 Barad, *Meeting the Universe Halfway*, 21.

29 Alaimo and Hekman, *Material Feminisms*, 7.

30 Vinesh Maharaj, in discussion with author in South Africa, February 12, 2015 (on file with author).

31 Maharaj, *Summary Reports for Key Hoodia Clinical Studies*.

32 Between October 8, 1998, and February 9, 1999, twenty obese males participated in a clinical study of Hoodia at the Covance Clinical Research Unit in Leeds, UK. The study was initially open to healthy obese male and female subjects between eighteen and fifty-five years of age, but only twenty males entered and completed it. The absence of female subjects may be partially explained by the requirement that they be surgically sterilized or post-menopausal and test negative for pregnancy. Obesity was defined as a body mass index (BMI) equal to or greater than 26 kg/m^2 and less than 45 kg/m^2, demonstrating the narrow conception of obesity in terms of body mass.

The male subjects were given daily either a placebo or a dosage of a dried extract of Hoodia's active chemical components formulated into a capsule. Clinicians measured their caloric intake, timed the duration of their meals, charted their hunger and moods, and calculated their body weight. Maharaj, *Summary Reports for Key Hoodia Clinical Studies*.

33 A few months later, between May 5, 1999, and June 2, 1999, thirty-two healthy male subjects agreed to participate in another Phytopharm-sponsored Hoodia clinical study at the PPD Development Clinic in Leicester, UK. "Healthy" was once again determined by BMI (between 21 kg/m^2 and 28 kg/m^2). The dosage levels in this study were much higher, ranging from 500 to 4000 mg. Seventeen of the subjects had some adverse effects, none of which were found to be serious or adverse or to produce changes in vital signs, although some subjects did experience a lack of appetite and headache. The study indicated that Hoodia was safe and reliable but found no clear effect on hunger, satiety, or mood at any dose level. These results were promising enough, however, to continue clinical studies. Maharaj, *Summary Reports for Key Hoodia Clinical Studies*.

34 This study included sixteen healthy male subjects who participated at the PPD Development Clinic, all of whom were between ages 18 and 50 with a body mass index between 21 kg/m^2 and 30 kg/m^2. Between August 20, 1999, and October 1, 1999, they stayed at the clinic for fourteen days and received daily doses of either a placebo or 500 mg of Hoodia in hard gelatin capsules. Although the study again found Hoodia capsules to be safe and reliable, it still showed no substantial differences between the treatment and placebo group in terms of appetite, calorie intake, or body weight. Maharaj, *Summary Reports for Key Hoodia Clinical Studies*.

35 In these second-stage trials, between February 16, 2001, and October 24, 2001, clinicians gave eighteen male volunteers with BMIs between 28 kg/m^2 and 36 kg/m^2 either a placebo or two Hoodia capsules a day for five days at a dosage level of 1200, 1600, or 2400 mg. This time they found that five-day repeated dosages of 2400 mg and 1600 mg of Hoodia significantly reduced calorie intake in comparison to the placebo and the 1200 mg dosage. Those who took the 1600 mg dosage also experienced a statistically significant greater reduction in body weight, although not in overall body fat content. Maharaj, *Summary Reports for Key Hoodia Clinical Studies*.

36 During the same period from February 16, 2001, to October 24, 2001, researchers also gave twenty male subjects within the same BMI parameters either a placebo or two Hoodia capsules a day for fifteen days at a dosage level of 1800 mg and found that this dosage was associated with a substantial reduction in calorie intake. Clinicians concluded that the Hoodia capsules reduced calorie intake but recommended a lower dosage because of the side effect of hyperbilirubinemia. Maharaj, *Summary Reports for Key Hoodia Clinical Studies*.

37 "Update on Development Programme for Appetite Suppressant P57" [press release, Phytopharm, London, March 12, 2003].

38 For more on Pfizer's termination of the project, see "Pfizer Returns Rights of P57" [press release, Phytopharm, London, July 30, 2003].

39 Jasjit S. Bindra, letter to the editor, *New York Times*, April 26, 2005.

40 Ibid.

41 "Phytopharm and Unilever Enter into a License and Joint Development Agreement for *Hoodia gordonii* Extract" [press release, Phytopharm, London, December 15, 2004]. A strong relationship between the companies prompted Sandy Morrison, former head of Lipton for Unilever, to join Phytopharm in 2006 as a nonexecutive director. David Blackwell, "Unilever Helps QCA in the Search for Experience," *Financial Times*, August 4, 2006. By April 2006, Phytopharm shares were up 10.2 percent, at 43P. The completion of first-stage clinical trials with Unilever were reported by Peter Garnham and Robert Orr in "Small-Caps: Plusnet Falls on Carphone Warehouse Plan," *Financial Times*, April 11, 2006. By May 6, 2006, Phytopharm shares had risen to 56.5P after the company received £10 million from Unilever to help develop a Hoodia product, as reported in Lisa Urquhart, "New Positive Alzheimer's Trial for Phytopharm," *Financial Times*, May 6, 2006. Although Phytopharm reported operating losses in the first part of 2006, attributed to the slow development of other products such as a treatment for Alzheimer's disease, the price of its shares remained steady, at 51.5P on April 26, 2007, and falling only slightly to 49P on May 2, 2007. Neil Hume and Robert Orr, "Boost for Clipper Windpower," *Financial Times*, April 26, 2007; Salamander Davoudi, "Phytopharm Narrows Losses Smallcap Briefing," *Financial Times*, May 2, 2007.

42 Unilever conducted several studies but published the results of only one clinical trial, which was conducted from March to October of 2008 at the Covance Clinical Research Unit in Madison, WI. Wendy A. M. Blom et al., "Effects of 15-D Repeated Consumption of *Hoodia Gordonii* Purified Extract on Safety, Ad Libitum Energy Intake, and Body Weight in Healthy Overweight Women: A Randomized Controlled Trial," *American Journal of Clinical Nutrition* 94, no. 5 (2011): 1171-81. The clinical trial included forty-nine healthy overweight women aged 18-50 with an average BMI of 24.9 kg/m²; as self-reported, the majority of the subjects were White (34), followed by Black (13), Asian (1), and Other (1). At mealtimes, researchers gave participants slightly larger portions than they would ordinarily consume and allowed them to ask for more, carefully measuring each participant's food intake and preventing them from seeing or talking to each other while eating to strictly control conditions.

43 "Unilever Returns Rights to *Hoodia* Extract" [press release, Phytopharm, London, December 12, 2008].

Chapter 5. Hoodia Growers and the Making of Hoodia as a Cultivated Plant

Cultivated *Hoodia gordonii* plants in Barrydale, South Africa (Photo by the author)

1   Robby Gass, in discussion with author in South Africa, February 26, 2009 (on file with author).

2   During our conversations, white Hoodia growers were not always forthcoming about Afrikaner ancestry. Perhaps not all of them were descendants of Afrikaner colonial settlers or perhaps they wanted to distance themselves from an Afrikaner identity because of the painful apartheid past. All those quoted here reviewed the chapter and approved of its characterization of them in terms of their self-identity. Situating SAHGA claims to Hoodia within Afrikaner histories is, however, just one way to understand San-SAHGA benefit sharing and changing notions of belonging in South Africa.

3   Lance Van Sittert, "From 'Mere Weeds' and 'Bosjes' to a Cape Floral Kingdom: The Re-Imagining of Indigenous Flora at the Cape, c. 1890–1939," *Kronos: South African Histories*, no. 28 (2002): 102–26; Penn, *The Forgotten Frontier*.

4   Saul Dubow, *A Commonwealth of Knowledge: Science, Sensibility, and South Africa, 1820-2000* (Oxford: Oxford University Press, 2006), 14.

5   T. Dunbar Moodie, *The Rise of Afrikanerdom: Power, Apartheid, and the Afrikaner Civil Religion* (Berkeley: University of California Press, 1975); Sarah Ives, "Uprooting 'Indigeneity' in South Africa's Western Cape: The Plant That Moves," *American Anthropologist* 116, no. 2 (2014): 310–23.

6   David McDermott Hughes, *Whiteness in Zimbabwe: Race, Landscape, and the Problem of Belonging* (New York: Palgrave Macmillan, 2010); Dominic Griffiths and Maria L. C. Prozesky, "The Politics of Dwelling: Being White/Being South African," *Africa Today* 56, no. 4 (2010): 22–41.

7   Griffiths and Prozesky, "The Politics of Dwelling."

8   Cornel Verwey and Michael Quayle, "Whiteness, Racism, and Afrikaner Identity in Post-Apartheid South Africa," *African Affairs* 111, no. 445 (2012): 551–75.

9   Steve Hurt, in discussion with author in South Africa, February 16, 2015 (on file with author).

10 Media attention and the patenting of Hoodia properties by CSIR scientists ignited demand for the plant, and the Hoodia botanical industry began to boom. In November 2004, a report by Leslie Stahl, a reporter for CBS's *60 Minutes*, brought international attention to Hoodia when it showed her in the Kalahari Desert eating Hoodia; www.cbsnews.com/news/african-plant-may-help-fight-fat/2/ (last accessed July 24, 2015). News of Hoodia weight-loss supplements further spread in the United States, including Katie Couric's

highlighting Hoodia on the *Today Show* (www.youtube.com/watch?v= jURXwmSHsDI) and Oprah's giving attention to it in *O: The Oprah Magazine* (Mary A. Fischer, "Diet Pills: The Next Generation," *O: The Oprah Magazine* 6, no. 7 [2005], 103). In the summer of 2005, *Radar* magazine reported that America was going mad over "Hoodia Love" and showed a picture of five smiling actresses from the popular show *Desperate Housewives* juxtaposed with an image of an elderly (supposedly San) woman opening her mouth to eat Hoodia. The article also displayed a bottle of Hoodia supplement from Steve Hurt's Afrigetics company. Andrew Goldman, "Hoodia Love," *Radar*, Summer 2005, 68–72.

11 For more on the San-SAHGA agreement, see Wynberg, Schroeder, and Chennells, *Indigenous Peoples, Consent, and Benefit Sharing*, 112.

12 According to an April 2009 press release from the US Federal Trade Commission (FTC), charges were filed against Nutraceuticals International, LLC, for deceptive advertising of *Hoodia gordonii* products; www.ftc.gov /news-events/press-releases/2009/04/ftc-charges-marketers-hoodia-weight -loss-supplements-deceptive (last accessed August 28, 2016). In April 2009, the Advertising Standards Authority of South Africa also issued a formal complaint against Planet Hoodia for claims that their Slender Gel containing *Hoodia gordonii* was scientifically proven to reduce weight; http://m .health24.com/health24/natural/news/hoodia-claims-retracted-20120721 (last accessed August 28, 2016).

13 Memorandum of Understanding between The San People of Southern Africa, Cape Ethnobotanical Growers Association, and South African Hoodia Growers Association with Cape Nature and Department of Tourism, Environment, and Conservation, December 7, 2006 (on file with author).

14 Constitution of the Southern African Hoodia Growers Association (on file with author).

15 For more on the San-SAHGA agreement, see Wynberg, Schroeder, and Chennells, *Indigenous Peoples, Consent, and Benefit Sharing*.

16 Hayden, "Taking as Giving."

17 Steve Hurt, in discussion with author in South Africa, February 16, 2015 (on file with author).

18 Letter of Receipt of Payment from Silke Felton, WIMSA Regional Coordinator, to Steve Hurt, July 30, 2008 (on file with author).

19 Hayden, "Taking as Giving," 746.

20 John L. Comaroff and Jean Comaroff, *Ethnicity, Inc.* (Chicago: University of Chicago Press, 2009).

21 Robby Gass, in discussion with author in South Africa, February 26, 2009 (on file with author). Gass launched his business in 2004 after leaving his position as general farm manager at another supplier of herbal medicines, Parceval Pharmaceuticals in Wellington. When I met Gass in 2009, he graciously agreed to show me his Zizamele operations, which were marketed under the slogan "God's Herbs for Your Health."

22 Robby Gass, in discussion with author in South Africa, February 26, 2009 (on file with author).

23 Steve Hurt, in discussion with author in South Africa, February 16, 2015 (on file with author).

24 Robby Gass, in discussion with author in South Africa, February 26, 2009 (on file with author).

25 Adolf Joubert, in discussion with author in South Africa, June 3, 2014 (on file with author); Steve Hurt, in discussion with author in South Africa, February 16, 2015 (on file with author).

26 For more information on rooibos farming, see www.sarooibos.org.za /rooibos-farming-factfile-75 (last accessed December 14, 2015).

27 Adolf Joubert, in discussion with author in South Africa, June 3, 2014 (on file with author).

28 In a deliberate moment of ethnographic refusal, I decline to include images of these websites with their racist content, knowing that some San peoples find these images highly insulting. I describe the images here in order to critique them with awareness that even doing the analysis here continues to reinscribe their meanings.

29 TraZic Hoodia Gordonii, www://www.trazic.com/hoodia-info.html (visited February 27, 2007) (on file with author).

30 Desert Burn, www://www.desertburn.com (accessed February 27, 2009) (on file with author).

31 Inderpal Grewal, *Transnational America: Feminisms, Diasporas, Neoliberalisms* (Durham, NC: Duke University Press, 2005), 23.

32 Becker, "The Least Sexist Society?," 23.

33 Arrie Tieties, in discussion with author in South Africa, March 3, 2009 (on file with author).

34 McClintock, *Imperial Leather*, 33.

35 For additional analysis of these images, see M. Neelika Jayawardane, "Impenetrable Bodies / Disappearing Bodies: Fat American Celebrities, Lean Indigenous People, and Multinational Pharmaceuticals in the Battle to Claim *Hoodia Gordonii*," *Popular Communication* 9, no. 2 (2011): 79–98.

36 For more on fat studies and fatphobia, see Anna Kirkland, "The Environmental Account of Obesity: A Case for Feminist Skepticism," *Signs: Journal of Women in Culture and Society* 36, no. 2 (2011): 463–85, and *Fat Rights: Dilemmas of Difference and Personhood* (New York: New York University Press, 2008).

37 Kevin Poovey, in discussion with author in South Africa over Skype, March 6, 2009 (on file with author).

38 Arrie Tieties, in discussion with author in South Africa, March 3, 2009 (on file with author).

39 Tommy Busakhwe, in discussion with author in South Africa, March 4, 2009 (on file with author).

40 Arrie Tieties, in discussion with author in South Africa, March 4, 2015 (on file with author).

41 Collin Louw, in discussion with author in South Africa, March 4, 2015 (on file with author).

42 Tasha, in discussion with author in South Africa, March 3, 2015 (on file with author).

43 Arrie Tieties, in discussion with author in South Africa, March 4, 2015 (on file with author).

44 Comaroff and Comaroff, "Naturing the Nation," 635.

45 Sarah Ives, "Farming the South African 'Bush': Ecologies of Belonging and Exclusion in Rooibos Tea," *American Ethnologist* 41, no. 4 (2014): 698–713, and "Uprooting 'Indigeneity' in South Africa's Western Cape."

Epilogue: Implications of a Feminist Decolonial Technoscience

1 See Chennells, "Traditional Knowledge and Benefit Sharing after the Nagoya Protocol"; Sean Carey, "A South African Herb That May Rival Prozac," *African Business*, no. 373 (2011), 52–54.

2 "Natural Justice Legally Supports the National Khoi-San Council in Historic Benefit Sharing Agreement," Natural Justice blog, August 22, 2013, http://natural-justice.blogspot.com/2013/08/natural-justice-legally-supports.html.

3 "Access and Benefit Sharing Meeting with Khoi-San Rooibos Farming Community in Wupperthal, Cedarburg Region," Natural Justice blog, May 17, 2016, http://natural-justice.blogspot.com/2016/05/access-and-benefit-sharing-meeting-with.html.

4 For more on biocultural community protocols, see Stephanie Booker et al., *Exploring the Development and Use of Biocultural Community Protocols to Help Secure Community Interests and Rights in Relation to Extractive Industries: A Framework Methodology* (Cape Town: Natural Justice, 2014); Jael Makagon et al., *Community Protocols Toolbox* (Cape Town: Natural Justice, 2016); Harry Jonas, Kabir Bavikatte, and Holly Shrumm, "Community Protocols and Access and Benefit Sharing," *Asian Biotechnology and Development Review* 13, no. 3 (2010): 49–76. For more on Bushbuckridge protocols, see Rodney Sibuye et al., "The Bushbuckridge BCP: Traditional Health Practitioners Organise for ABS in South Africa," *Participatory Learning and Action* 65 (2012): 101–8. For more on community-led protocols, see Ilse Köhler-Rollefson et al., "Biocultural Community Protocols: Tools for Securing the Assets of Livestock Keepers," ibid., 109–18.

5 For more information on the 2015 amendments, see Foster, "The Making and Unmaking of Patent Ownership."

6 Ives, "Uprooting 'Indigeneity' in South Africa's Western Cape" and "Farming the South African 'Bush'"; Comaroff and Comaroff, "Naturing the

Nation"; Richard B. Lee, "Indigenous Rights and the Politics of Identity in Post-Apartheid Southern Africa," in *At the Risk of Being Heard: Identity, Indigenous Rights, and Postcolonial States*, ed. Bartholomew C. Dean and Jerome M. Levi (Ann Arbor: University of Michigan Press, 2003), 80–81.

Appendix 2

1   *Graham v. John Deere Co.*, 383 U.S. 1 (1966).
2   *In re Klein* 647 F.3d 1343 (Fed. Cir. 2011); *KSR International Co. v. Teleflex, Inc.*, 127 S. Ct. 1727 (2007).
3   For critiques of the "reasonable person" standard in rape law, see Susan Estrich, "Rape," *Yale Law Journal* 95, no. 6 (1986); 1087–184; in sexual harassment law, see Martha Chamallas, "Feminist Constructions of Objectivity: Multiple Perspectives on Sexual and Racial Harassment Litigation," in *Applications of Feminist Legal Theory to Women's Lives: Sex, Violence, Work, and Reproduction*, ed. D. Kelly Weisberg (Philadelphia: Temple University Press, 1996), 808–25; in intellectual property law, see Ann Bartow, "Women in the Web of Secondary Copyright Liability and Internet Filtering," *Northern Kentucky Law Review* 33, no. 3 (2005): 449–93; and Burk, "Do Patents Have Gender?"

Bibliography

Abraham, Itty. "The Contradictory Spaces of Postcolonial Techno-Science." *Economic and Political Weekly* 41, no. 3 (2006): 210–17.

Abrahams, Yvette. "Gender and Locating Sarah Baartman in the Present." In *Democracy X: Marking the Present, Re-Presenting the Past*, edited by Andries Walter Oliphant, Peter Delius, and Lalou Meltzer, 151-62. Pretoria: University of South Africa, 2004.

Abrell, Elan, Kabir Bavikatte, Gino Cocchiaro, Harry Jonas, and Andrew Rens. *Imagining a Traditional Knowledge Commons: A Community Approach to Ensuring the Local Integrity of Environmental Law and Policy*. Rome: Natural Justice, 2009.

Ahmed, Sara. "Open Forum Imaginary Prohibitions: Some Preliminary Remarks on the Founding Gestures of the 'New Materialism.'" *European Journal of Women's Studies* 15, no. 1 (2008): 23–39.

Alaimo, Stacy, and Susan J. Hekman, eds. *Material Feminisms*. Bloomington: Indiana University Press, 2008.

Allen, Paula Gunn. *Grandmothers of the Light: A Medicine Woman's Sourcebook*. Boston: Beacon Press, 1991.

Andanda, Pamela, Doris Schroeder, Sachin Chaturvedi, Emezat Mengesha, and Tim Hodges. "Legal Frameworks for Benefit Sharing: From Biodiversity to Human Genomics." In *Benefit Sharing: From Biodiversity to Human Genetics*, edited by Doris Schroeder and Julie Cook Lucas, 33–64. New York: Springer, 2013.

Anderson, Jane E. *Law, Knowledge, Culture: The Production of Indigenous Knowledge in Intellectual Property Law*. Cheltenham, UK: Edward Elgar, 2009.

Badenhorst, P. J., Juanita M. Pienaar, and Hanri Mostert, eds. *Silberberg and Schoeman's The Law of Property*. Durban: LexisNexis Butterworths, 2006.

Barad, Karen Michelle. *Meeting the Universe Halfway: Quantum Physics and the Entanglement of Matter and Meaning*. Durham, NC: Duke University Press, 2007.

Barnard, Alan. "Laurens Van Der Post and the Kalahari Debate." In *Miscast:*

Negotiating the Presence of the Bushmen, edited by Pippa Skotnes, 239–47. Cape Town: University of Cape Town Press, 1996.

Barnard, David. "In the High Court of South Africa, Case No. 4138/98: The Global Politics of Access to Low-Cost AIDS Drugs in Poor Countries." *Kennedy Institute of Ethics Journal* 12, no. 2 (2002): 159–74.

Bartow, Ann. "Women in the Web of Secondary Copyright Liability and Internet Filtering." *Northern Kentucky Law Review* 33, no. 3 (2005): 449–93.

Becker, Heike. "'The Least Sexist Society? Perspectives on Gender, Change, and Violence among Southern African San." *Journal of Southern African Studies* 29, no. 1 (2003): 5–23.

Beinart, William. *Twentieth-Century South Africa*, 2nd ed. Oxford: Oxford University Press, 2001.

Benjamin, Ruha. "Informed Refusal: Toward a Justice-Based Bioethics." *Science, Technology, and Human Values* 41, no. 6 (2016): 967–90.

———. "A Lab of Their Own: Genomic Sovereignty as Postcolonial Science Policy." *Policy and Society* 28, no. 4 (2009): 341–55.

Bhatt, Amy, Madhavi Murty, and Priti Ramamurthy. "Hegemonic Developments: The New Indian Middle Class, Gendered Subalterns, and Diasporic Returnees in the Event of Neoliberalism." *Signs: Journal of Women in Culture and Society* 36, no. 1 (2010): 127–52.

Blackwell, David. "Unilever Helps QCA in the Search for Experience." *Financial Times*, August 4, 2006.

Bleier, Ruth. *Feminist Approaches to Science*. New York: Pergamon Press, 1986.

———. *Science and Gender: A Critique of Biology and Its Theories on Women*. New York: Pergamon Press, 1984.

Blom, Wendy A. M., Salomon L. Abrahamse, Roberta Bradford, Guus SMJE Duchateau, Winfried Theis, Antonia Orsi, Caroline L. Ward, and David J. Mela. "Effects of 15-D Repeated Consumption of *Hoodia Gordonii* Purified Extract on Safety, Ad Libitum Energy Intake, and Body Weight in Healthy Overweight Women: A Randomized Controlled Trial." *American Journal of Clinical Nutrition* 94, no. 5 (2011): 1171–81.

Boateng, Boatema. *The Copyright Thing Doesn't Work Here: Adinkra and Kente Cloth and Intellectual Property in Ghana*. Minneapolis: University of Minnesota Press, 2011.

Bond, Patrick. *Elite Transition: From Apartheid to Neoliberalism in South Africa*. Pietermaritzburg, South Africa: University of Natal Press, 2000.

Booker, Stephanie, Holly Jonas, Eli Makagon, Johanna von Braun, and Marie Wilke. *Exploring the Development and Use of Biocultural Community Protocols to Help Secure Community Interests and Rights in Relation to Extractive Industries: A Framework Methodology*. Cape Town: Natural Justice, 2014.

Boyle, James. *The Public Domain: Enclosing the Commons of the Mind*. New Haven, CT: Yale University Press, 2008.

———. *Shamans, Software, and Spleens: Law and the Construction of the Information Society*. Cambridge, MA: Harvard University Press, 1996.

Bradlow, Frank R. *Francis Masson's Account of Three Journeys at the Cape of Good Hope, 1772-1775*. Cape Town: Tablecloth Press, 1994.

Braidotti, Rosi. *Women, the Environment, and Sustainable Development: Towards a Theoretical Synthesis*. London: Zed Books, 1994.

Brighton Women and Science Group and Lynda I. A. Birke, eds. *Alice through the Microscope: The Power of Science over Women's Lives*. London: Virago, 1980.

Brockway, Lucile. *Science and Colonial Expansion: The Role of the British Royal Botanic Gardens*. New York: Academic Press, 1979.

Brown, Michael F. "Can Culture Be Copyrighted?" *Current Anthropology* 39, no. 2 (1998): 193–222.

———. *Who Owns Native Culture?* Cambridge, MA: Harvard University Press, 2003.

Brown, N. E. "Asclepiadeae." In *Flora Capensis: Being a Systematic Description of the Cape Colony, Caffrara, and Port Natal*, edited by Sir William T. Thiselton-Dyer, 518–1036. London: Lovell Reeve and Co., 1909.

Brush, Stephen B., and Doreen Stabinsky. *Valuing Local Knowledge: Indigenous People and Intellectual Property Rights*. Washington, DC: Island Press, 1996.

Bruyns, Peter V. *Stapeliads of Southern Africa and Madagascar*. Hatfield, South Africa: Umdaus Press, 2005.

Burk, Dan L. "Do Patents Have Gender?" *Journal of Gender, Social Policy, and the Law* 19, no. 3 (2011): 881–919.

———. "Feminism and Dualism in Intellectual Property." *Journal of Gender, Social Policy, and the Law* 15, no. 2 (2007): 183–206.

Burrell, Timothy Donald. *Burrell's South African Patent and Design Law*, 3rd ed. Durban: Butterworths, 1999.

Callon, Michel. "Some Elements of a Sociology of Translation: Domestication of the Scallops and the Fishermen of St. Brieuc Bay." In *Power, Action, and Belief: A New Sociology of Knowledge?*, edited by John Law, 196–223. London: Routledge, 1986.

Carey, Sean. "A South African Herb That May Rival Prozac." *African Business*, no. 373 (2011), 52–54.

Carney, Judith Ann. *Black Rice: The African Origins of Rice Cultivation in the Americas*. Cambridge, MA: Harvard University Press, 2001.

Chamallas, Martha. "Feminist Constructions of Objectivity: Multiple Perspectives on Sexual and Racial Harassment Litigation." In *Applications of Feminist Legal Theory to Women's Lives: Sex, Violence, Work, and Reproduction*, edited by D. Kelly Weisberg, 808–25. Philadelphia: Temple University Press, 1996.

Chennells, Roger. "Ethics and Practice in Ethnobiology: The Experience of the San Peoples of Southern Africa." In *Biodiversity and the Law: Intellectual Property, Biotechnology, and Traditional Knowledge*, edited by Charles R. McManis, 413–27. London: Earthscan, 2007.

———. "The ≠Khomani San of South Africa." In *Indigenous Peoples Protected Areas in Africa: From Principles to Practice*, edited by John Nelson and

Lindsay Hossack, 269–93. Moreton-in-Marsh, UK: Forest Peoples Programme, 2003.

———. "Toward Global Justice through Benefit Sharing." *Hastings Center Report* 40, no. 1 (2010): 3.

———. "Traditional Knowledge and Benefit Sharing after the Nagoya Protocol: Three Cases from South Africa." *Law, Environment, and Development Journal* 9, no. 2 (2013): 165–84.

———. "Vulnerability and Indigenous Communities: Are the San of South Africa a Vulnerable People?" *Cambridge Quarterly of Healthcare Ethics* 18, no. 2 (2009): 147–54.

Chidester, David. "Bushmen Religion: Open, Closed, and New Frontiers." In *Miscast: Negotiating the Presence of the Bushmen*, edited by Pippa Skotnes, 51–60. Cape Town: University of Cape Town Press, 1996.

Clarke, Adele E. *Disciplining Reproduction: Modernity, American Life Sciences, and "the Problems of Sex."* Berkeley: University of California Press, 1998.

Clarke, Adele E., and Theresa Montini. "The Many Faces of RU486: Tales of Situated Knowledges and Technological Contestations." *Science, Technology, and Human Values* 18, no. 1 (1993): 42–78.

Clarke, Adele E., and Susan Leigh Star. "The Social Worlds Framework: A Theory/Methods Framework." In *The Handbook of Science and Technology Studies*, edited by Edward J. Hackett, Olga Amsterdamska, Michael Lynch, and Judy Wajcman, 113–38. Cambridge, MA: MIT Press, 2008.

Collins, Patricia Hill, and Sirma Bilge. *Intersectionality.* Malden, MA: Polity Press, 2016.

Comaroff, Jean, and John L. Comaroff. *Ethnicity, Inc.* Chicago: University of Chicago Press, 2009.

———. "Naturing the Nation: Aliens, Apocalypse, and the Postcolonial State." *Journal of Southern African Studies* 27, no. 3 (2001): 627–51.

———. *Theory from the South, or How Euro-America Is Evolving toward Africa.* Boulder, CO: Paradigm, 2012.

Coombe, Rosemary J. *The Cultural Life of Intellectual Properties: Authorship, Appropriation, and the Law.* Durham, NC: Duke University Press, 1998.

Cooper, Melinda. *Life as Surplus: Biotechnology and Capitalism in the Neoliberal Era.* Seattle: University of Washington Press, 2008.

Crais, Clifton C., and Pamela Scully. *Sara Baartman and the Hottentot Venus: A Ghost Story and a Biography.* Princeton: Princeton University Press, 2009.

Crenshaw, Kimberlé. "Mapping the Margins: Intersectionality, Identity Politics, and Violence against Women of Color." *Stanford Law Review* 43, no. 6 (1991): 1241–99.

Curtis, William, and John Sims. *Curtis's Botanical Magazine or Flower-Garden Displayed*, vol. 51. London: T. Curtis, 1824.

Daston, Lorraine, and Peter Galison. "The Image of Objectivity." *Representations*, no. 40 (1992): 81–128.

Davoudi, Salamander. "Phytopharm Narrows Losses Smallcap Briefing." *Financial Times*, May 2, 2007.

Deloria Jr., Vine. *Custer Died for Your Sins: An Indian Manifesto*. New York: Macmillan, 1969.

Derrida, Jacques. "Force of Law: The 'Mystical Foundation of Authority.'" *Cardozo Law Review* 11, nos. 5-6 (1990): 919–1046.

de Sousa Santos, Boaventura. "A Map of Misreading: Toward a Postmodern Conception of Law." *Journal of Law and Society* 14, no. 3 (1987): 279–302.

Ding, Waverly W., Fiona Murray, and Toby E. Stuart. "Gender Differences in Patenting in the Academic Life Sciences." *Science* 313, no. 5787 (2006): 665–67.

Drahos, Peter. *A Philosophy of Intellectual Property*. Dartmouth, MA: Dartmouth Publishing Group, 1996.

Drahos, Peter, and Ruth Mayne, eds. *Global Intellectual Property Rights: Knowledge, Access, and Development*. New York: Palgrave Macmillan, 2002.

Dreyfuss, Rochelle. "Protecting the Public Domain of Science: Has the Time for an Experimental Use Defense Arrived?" *Arizona Law Review* 46, no. 3 (2004): 457–72.

Dube, Ernest F. "Racism and Education in South Africa." In *The Anti-Apartheid Reader: The Struggle against White Racist Rule in South Africa*, edited by David Mermelstein, 177–84. New York: Grove Press, 1987.

du Bois, François, ed. *Wille's Principles of South African Law*. Cape Town: Juta and Co., 2007.

Dubow, Saul. *A Commonwealth of Knowledge: Science, Sensibility, and South Africa, 1820-2000*. Oxford: Oxford University Press, 2006.

———. *Scientific Racism in Modern South Africa*. Cambridge: Cambridge University Press, 1995.

Endress, Mary E., and Peter V. Bruyns. "A Revised Classification of the Apocynaceae S.L." *Botanical Review* 66, no. 1 (2000): 1–56.

Estrich, Susan. "Rape." *Yale Law Journal* 95, no. 6 (1986): 1087–184.

Fanon, Frantz. *The Wretched of the Earth*. Translated by Richard Philcox. New York: Grove Press, 2004.

Fausto-Sterling, Anne. *Myths of Gender: Biological Theories about Women and Men*. New York: Basic Books, 1985.

Felton, Silke, and Heike Becker. *A Gender Perspective on the Status of the San in Southern Africa*. Windhoek, Namibia: Legal Assistance Centre, 2001.

Ferguson, James. *Global Shadows: Africa in the Neoliberal World Order*. Durham, NC: Duke University Press, 2006.

Finger, J. M., and Philip Schuler, eds. *Poor People's Knowledge: Promoting Intellectual Property in Developing Countries*. Washington, DC: World Bank and Oxford University Press, 2004.

Fiorella, Kathryn Joan. "The Researcher's Personal Pursuit of Balance between Academic and Practical Contributions." *Journal of Research Practice* 10, no. 2 (2014): N11.

Firn, David. "African Cactus Could Help Fight Obesity." *London Financial Times*, April 11, 2001, 2.

Fischer, Mary A. "Diet Pills: The Next Generation." *O: The Oprah Magazine* 6, no. 7 (2005), 103.

Foster, Laura A. "Decolonizing Patent Law: Postcolonial Technoscience and Indigenous Knowledge in South Africa." *Feminist Formations* 28, no. 3 (2016): 148–73.

———. "The Making and Unmaking of Patent Ownership: Technicalities, Materialities, and Subjectivities." *PoLAR: Political and Legal Anthropology Review* 39, no. 1 (2016): 127–43.

———. "Patents, Biopolitics, and Feminisms: Locating Patent Law Struggles over Breast Cancer Genes and the *Hoodia* Plant." *International Journal of Cultural Property* 19, no. 3 (2012): 371–400.

———. "A Postapartheid Genome: Genetic Ancestry Testing and Belonging in South Africa." *Science, Technology, and Human Values* 41, no. 6 (2016): 1015–36.

———. "Situating Feminisms, Patent Law, and the Public Domain." *Columbia Journal of Gender and Law* 20, no. 2 (2011): 261–347.

Foucault, Michel. *The Order of Things: An Archaeology of the Human Sciences*. New York: Vintage Books, 1973.

Friese, Carrie. *Cloning Wild Life: Zoos, Captivity, and the Future of Endangered Animals*. New York: New York University Press, 2013.

Frietsch, Rainer, Inna Haller, Melanie Funken-Vrohlings, and Harloff Grupp. "Gender-Specific Patterns in Patenting and Publishing." *Research Policy* 38, no. 4 (2009): 590–99.

Garnham, Peter, and Robert Orr. "Small-Caps: Plusnet Falls on Carphone Warehouse Plan." *Financial Times*, April 11, 2006.

Gelb, Stephen. "Macroeconomic Policy in South Africa: From RDP through GEAR to ASGISA." In *At the End of the Rainbow? Social Welfare in the New South Africa*, edited by Gorm Gunnarsen, Patrick Mac Manus, Morten Nielsen, and Hans Erik Stolten, 17–28. Copenhagen: Southern Africa Contact, 2007.

Goldman, Andrew. "Hoodia Love." *Radar*, Summer 2005, 68–72.

Gould, Stephen Jay. "American Polygeny and Craniometry before Darwin: Blacks and Indians as Separate, Inferior Species." In *The "Racial" Economy of Science: Toward a Democratic Future*, edited by Sandra G. Harding, 84–115. Bloomington: Indiana University Press, 1993.

Govender, Pregs. *Love and Courage: A Story of Insubordination*. Auckland Park, South Africa: Jacana Media, 2007.

Green, Joyce. "Taking Account of Aboriginal Feminism." In *Making Space for Indigenous Feminism*, edited by Joyce Green, 20–31. Black Point, NS: Fernwood, 2007.

Greene, Shane. "Indigenous People Incorporated? Culture as Politics, Culture as Property in Pharmaceutical Bioprospecting." *Current Anthropology* 45, no. 2 (2004): 211–37.

Grewal, Inderpal. *Transnational America: Feminisms, Diasporas, Neoliberalisms*. Durham, NC: Duke University Press, 2005.

Griffin, Susan. *Woman and Nature: The Roaring Inside Her*. New York: Harper and Row, 1978.

Griffiths, Dominic, and Maria L. C. Prozesky. "The Politics of Dwelling: Being White / Being South African." *Africa Today* 56, no. 4 (2010): 22–41.

Halbert, Debora J. "Feminist Interpretations of Intellectual Property." *Journal of Gender, Social Policy, and the Law* 14, no. 3 (2006): 431–60.

Hamilton, Jennifer A. *Indigeneity in the Courtroom: Law, Culture, and the Production of Difference in North American Courts*. New York: Routledge, 2009.

Hammonds, Evelynn. "Race, Sex, AIDS: The Construction of 'Other.'" In *Race, Class, and Gender: An Anthology*, edited by Margaret Anderson and Patricia Hill Collins, 402–13. Belmont, CA: Wadsworth, 1995 [1987].

Haraway, Donna J. *The Companion Species Manifesto: Dogs, People, and Significant Otherness*. Chicago: Prickly Paradigm Press, 2003.

———. *Modest_Witness@Second_Millennium.FemaleMan_Meets_OncoMouse: Feminism and Technoscience*. New York: Routledge, 1997.

———. *Primate Visions: Gender, Race, and Nature in the World of Modern Science*. New York: Routledge, 1989.

———. *When Species Meet*. Minneapolis: University of Minnesota Press, 2008.

Harding, Sandra. *Is Science Multicultural? Postcolonialisms, Feminisms, and Epistemologies*. Bloomington: Indiana University Press, 1998.

———. "Latin American Decolonial Social Studies of Scientific Knowledge: Alliances and Tensions." *Science, Technology, and Human Values* 41, no. 6 (2016): 1063–87.

———. "Postcolonial and Feminist Philosophies of Science and Technology: Convergences and Dissonances." *Postcolonial Studies* 12, no. 4 (2009): 401–21.

———. *The Postcolonial Science and Technology Studies Reader*. Durham, NC: Duke University Press, 2011.

———. *The Science Question in Feminism*. Ithaca, NY: Cornell University Press, 1986.

———. *Sciences from Below: Feminisms, Postcolonialities, and Modernities*. Durham, NC: Duke University Press, 2008.

———. *Whose Science? Whose Knowledge? Thinking from Women's Lives*. Ithaca, NY: Cornell University Press, 1991.

Harrison, Graham. "Post-Neoliberalism?" *Review of African Political Economy* 37, no. 123 (2010): 1–5.

Harry, Debra, and Le`a Malia Kanehe. "The BS in Access and Benefit Sharing (ABS): Critical Questions for Indigenous Peoples." In *The Catch: Perspectives in Benefit Sharing*, edited by Beth Burrows, 81-120. Edmonds, WA: Edmonds Institute, 2005.

———. "The Right of Indigenous Peoples to Permanent Sovereignty over Genetic Resources and Associated Indigenous Knowledge." *Journal of Indigenous Policy*, no. 6 (2007): 28–43.

Harvey, David. *A Brief History of Neoliberalism*. Oxford: Oxford University Press, 2005.

Haupt, Adam. *Stealing Empire: P2P, Intellectual Property, and Hip-Hop Subversion*. Cape Town: Human Sciences Research Council, 2008.

Hayden, Cori. "Taking as Giving: Bioscience, Exchange, and the Politics of Benefit-Sharing." *Social Studies of Science* 37, no. 5 (2007): 729–58.

———. *When Nature Goes Public: The Making and Unmaking of Bioprospecting in Mexico*. Princeton, NJ: Princeton University Press, 2003.

Hecht, Gabrielle. *Being Nuclear: Africans and the Global Uranium Trade*. Cambridge, MA: MIT Press, 2012.

Holden, Phillipa. "Conservation and Human Rights: The Case of the Khomani San (Bushmen) and the Kgalgadi Transfrontier Park, South Africa." *Policy Matters* 15 (2007): 57–68.

Hubbard, Ruth, Mary Sue Henifin, and Barbara Fried, eds. *Biological Woman—the Convenient Myth: A Collection of Feminist Essays and a Comprehensive Bibliography*. Cambridge, MA: Schenkman, 1982.

———, eds. *Women Look at Biology Looking at Women: A Collection of Feminist Critiques*. Boston: G. K. Hall, 1979.

Hughes, David McDermott. *Whiteness in Zimbabwe: Race, Landscape, and the Problem of Belonging*. New York: Palgrave Macmillan, 2010.

Hume, Neil, and Robert Orr. "Boost for Clipper Windpower." *Financial Times*, April 26, 2007.

Ives, Sarah. "Farming the South African 'Bush': Ecologies of Belonging and Exclusion in Rooibos Tea." *American Ethnologist* 41, no. 4 (2014): 698–713.

———. "Uprooting 'Indigeneity' in South Africa's Western Cape: The Plant That Moves." *American Anthropologist* 116, no. 2 (2014): 310–23.

Jackson, Shannon, and Steven Robins. "Miscast: The Place of the Museum in Negotiating the Bushman Past and Present." *Critical Arts* 13, no. 1 (1999): 69–101.

Jaimes, M. A. "Savage Hegemony: From 'Endangered Species' to Feminist Indiginism." In *Talking Visions: Multicultural Feminism in Transnational Age*, edited by Ella Shohat, 413–39. New York: New Museum of Contemporary Art, 1998.

Jasanoff, Sheila. "The Idiom of Co-Production." In *States of Knowledge: The Co-Production of Science and Social Order*, edited by Sheila Jasanoff, 1–12. London: Routledge, 2004.

Jayawardane, M. Neelika. "Impenetrable Bodies / Disappearing Bodies: Fat American Celebrities, Lean Indigenous People, and Multinational Pharmaceuticals in the Battle to Claim *Hoodia Gordonii*." *Popular Communication* 9, no. 2 (2011): 79–98.

Jen, Clare Ching. "How to Survive Contagion, Disease, and Disaster: The 'Masked Asian/American Woman' as Low-Tech Specter of Emergency Preparedness." *Feminist Formations* 25, no. 2 (2013): 107–28.

Jenkins, Patrick. "Pfizer Set to Bolster Phytopharm Programme." *Financial Times,* April 12, 2002.

Jonas, Harry, Kabir Bavikatte, and Holly Shrumm. "Community Protocols and Access and Benefit Sharing." *Asian Biotechnology and Development Review* 13, no. 3 (2010): 49–76.

Kahler, Annette I. "Examining Exclusion in Woman-Inventor Patenting: A Comparison of Educational Trends and Patent Trends and Patent Data in the Era of Computer Engineer Barbie®." *Journal of Gender, Social Policy, and the Law* 19, no. 3 (2011): 773–98.

Kahn, Jonathan. "Exploiting Race in Drug Development: BiDil's Interim Model of Pharmacogenomics." *Social Studies of Science* 38, no. 5 (2008): 737–58.

———. "Race-ing Patents / Patenting Race: An Emerging Political Geography of Intellectual Property in Biotechnology." *Iowa Law Review* 92, no. 1 (2007): 353–402.

Kane, Eileen. "Molecules and Conflict: Cancer, Patents, and Women's Health." *Journal of Gender, Social Policy, and the Law* 15, no. 2 (2007): 305–35.

Kang, Hyo Yoon. "An Exploration into Law and Narratives: The Case of Intellectual Property Law of Biotechnology." *Law Critique* 17, no. 1 (2006): 239–65.

Karsten, Mia C. "Francis Masson, a Gardener-Botanist Who Collected at the Cape." In *Francis Masson's Account of Three Journeys at the Cape of Good Hope, 1772-1775,* edited by Frank R. Bradlow, 203–14. Cape Town: Tablecloth Press, 1994.

Keller, Evelyn Fox. "Feminism and Science." *Signs: Journal of Women in Culture and Society* 7, no. 3 (1982): 598–602.

Khan, B. Zorina. "Married Women's Property Laws and Female Commercial Activity: Evidence from United States Patent Records, 1790-1895." *Journal of Economic History* 56, no. 2 (1996): 356–88.

———. "'Not for Ornament': Patenting Activity by Nineteenth-Century Women Inventors." *Journal of Interdisciplinary History* 31, no. 2 (2000): 159–95.

Kirby, Vicki. *Quantum Anthropologies: Life at Large.* Durham, NC: Duke University Press, 2011.

Kirkland, Anna. "The Environmental Account of Obesity: A Case for Feminist Skepticism." *Signs: Journal of Women in Culture and Society* 36, no. 2 (2011): 463–85.

———. *Fat Rights: Dilemmas of Difference and Personhood.* New York: New York University Press, 2008.

Köhler-Rollefson, Ilse, Abdul Raziq Kakar, Evelyn Mathias, Hanwant Singh Rathore, and Jacob Wanyama. "Biocultural Community Protocols: Tools for Securing the Assets of Livestock Keepers." *Participatory Learning and Action* 65 (2012): 109–18.

LaDuke, Winona. *Recovering the Sacred: The Power of Naming and Claiming.* Cambridge, MA: South End Press, 2005.

Lalu, Premesh. *The Deaths of Hintsa: Postapartheid South Africa and the Shape of Recurring Pasts.* Cape Town: HSRC Press, 2009.

———. "When Was South African History Ever Postcolonial?" *Kronos* 34, no. 1 (2008): 267–81.

Larner, Wendy. "Neo-Liberalism: Policy, Ideology, Governmentality." *Studies in Political Economy* 63 (2000): 5–25.

Latour, Bruno. *Science in Action: How to Follow Scientists and Engineers through Society.* Cambridge, MA: Harvard University Press, 1987.

Latour, Bruno, and Steve Woolgar. *Laboratory Life: The Construction of Scientific Facts.* Princeton, NJ: Princeton University Press, 1986.

Lee, Richard B. *The Dobe Ju/'hoansi*, 3rd ed. Belmont, CA: Wadsworth Thomson Learning, 2003.

———. "Indigenous Rights and the Politics of Identity in Post-Apartheid Southern Africa." In *At the Risk of Being Heard: Identity, Indigenous Rights, and Postcolonial States*, edited by Bartholomew C. Dean and Jerome M. Levi, 80–111. Ann Arbor: University of Michigan Press, 2003.

Le Fleur, Andrew, and Lesle Jansen. "Country Report: The Khoisan in Contemporary South Africa: Challenges of Recognition as an Indigenous Peoples." Cape Town: Konrad-Adenauer-Stiftung, 2013.

le Roux, Willemien, and Alison White, eds. *Voices of the San: Living in Southern Africa Today.* Cape Town: Kwela Books, 2004.

Lessig, Lawrence. *The Future of Ideas: The Fate of the Commons in a Connected World.* New York: Random House, 2001.

Linnaeus, Carl. *Systema Naturae*, vol. 1, 10th ed. Stockholm: Laurentii Salvii, 1758.

Longino, Helen E. *Science as Social Knowledge: Values and Objectivity in Scientific Inquiry* Princeton, NJ: Princeton University Press, 1990.

MacKinnon, Catharine A. "Feminism, Marxism, Method, and the State: An Agenda for Theory." *Signs: Journal of Women in Culture and Society* 7, no. 3 (1982): 515–44.

Makagon, Jael, Johanna von Braun, Gino Cocchiaro, Stella James, and Jochen Luckscheiter. *Community Protocols Toolbox.* Cape Town: Natural Justice, 2016.

Marais, Hein. *South Africa Pushed to the Limit: The Political Economy of Change.* London: Zed Books, 2011.

Marloth, Rudolf. *The Flora of South Africa with Synopsis of the South African Genera of Phanerogamous Plants*, vol. 3. London: Wheldon and Wesley, 1932.

Masson, Francis. *An Account of Three Journeys from the Cape Town into the Southern Parts of Africa; Undertaken for the Discovery of New Plants, Towards the Improvement of the Royal Botanical Gardens at Kew.* London: Royal Society of London, 1776.

———. *Stapeliae Novae: Or, a Collection of Several New Species of That Genus; Discovered in the Interior Parts of Africa.* London: W. Bulmer and Co., 1796.

May, Christopher, and Susan K. Sell. *Intellectual Property Rights: A Critical History.* Boulder, CO: Lynne Rienner, 2006.

May, Vivian M. *Pursuing Intersectionality, Unsettling Dominant Imaginaries.* New York: Routledge, 2015.

Mbembe, Achille. *On the Postcolony.* Berkeley: University of California Press, 2001.

McCann, Carole R. "Malthusian Men and Demographic Transitions: A Case Study of Hegemonic Masculinity in Mid-Twentieth-Century Population Theory." *Frontiers: A Journal of Women's Studies* 30, no. 1 (2009): 142–71.

McClintock, Anne. *Imperial Leather: Race, Gender, and Sexuality in the Colonial Contest.* New York: Routledge, 1995.

McGrath, Steve. "Phytopharm Shares Leap as Trading Resumes after Merger Deal." *Alliance News,* September 24, 2013, www.lse.co.uk/AllNews.asp?code=t5lq3wdy.

McLachlan, Fiona. "The Apartheid Laws in Brief." In *The Anti-Apartheid Reader: The Struggle against White Racist Rule in South Africa,* edited by David Mermelstein, 76–98. New York: Grove Press, 1987.

Medina, Eden, Ivan da Costa Marques, and Christina Holmes. *Beyond Imported Magic: Essays on Science, Technology, and Society in Latin America.* Cambridge, MA: MIT Press, 2014.

Merchant, Carolyn. *The Death of Nature: Women, Ecology, and the Scientific Revolution.* San Francisco: Harper and Row, 1980.

Merritt, Deborah J. "Hypatia in the Patent Office: Women Inventors and the Law, 1865-1900." *American Journal of Legal History* 35, no. 3 (1991): 235–306.

Merry, Sally Engle. "Legal Pluralism." *Law and Society Review* 22, no. 5 (1988): 869–96.

Mgbeoji, Ikechi. *Global Biopiracy: Patents, Plants, and Indigenous Knowledge.* Vancouver: UBC Press, 2006.

Mirowski, Philip, and Dieter Plehwe. *The Road from Mont Pèlerin: The Making of the Neoliberal Thought Collective.* Cambridge, MA: Harvard University Press, 2009.

Moodie, T. Dunbar. *The Rise of Afrikanerdom: Power, Apartheid, and the Afrikaner Civil Religion.* Berkeley: University of California Press, 1975.

Moran, Shane. *Representing Bushmen: South Africa and the Origin of Language.* Rochester, NY: University of Rochester Press, 2009.

Mudimbe, V. Y. *The Invention of Africa: Gnosis, Philosophy, and the Order of Knowledge.* Bloomington: Indiana University Press, 1988.

Mukuka, George Sombe. *Reap What You Have Not Sown: Indigenous Knowledge Systems and Intellectual Property Laws in South Africa.* Pretoria: Pretoria University Law Press, 2010.

Murphy, Michelle. *Seizing the Means of Reproduction: Entanglements of Feminism, Health, and Technoscience.* Durham, NC: Duke University Press, 2012.

Ncube, Caroline B. "The Development of Intellectual Property Policies in Africa: Some Key Considerations and a Research Agenda." *Intellectual Property Rights* 1, no. 1 (2013): 1–5.

Ncube, Caroline B., and Tobias Schonwetter. "New Hope for Africa? Copyright and Access to Knowledge in the Digital Age." *Info* 13, no. 3 (2011): 64–74.

Nelson, Alondra. "Bio Science: Genetic Genealogy Testing and the Pursuit of African Ancestry." *Social Studies of Science* 38, no. 5 (2008): 759–83.

Nuttall, Sarah. "Subjectivities of Whiteness." *African Studies Review* 44, no. 2 (2001): 115–40.

Ong, Aihwa. *Neoliberalism as Exception: Mutations in Citizenship and Sovereignty.* Durham, NC: Duke University Press, 2006.

Osseo-Asare, Abena Dove. *Bitter Roots: The Search for Healing Plants in Africa.* Chicago: University of Chicago Press, 2014.

Park, Sandra S. "Gene Patents and the Public Interest: Litigating *Association for Molecular Pathology v. Myriad Genetics* and Lessons Moving Forward." *North Carolina Journal of Law and Technology* 15, no. 4 (2014): 519–36.

Parkington, John, David Morris, and Neil Rusch. *Karoo Rock Engravings.* Cape Town: Creda Communications, 2008.

Parthasarathy, Shobita. "Whose Knowledge? Whose Values? The Comparative Politics of Patenting Life Forms in the United States and Europe." *Policy Sciences* 44, no. 3 (2011): 267–88.

Peck, Jamie, and Adam Tickell. "Neoliberalizing Space." *Antipode* 34, no. 3 (2002): 380–404.

Penn, Nigel. "'Fated to Perish': The Destruction of the Cape San." In *Miscast: Negotiating the Presence of the Bushmen,* edited by Pippa Skotnes, 81–92. Cape Town: University of Cape Town Press, 1996.

———. *The Forgotten Frontier: Colonist and Khoisan on the Cape's Northern Frontier in the Eighteenth Century.* Athens: Ohio University Press, 2005.

Petryna, Adriana. *Life Exposed: Biological Citizens after Chernobyl.* Princeton, NJ: Princeton University Press, 2002.

Pettitt, Clare. *Patent Inventions: Intellectual Property and the Victorian Novel.* Oxford: Oxford University Press, 2004.

Philip, Kavita. *Civilizing Natures: Race, Resources, and Modernity in Colonial South India.* New Brunswick, NJ: Rutgers University Press, 2004.

Pollack, Malla. "Towards a Feminist Theory of the Public Domain, or Rejecting the Gendered Scope of United States Copyrightable and Patentable Subject Matter." *Journal of Women and Law* 12 (2006): 603–26.

Pollock, Anne. "Places of Pharmaceutical Knowledge-Making: Global Health, Postcolonial Science, and Hope in South African Drug Discovery." *Social Studies of Science* 44, no. 6 (2014): 848–73.

Pollock, Anne, and Banu Subramaniam. "Resisting Power, Retooling Justice: Promises of Feminist Postcolonial Technosciences." *Science, Technology, and Human Values* 41, no. 6 (2016): 951–966.

Posel, Deborah. "Race as Common Sense: Racial Classification in Twentieth-Century South Africa." *African Studies Review* 44, no. 2 (2001): 87–113.

Pottage, Alain. "The Inscription of Life in Law: Genes, Patents, and Bio-Politics." *Modern Law Review* 61, no. 5 (1998): 740–65.

Povinelli, Elizabeth A. *The Cunning of Recognition: Indigenous Alterities and the*

Making of Australian Multiculturalism. Durham, NC: Duke University Press, 2002.

Pratt, Mary Louise. *Imperial Eyes: Travel Writing and Transculturation*, 2nd ed. New York: Routledge, 2008.

Rai, Arti K., and Rebecca S. Eisenberg. "Bayh-Dole Reform and the Progress of Biomedicine." *Law and Contemporary Problems* 66, nos. 1-2 (2003): 289–314.

Reardon, Jenny. *Race to the Finish: Identity and Governance in an Age of Genomics*. Princeton, NJ: Princeton University Press, 2005.

Reed, Evelyn. *Is Biology Woman's Destiny?* 2nd ed. New York: Pathfinder Press, 1985.

———. *Sexism and Science*. New York: Pathfinder Press, 1978.

Riles, Annelise. *Collateral Knowledge: Legal Reasoning in the Global Financial Markets*. Chicago Series in Law and Society. Chicago: University of Chicago Press, 2011.

———. "A New Agenda for the Cultural Study of Law: Taking on the Technicalities." *Buffalo Law Review* 53, no. 3 (2005): 979–1033.

Robertson, Emma. *Chocolate, Women, and Empire: A Social and Cultural History*. Manchester: Manchester University Press, 2013.

Robins, Steven. *Limits to Liberation after Apartheid: Citizenship, Governance, and Culture*. Athens: Ohio University Press, 2005.

———. "NGOs, 'Bushmen,' and Double Vision: The p khomani San Land Claim and the Cultural Politics of 'Community' in the Kalahari." *Journal of Southern African Studies* 27, no. 4 (2001): 833–53.

Robins, Steven, Elias Madzudzo, and Matthias Brenzinger. *An Assessment of the Status of the San in South Africa, Angola, Zambia, and Zimbabwe*. Windhoek: Legal Assistance Centre, 2001.

Rofel, Lisa. *Desiring China: Experiments in Neoliberalism, Sexuality, and Public Culture*. Durham, NC: Duke University Press, 2007.

Romm, Jeffrey M. "The Researcher's Personal Pursuit of Balance between Academic and Practical Contributions." *Journal of Research Practice* 10, no. 2 (2014): N10.

Rose, Nikolas. *The Politics of Life Itself: Biomedicine, Power, and Subjectivity in the Twenty-First Century*. Princeton, NJ: Princeton University Press, 2006.

Rosenthal, Joshua. "Integrating Drug Discovery, Biodiversity Conservation, and Economic Development: Early Lessons from the International Cooperative Biodiversity Groups." In *Biodiversity and Human Health*, edited by Grifo Francesca and Joshua Rosenthal, 281–301. Washington, DC: Island Press, 1997.

Rosser, Sue. "The Gender Gap in Patents." In *Women, Science, and Technology: A Reader in Feminist Science Studies*, edited by Mary Wyer, Mary Barbercheck, Donna Cookmeyer, Hatice Örün Öztürk, and Marta Wayne, 111–32. New York: Routledge, 2014.

Roy, Deboleena, and Banu Subramaniam. "Matter in the Shadows: Feminist

New Materialism and the Practices of Colonialism" In *Mattering: Feminism, Science, and Materialism*, edited by Victoria Pitts-Taylor, 23–42. New York: New York University Press, 2016.

Salo, Elaine, and Benita Moolman. "Introduction: Biology, Bodies, and Human Rights." *Agenda: Empowering Women for Gender Equity* 27, no. 4 (2013): 3–9.

Sasser, Jade. "The Limits to Giving Back." *Journal of Research Practice* 10, no. 2 (2014): M7.

Sawyer, Sarah Cahill "Failing to Give Enough: When Researcher Ideas about Giving Back Fall Short." *Journal of Research Practice* 10, no. 2 (2014): N12.

Schiebinger, Londa. "The Loves of the Plants." *Scientific American*, February 1996: 110–15.

———. *Plants and Empire: Colonial Bioprospecting in the Atlantic World*. Cambridge, MA: Harvard University Press, 2004.

Schroeder, Doris. "Informed Consent: From Medical Research to Traditional Knowledge." In *Indigenous Peoples, Consent and Benefit Sharing*, edited by Rachel Wynberg, Doris Schroeder, and Roger Chennells, 27–52. New York: Springer, 2009.

Scott, Catherine V. *Gender and Development: Rethinking Modernization and Dependency Theory*. Boulder, CO: Lynne Rienner, 1995.

Sell, Susan K. *Private Power, Public Law: The Globalization of Intellectual Property Rights*. Cambridge: Cambridge University Press, 2003.

Shapin, Steven, and Simon Schaffer. *Leviathan and the Air-Pump: Hobbes, Boyle, and the Experimental Life*. Princeton, NJ: Princeton University Press, 1985.

Sharp, John, and Stuart Douglas. "Prisoners of Their Reputation? The Veterans of the 'Bushman' Battalions in South Africa." In *Miscast: Negotiating the Presence of the Bushmen*, edited by Pippa Skotnes, 323–29. Cape Town: University of Cape Town Press, 1996.

Shelley, Mary Wollstonecraft, and J. Paul Hunter. *Frankenstein: The 1818 Text, Contexts, Nineteenth-Century Responses, Modern Criticism*. New York: W.W. Norton, 1996.

Shepard, Nick. "Disciplining Archaeology: The Invention of South African Prehistory, 1923-1953." *Kronos* 28, no. 1 (2002): 127–45.

Shiva, Vandana. *Biopiracy: The Plunder of Nature and Knowledge*. Boston: South End Press, 1997.

Shiva, Vandana, and Ingunn Moser. *Biopolitics: A Feminist and Ecological Reader on Biotechnology*. London: Zed Books.1995.

Sibuye, Rodney, Marie-Tinka Uys, Gino Cocchiaro, and Johan Lorenzen. "The Bushbuckridge BCP: Traditional Health Practitioners Organise for ABS in South Africa." *Participatory Learning and Action* 65 (2012): 101–8.

Simpson, Audra. "On Ethnographic Refusal: Indigeneity, 'Voice,' and Colonial Citizenship." *Junctures* 9 (2007): 67–80.

Sittert, Lance Van. "From 'Mere Weeds' and 'Bosjes' to a Cape Floral Kingdom: The Re-Imagining of Indigenous Flora at the Cape, c. 1890-1939." *Kronos: South African Histories*, no. 28 (2002): 102–26.

Smith, Andrea. "Native American Feminism, Sovereignty, and Social Change." In *Making Space for Indigenous Feminism*, edited by Joyce Green, 93–107. Black Point, NS: Fernwood, 2007.

———. "Native Studies at the Horizon of Death: Theorizing Ethnographic Entrapment and Settler Self-Reflexivity." In *Theorizing Native Studies*, edited by Andrea Smith and Audra Simpson, 207–34. Durham, NC: Duke University Press, 2014.

Smith, Andy, Candy Malherbe, Mat Guenther, and Penny Berens. *The Bushmen of Southern Africa: A Foraging Society in Transition*. Cape Town: David Philip, 2000.

Smith, Linda Tuhiwai. *Decolonizing Methodologies: Research and Indigenous Peoples*. London: Zed Books, 1999.

Smith, Lindsay Adams. "Identifying Democracy: Citizenship, DNA, and Identity in Postdictatorship Argentina." *Science, Technology, and Human Values* 41, no. 6 (2016): 1037–62.

Strathern, Marilyn. "Cutting the Network." *Journal of the Royal Anthropological Institute* 2, no. 3 (1996): 517–35.

Subramaniam, Banu. *Ghost Stories for Darwin: The Science of Variation and the Politics of Diversity*. Urbana: University of Illinois Press, 2014.

Subramaniam, Banu, Laura Foster, Sandra Harding, Deboleena Roy, and Kim TallBear. "Feminism, Postcolonialism, and Technoscience." In *Handbook of Science and Technology Studies*, edited by Clark Miller, Laurel Smith-Doerr, Ulrike Felt, and Rayvon Fouché. Cambridge, MA: MIT Press, 2016.

Sugimoto, Cassidy R., Chaoqun Ni, Jevin D. West, and Vincent Larivière. "The Academic Advantage: Gender Disparities in Patenting." *PLOS One* 10, no. 5 (2015): 1–10.

Sunder, Madhavi. "The Invention of Traditional Knowledge." *Law and Contemporary Problems* 70, no. 2 (2007): 97–124.

Swanson, Kara W. "Getting a Grip on the Corset: Gender, Sexuality, and Patent Law." *Yale Journal of Law and Feminism* 23, no. 1 (2011): 57–115.

———. "Intellectual Property and Gender: Reflections on Accomplishments and Methodology." *Journal of Gender, Social Policy and the Law* 43, no. 1 (2015): 175–98.

Swarr, Amanda Lock, and Richa Nagar. *Critical Transnational Feminist Praxis*. Albany: SUNY Press, 2010.

Swart, Elsabe. "Hoodia Gordonii in Southern Africa." Department of Tourism, Environment, and Conservation, 2008.

Sweet, Robert. *Hortus Britannicus: Or, a Catalogue of Plants, Indigenous, or Cultivated in the Gardens of Great Britain; Arranged According to Their Natural Orders*. London: James Ridgway, 1830.

Sylvain, Renée. "At the Intersections: San Women and the Rights of Indigenous Peoples in Africa." *International Journal of Human Rights* 15, no. 1 (2011): 89–110.

———. "San Women Today: Inequality and Dependency in a Post-Foraging World." *Indigenous Affairs* 1-2, no. 4 (2004): 89–110.

Takeshita, Chikako. *The Global Biopolitics of the IUD: How Science Constructs Contraceptive Users and Women's Bodies*. Cambridge, MA: MIT Press, 2012.

TallBear, Kim. *Native American DNA: Tribal Belonging and the False Promise of Genetic Science*. Minneapolis: University of Minnesota Press, 2013.

———. "Native-American DNA.Com: In Search of Native American Race and Tribe." In *Revisiting Race in a Genomic Age*, edited by Barbara A. Koenig, Sandra Soo-Jin Lee, and Sarah S. Richardson, 235–52. New Brunswick, NJ: Rutgers University Press, 2008.

———. "Standing with and Speaking as Faith: A Feminist-Indigenous Approach to Inquiry." *Journal of Research Practice* 10, no. 2 (2014): N17.

Tauli-Corpuz, Victoria. "Is Biopiracy an Issue for Feminists in the Philippines?" *Signs: Journal of Women in Culture and Society* 32, no. 2 (2007): 332–37.

Terrall, Mary. "Heroic Narratives of Quest and Discovery." In *The Postcolonial Science and Technology Studies Reader*, edited by Sandra G. Harding, 84–102. Durham, NC: Duke University Press, 2011.

Thompson, Leonard. *A History of South Africa*, 4th ed. New Haven, CT: Yale University Press, 2014.

Thursby, Jerry G., and Marie C. Thursby. "Gender Patterns of Research and Licensing Activity of Science and Engineering Faculty." *Journal of Technology Transfer* 30, no. 4 (2005): 343–53.

Tilley, Helen. *Africa as a Living Laboratory: Empire, Development, and the Problem of Scientific Knowledge, 1870-1950*. Chicago: University of Chicago Press, 2011.

Traweek, Sharon. *Beamtimes and Lifetimes: The World of High Energy Physicists*. Cambridge, MA: Harvard University Press, 1988.

Tuana, Nancy, ed. *Feminism and Science*. Bloomington: Indiana University Press, 1989.

United Nations Environmental Programme. "Convention on International Trade in Endangered Species," July 1, 1975, www.cites.org/eng/disc/text.php.

Urquhart, Lisa. "New Positive Alzheimer's Trial for Phytopharm." *Financial Times*, May 6, 2006.

Valverde, Mariana. "Jurisdiction and Scale: Legal 'Technicalities' as Resources for Theory." *Social and Legal Studies* 18, no. 2 (2009): 139–57.

van Dooren, Thom. "Inventing Seed: The Nature(s) of Intellectual Property in Plants." *Environment and Planning D: Society and Space* 26, no. 4 (2008): 676–97.

Vermeylen, Saskia. "Contextualizing 'Fair' and 'Equitable': The San's Reflections on the Hoodia Benefit-Sharing Agreement." *Local Environment* 12, no. 4 (2007): 423–36.

———. "From Life Force to Slimming Aid: Exploring Views on the Commodification of Traditional Medicinal Knowledge." *Applied Geography* 28, no. 3 (2008): 224–35.

Verwey, Cornel, and Michael Quayle. "Whiteness, Racism, and Afrikaner

Identity in Post-Apartheid South Africa." *African Affairs* 111, no. 445 (2012): 551–75.

Visvanathan, Nalini, Lynn Duggan, Laurie Nisonoff, and Nan Wiegersma, eds. *The Women, Gender, and Development Reader.* London: Zed Books, 1997.

Walwyn, D., and P. Steyn. *A Short History of Natural Product Research in the CSIR.* Pretoria, South Africa: CSIR, 2006.

wa Thiong'o, Ngũgĩ. *Decolonising the Mind: The Politics of Language in African Literature.* London: James Currey, 1986.

White, Alain, and Boyd L. Sloane. *The Stapelieae,* vol. 3, 2nd ed. Pasadena, CA: Abbey San Encino Press, 1937.

———. *The Stapelieae: An Introduction to the Study of This Tribe of Asclepiadaceae.* Pasadena, CA: Abbey San Encino Press, 1933.

Whittington, Kjersten Bunker. "Mothers of Invention? Gender, Motherhood, and New Dimensions of Productivity in the Science Profession." *Work and Occupations* 38, no. 3 (2011): 417–56.

Whittington, Kjersten Bunker, and Laurel Smith-Doerr. "Gender and Commercial Science: Women's Patenting in the Life Sciences." *Journal of Technology Transfer* 30, no. 4 (2005), 355–70.

———. "Women Inventors in Context: Disparities in Patenting across Academia and Industry." *Gender and Society* 22, no. 2 (2008): 194–218.

Willey, Angela. *Undoing Monogamy: The Politics of Science and the Possibilities of Biology.* Durham, NC: Duke University Press, 2016.

———. "A World of Materialisms: Postcolonial Feminist Science Studies and the New Natural." *Science, Technology, and Human Values* 41, no. 6 (2016): 991–1014.

Williams, Patricia A. *The Alchemy of Race and Rights.* Cambridge, MA: Harvard University Press, 1991.

Williams, Paul, and Ian Taylor. "Neoliberalism and the Political Economy of the 'New' South Africa." *New Political Economy* 5, no. 1 (2010): 21–40.

Wilson, Elizabeth A. *Gut Feminism.* Durham, NC: Duke University Press, 2015.

Wynberg, Rachel P. "Navigating a Way through Regulatory Frameworks for Hoodia Use, Conservation, Trade, and Benefit Sharing." In *Wild Product Governance: Finding Policies That Work for Non–Timber Forest Products,* edited by Sarah A. Laird, Rebecca McLain, and Rachel P. Wynberg, 309–26. London: Earthscan, 2010.

———. "Rhetoric, Realism, and Benefit Sharing: Use of Traditional Knowledge of Hoodia Species in the Development of Appetite Suppressant." *Journal of World Intellectual Property* 7, no. 6 (2004): 851–76.

Wynberg, Rachel P., and Sarah A. Laird. "Bioprospecting: Tracking the Policy Debate." *Environment: Science and Policy for Sustainable Development* 49, no. 10 (2007): 20–32.

Wynberg, Rachel P., Sarah Laird, Jaci van Niekerk, and Witness Kozanayi. "Formalization of the Natural Product Trade in Southern Africa: Unintended

Consequences and Policy Blurring in Biotrade and Bioprospecting." *Society and Natural Resources* 28 (2015): 559–74.

Wynberg, Rachel P., Doris Schroeder, and Roger Chennells. *Indigenous Peoples, Consent and Benefit Sharing: Lessons from the San-Hoodia Case.* New York: Springer, 2009.

Ybarra, Megan. "Don't Just Pay It Back, Pay It Forward: From Accountability to Reciprocity in Research Relationships." *Journal of Research Practice* 10, no. 2 (2014): N5.

Index

Beijing Declaration of Indigenous Women (1995), 8
belonging: Afrikaners and, 104–6, 107, 124, 173n2; benefit sharing and, 6, 64, 110–11, 127; autochthony and, 62; as framework for discussion, 16–17; indigeneity and, 6, 124–25; law and, 15; and materialities of Hoodia, 26, 30, 64; in postapartheid South Africa, 17, 48, 84, 104, 107, 111, 124–25, 127, 148n49; and stereotypical images, 122; unequal modes of, 6, 11, 24, 76, 101, 119, 129, 130; and ways of knowing, 104, 129–31
benefit sharing: as belonging, 6, 64, 110–11, 127; in Biodiversity Act of 2004, 53; in Media and Research Contract, 20; in Regulations of 2008, 110; scholarship on, 7, 8, 109; by scientists and indigenous peoples, 127–28. See also San-CSIR benefit-sharing agreement; San-SAHGA benefit-sharing agreement
Benjamin, Miriam E., 141n17
Benjamin, Ruha, 21, 101
Berne Declaration, 158n17
Big Bang Theory (television show), 13
Bindra, Jasjit S., 98
biocultural community protocols, 128
biodiversity, 161n31. See also Biodiversity Act; Convention on Biological Diversity
Biodiversity Act (2004), 53, 60, 157n13
biological citizenship, 16, 147n46
biopiracy, 8, 53–54
bioprospecting, 35, 59, 161n31. See also Regulations on Bio-Prospecting, Access, and Benefit-Sharing
Biowatch South Africa, 53
Black women, patents owned by, 141n17
Bleek, Wilhelm, 38
Boers, 33, 39

Bohr, Niels, 146n40
Boone, Sarah, 141n17
botanists, 36, 37, 38, 70–71
Botswana, 43, 63
British colonization, 33–35, 105, 151–52n35
British patent law, 34–35
Brou, Keis, 39
Brown, Nicholas Edward, 38–39, 71, 154n54
Bruyns, Peter V., 31, 70, 71, 151n34, 152–53n45
Buchu plant, 128
Busakhwe, Tommy, 49–50, 62, 76, 81, 122
Bushbuckridge (South Africa), 128
Bushman Secrets Health Products Store, 51
Bushmen: claimed as identity, 23, 42, 49; described by Dickens, 38; displayed in London, 38; term used by Dutch settlers, 33; term used by Masson, 152nn37, 39
Bushmen Hoodia, 119

Cape Coloured People, 34
Cape Ethnobotanical Growers Association (CEGA), 107, 108, 109
Cape Khoi, 23, 32
Cape Kingdom Nutraceuticals, 128
Cape Nature, 108, 109
Carallumas, 40
cattle, 31
CBD (UN Convention on Biological Diversity), 48, 53, 54, 60, 157n13
Central Kalahari Game Reserve, 18
Chennells, Roger: acquaintance with, 19; approached by Steve Hurt, 107; invited by Poovey, 169n22; as lawyer for San peoples, 19, 55, 148n52, 159–60n30; and negotiations with CSIR, 56, 57; quoted on biopiracy, 54; on strategy for addressing CSIR patents, 158n17

Chernobyl, 147n46
CITES (Convention on International Trade in Endangered Species), 109, 137–38n3, 168n1
citizenship, 16, 147n46
classification, 37–38, 39
clinical studies, 97–98, 99, 100, 170–71n32, 171nn33–36, 172nn41–42
Cocchiaro, Gino, 7
Coetzee, Sophia Katrina, 155n79
colonialism: gender and, 44; histories of, 30–35, 37, 60, 104–6, 119, 123; Hoodia advertising and, 120; patent law and, 34–35; and relationships among indigenous peoples, 33; and resource extraction, 74–75; science and, 8–9, 26, 29, 30, 33, 35–37, 74–75
Comaroff, John, 111, 124
Comaroff, Jean, 111, 124
Committee on Women (South African Parliament), 165n13
"commodity racism" (McClintock), 120
Community Properties Association Act of 1996, 155n80
Companies and Intellectual Property Commission (CIPC), 163n9
contact zones (Pratt), 76
Convention on Biological Diversity (CBD), 48, 53, 54, 60, 157n13
Convention on International Trade in Endangered Species (CITES), 109, 137–38n3, 168n1
Cooper, Dr. Sheldon (fictional character), 13
Council for Science and Industrial Research. See CSIR
Couric, Katie, 173–74n10
Covance Clinical Research Unit (Leeds, UK), 170–71n32
Covance Clinical Research Unit (Madison, WI), 172n42
coverture laws, 140n17
Crenshaw, Kimberlé, 16, 148n48

CSIR (Council for Scientific and Industrial Research, South Africa): anti-obesity research, 75; complex in Pretoria, 69; construction of Hoodia and San peoples as scientific objects, 37; extraction of chemicals from Hoodia, 67, 82–83, 84; Hoodia farms managed by, 95, 170n27; Hoodia labs, 69; Hoodia patents, 3, 55, 75, 77, 80, 158n17; mission of, 69, 162n1; partnership with Phytopharm, 88–89, 90–91; patent application in United Kingdom, 163n9; provisional patent of 1994, 67–68, 73, 163n9; research funding of, 162n1; research on nutrition, 69–70; traditional knowledge of, 80; unequal partnership of, 101; unit established by Pfizer, 99. See also Hoodia: at the scale of molecule; San-CSIR benefit-sharing agreement
Curtis, William, 153n46

Daston, Lorraine, 152n36
Deloria Jr., Vine, 13
Department of Environmental Affairs and Tourism (DEAT), 110, 161n31
Department of Science and Technology (DST), 160n31, 162n1
Department of Tourism, Environment, and Conservation, 63, 108, 109
Derrida, Jacques, 15, 77
Desert Burn, 122–23
Desperate Housewives (television show), 174n10
diabetes, 81, 166n33
Dickens, Charles, 38
Didiza, Angela Thokozile, 155n79
dioramas, 30
discovery: and classification, 24, 26, 35; and invention, 12–14, 75, 82; Masson and, 29

Growth, Equity, and Reconstruction
Programme (GEAR), 73, 164n11
Gunn Allen, Paula, 149n2

Hamilton, Jennifer, 57
Hammonds, Evelynn, 16, 148n48
Haraway, Donna, 8, 142n22
Harding, Sandra, 7, 8, 16, 35, 144n28,
148n48
Harry, Debra, 8, 18, 61
Harvard Kalahari Research Group,
150n4
Haupt, Adam, 7, 60
Hayden, Cori, 109, 110
Health Synergetics, 106, 121
Hekman, Susan, 14, 63, 95, 146n40
herbal supplement industry, 4, 18,
88, 104, 167–68n1. *See also* Hoodia
growers; San-SAHGA benefit-
sharing agreement; South African
Hoodia Growers Association
HGH Pharmaceuticals, 128
histories: colonial, 30–35, 37, 60, 104–
6, 119, 123; and Hoodia patent
struggles, 44–45; of Hoodia plants,
40–41, 123–24; of San Hoodia
knowledge, 64, 75, 81; of San peoples, 37, 41–44, 48, 56, 119, 123–24
HIV/AIDS drugs, 74, 164–65n13
homelands, 41
Homo monstrosis monorchidei, 38
Homo sapiens, 38
Hood, Mr. (grower of exotic plants),
37, 153n46
Hoodia: as agents 25, 26, 39–40, 95–
96; as antiobesity drug, 3–4, 14, 68,
81, 87, 91–92; as appetite suppressant, 3, 67, 72–73, 74, 75, 82, 91, 98,
137n2; botanical industry, 173n10,
174n10; chemistry of, 14, 68, 70,
71–73, 96, 97, 98, 99; clinical studies, 97–98, 99, 100, 170–71n32,
171nn33–36, 172nn41–42; dried, 4,
104, 114, 117; effectiveness of, 97–

98, 100, 171nn33–36; endangerment of, 4, 112; as energy source,
81, 111; ethnographic account of,
10; as food ingredient, 93–94; and
gastric acid secretion, 81, 166n32;
and gender, 111, 114–15, 119–20; as
herbal weight-control supplement,
4, 18, 88, 104, 167–68n1; as indigenous knowledge, 17, 25, 52–53, 64,
81, 160n31; market for, 109, 110;
marketing of, 4, 18, 25, 31, 91, 108,
111, 118, 120–24, 174n12; materialities of, 5–6, 14, 51, 58, 64, 65, 87, 91,
114, 125, 129, 130; media attention
to, 173–74n10; microscopic study
of, 38–39; as patented molecules,
50, 51; physical scales of, 10–11;
pill/plant amalgamation, 86*fig.*, 87;
resistance to commercial desires,
88, 99, 100–101; at the scale of colonial scientific object, 26, 29, 37,
71; at the scale of cultivated plant,
27, 95, 101, 102*fig.*, 103–4, 111–15,
115–18, 121, 124, 125, 130; at the
scale of molecule, 26, 50, 65, 68,
71–73, 74, 76, 80, 82–83, 101, 113,
125, 130; at the scale of plant from
nature, 3, 25, 26, 47, 48–51, 58, 64,
91, 118, 121, 125, 130; at the scales
of solid drug and liquid food, 26;
seed production, 116–17; side effects of, 97–98, 100, 171n33; as
source of food and water, 69; studies with rats, 72–73; supply of
plants, 91, 94; unpredictability of,
115–18; as weight-loss drink, 99–
100. See also *Hoodia gordonii*;
!Khoba plant; P57
Hoodia farms, 94–95, 102*fig.*, 103–4,
170n27. *See also* Hoodia growers
Hoodia genus, 37, 39, 40, 71, 137n2,
153n45
Hoodia gordoni, 154n54. See also
Hoodia gordonii

Hoodia gordonii: chemical structure of, from patent application, 66*fig.*; classification of, 37–38, 39, 71; cultivated in Barrydale, South Africa, 102*fig.*; deceptive advertising of, 174n12; drawings of, 28*fig.*, 29, 36, 151n34; habitat and distribution of, 63–64; as historical actor, 40–41; material-discursive meanings of, 3–4; in Phytopharm's Factfile, 167–68n1; as scientific object of study, 71. *See also* Hoodia; *Stapelia Gordoni*

Hoodia growers: and belonging in postapartheid South Africa, 104, 107, 111, 124–25; benefit sharing with San peoples, 107–9; contracts with Unilever, 94–95; knowledge of Hoodia as a cultivated plant, 111–13, 121; marketing of Hoodia, 27; views on Hoodia patents, 113–14. *See also* Gass, Robby; Hurt, Steve; Joubert, Albert; South African Hoodia Growers Association

Hoodia piliferum, 137n2. See also *Trichocaulon piliferum*

"Hottentots," 33, 70, 71, 152nn37, 39

Huernia genus, 40

human/nonhuman binary, 11, 25, 38

human-nonhuman relationships, 6, 11, 14, 77, 104–5, 146n42

human-plant relationships, 16, 26, 41, 50, 65, 125

human rights, 9

human subjects, 21

hunting, 81, 111, 115, 119–20; and gathering, 31–32, 44, 159n30

Hurt, Steve, 106–7, 109–10, 113–14, 116. *See also* Health Synergetics

hyperbilirubinemia, 98, 100, 171n36

Immorality Act of 1950, 154n67

India, patents in, 8

Indians (racial classification), 70

indigeneity: "acquired indigeneity" (Dubow), 105; belonging and, 124–25; definition of, 23–24; use of the term *indigenous*, 22–23

Indigenous Knowledge Systems (IKS), 160–61n31, 170n27

indigenous peoples: challenges to patents, 135–36; closeness to nature, 83, 157n13; community protocols and research guidelines for working with, 133–34; as raw materials, 27. *See also* San peoples

Indigenous Peoples' Council on Biocolonialism, 18

Indigenous People's Permanent Forum, 8

indigenous peoples' self-determination, 3, 53, 127, 128–29

"informed refusal" (Ruha Benjamin), 21

Intellectual Property Rationalisation Act, 73

intellectual property rights: contrasted with indigenous knowledge, 160n31; critical frameworks for, 7; and images of San peoples, 122–23; ≠Khomani San views of, 76; San training session regarding, 55–56; as threat to indigenous women's lives, 8; TRIPs, 74, 164n13. *See also* patent law; patents

Internet marketing of Hoodia, 27, 31, 111, 118–20, 121, 122–24, 167–68n1, 175n28

interracial marriage, 154n67

intersectional analysis, 11, 25, 30, 131

invention: discovery and, 12–14, 75, 82; masculinity and, 34; patents and, 34–35, 130; use of the term, 6

"invention of traditional knowledge" (Sunder), 82

Ives, Sarah, 125

IXICO, 168n2

Jackson, Shannon, 149–50n2

Jacobs, Rykes, 20, 49

Jaimes, M. Annette, 44
Jansen, Lesle, 21, 23. *See also* Natural Justice
Jonas, Harry, 7
Jones, Indiana (fictional character), 12–13
Joubert, Albert, 107, 116, 117

Kabembe, Likua, 119
Kalahari Desert, 30, 47, 92, 115, 116, 167n1; game reserve, 18; !Khoba plant in, 46*fig.*; Molopo Lodge, 3, 62, 127
Kalahari Gemsbok National Park, 41, 52. *See also* !Ae!Hai Kalahari Heritage Park Agreement
Kanehe, Le'a, 8, 18, 61
Kew Gardens, 29, 36, 38
Kgalagadi Transfrontier Park, 49
Khan, B. Zorina, 140n17
!Khoba plant: in Kalahari Desert, 46*fig.*, 47; ≠Khomani San descriptions of, 49–50; San name for *Hoodia gordonii*, 137n2; traditional knowledge of, 50, 58–59, 62–63, 64, 81, 159n30. *See also* Hoodia
Khoi peoples, 23, 30, 31–33, 104
Khoisan, 23
≠Khomani San: contacts with, 20–21; criteria for membership, 43, 155n80; displaced from Kalahari Gemsbok National Park, 41; as group included in San, 23, 32; land claims, 43, 53, 55, 155n80; posters on history and culture, 48; representation of, 20; revitalization movements, 52–53. *See also* San peoples
Khwe, 21, 23, 32, 42, 43, 44
Kirby, Vicky, 14, 146n40
Kock, Hans Johannes, 68
Koranna, 23, 32

LaDuke, Winona, 8, 33
Lalu, Premesh, 34

land claims, 43, 53, 55, 155n80
landownership by females, 155n80
language and terminology, 22–24
law, materiality of, 15, 147n45
Leahy-Smith America Invents Act, 135
Le Fleur, Andrew, 23
Linnaeus, Carl, 30, 36, 37, 38, 153n45
Lloyd, Lucy, 38
Locke, John, 34, 68
London Financial Times, 54, 168n13, 172n41
London Observer, 31, 53–54
Louw, Collin, 19–20, 48, 51, 122–24

MacKinnon, Catherine, 16, 148n48
Mahango, Mario Kapilolo, 30
Maharaj, Dr. Vinesh, 70–73, 74, 96, 97, 99
malnutrition, 69
Mandela, Nelson, 23, 43
Manukan Declaration of the Indigenous Women's Biodiversity Network (2004), 8
Marais, Hein, 164n11
Marloth, Rudolf, 70, 71
Masson, Francis, 29, 36–37, 71, 152nn37, 39; drawing of Hoodia, 28*fig.*, 36, 151n34; *Stapeliae Novae*, 29, 151nn34–35
materialist feminist scholarship, 14, 63, 95, 146nn40, 42
materiality, 14–16; of law, 15, 147n45; multiple modalities of, 15, 131–32; of nature, 14–15, 146n42; of plants, 64. *See also* Hoodia: materialities of
May, Christopher, 164n12
McClintock, Anne, 37, 120
"mechanical objectivity" (Daston and Galison), 152n36
Media and Research Contract, 19–20
medicine, traditional and Western, 51
Meneputo, 88
Merritt, Deborah J., 140n17
Mgbeoji, Ikechi, 35

Mgoqi, Wallace Amos, 155n79
microscope, 38, 152n36
missionaries, 38
Mochudi, legal clinic in, 18
modernity, notions of, 144n28
modern/nonmodern binary, 25, 26, 45, 57, 81, 84–85. *See also* San peoples: as modern and nonmodern
Molopo Lodge (Kalahari Desert), signing ceremony at, 3–4, 59–60, 62, 127
monogenism, 38
mood-enhancing plants, 128
Morrison, Sandy, 172n41
Moses, Kxao, 4, 59–60, 159–60n30
Msimang, Mavuso, 155n79
Mudimbe, Valentin-Yves, 13
Murphy, Michele, 10
Myriad Genetics, 142n17

Nagar, Richa, 21
Nagoya Protocol on Access and Benefit Sharing (ABS), 128, 157n13
Nama, 23, 32, 64
Namibia, 32, 41, 43, 63, 64
naming and claiming, 33, 37
Natal, 35
National Advisory Council on Innovation Act, 74
National Environmental Management: Biodiversity Bill, 161n31
National House of Traditional Leaders, 23, 32, 128
National Khoisan Council (NKC), 21, 23, 128
National Research and Development Strategy, 160n31
nation-state: belonging and, 17, 84, 148n49; patent law and, 79–80; rights claims and, 61; sovereignty over natural resources, 157n13
Natural Justice, 19, 20, 21, 128
natural property rights, 13, 68
nature: Hoodia patents and, 94, 113, 114; multiple meanings of, 6; as

property, 68. *See also* Hoodia: at the scale of plant from nature; nature and culture
nature and culture: as binary, 25, 49–52, 65, 83, 84, 88, 101; in feminist theory, 146nn40, 42; in the marketing of Hoodia, 91, 92–93; in Unilever's construction of Hoodia, 94, 95
Ncube, Caroline, 7
neem tree, patents on, 8
neoliberal governance, 73–74, 163–64n10, 164nn11, 13
New York Times, 98
Ngubane, Ben, 59–60, 160–61n31
Nguni language, 32
nuclear magnetic resonance spectrometry, 67, 70
Nutraceuticals International, 174n12
Nuttall, Sarah, 17, 148n49
Nyae Nyae, 41

obesity, 69, 75, 80, 91, 170n32
Oldenburg, D., 151n34
Olyn, Andries, 39, 41
Onseepkans farm, 95, 170n27
Oompa-Loompas, 12–13, 130
Oprah, 174n10
Orange Free State, 35
Osseo-Asare, Abena Dove, 10
oxetanones, 80

Parceval Pharmaceuticals, 174n21
paresthesia, 98
Parthasarathy, Shobita, 142n22
patentability, 11–14
patent law: British, 34–35; colonialism and, 34–35; contingency in, 83, 84; discovery and invention in, 12–14, 24, 75, 82, 130; examining and nonexamining offices, 79, 163n9.; extraction processes and, 82–83, 84; feminist science studies of, 7–8, 140–42n17; and Hoodia materiali-

ties, 26, 68; and indigenous knowledge, 57–58; litigation strategies, 135–36; nation-states and, 79–80; novelty and nonobviousness in, 24, 78–79, 135–36, 166n26; opposition to, 74, 164n13, 165n13; patriarchy and, 25; prior art, 78, 79, 80, 135–36, 165n25; provisional patents, 82, 163n9; "reasonable person" standard in, 136; requirement to "isolate and purify," 82; in South Africa, 74, 163n9; as taught in US law schools, 12–14, 24, 130; U.S. and South African, 77–79, 82; and ways of knowing, 80–81, 83. *See also* intellectual property rights; patents

patents: and belonging, 84; as drivers of economic growth, 164n12; effects on indigenous peoples, 7, 8; expertise barriers in, 142n22; in fifteenth-century Venice, 34; gender and, 8, 140–42n17; Hoodia-related, 3, 55, 75, 77, 79, 80–81, 82–84, 158n17, 166nn31–33; in India, 8; and natural rights, 34; nature and, 113; owned by women, 140–41n17; and women's health care, 141–42n17

Patents, Designs, Trade Marks, and Copyright Act of 1916, 35
Pedi language, 32
Pella farm, 95, 170n27
Pentandria Digynia, 153n45
Petryna, Adriana, 147n46
P57, 91–92, 99, 114, 116, 168n13
Pfizer: accused of biopiracy, 53–54; claims regarding Hoodia, 26; as commercial partner of CSIR, 4, 90–91, 99; dropped plans to develop Hoodia in 2003, 5, 87, 93, 98, 99; growers' view of, 113–14; mentioned, 75; Natureceuticals group, 93, 99

Pharmaceutical Manufacturers Association of South Africa, 164n13
phenylglycines, 80
Philip, Kavita, 35
photography, 152n36
Phytopharm: accused of biopiracy, 53–54; claimed San peoples as extinct, 31, 54; claims regarding Hoodia, 26; clinical studies of Hoodia, 97, 170–71n32, 171nn33–36; collaboration with CSIR on gastric acid secretion, 81; as commercial partner of CSIR, 4, 88–89, 90–91, 168n2; Hoodia-based patents of, 81; image of Hoodia as pill and plant, 87, 167n1; mentioned, 75; merger with IXICO, 168n2; milestone payments, 57; P57 research, 90–91, 168n13; partnership with Unilever, 5, 87, 94, 99, 169n22, 172n41; stock of, 91, 99, 168n2, 172n41; website and Factfile of, 87, 91, 167–68n1, 169n14. *See also* P57

Planet Hoodia Slender Gel, 174n12
plants: as agents, 95–96; cultivation of, 32, 37, 111–13; as historical actors, 40–41, 63; materiality of, 64, 104; relationships with humans, 16, 26, 41, 50, 65, 125; unpredictability of, 7, 96. *See also* Hoodia: at the scale of cultivated plant; Hoodia: at the scale of plant from nature

Pollock, Anne, 74
polygenism, 38
Poovey, Kevin, 93–95, 120–21, 169n22
Population Registration Act of 1950, 41, 154n67
postcolonial studies, 9, 144n28
PPD Development Clinic (Leicester, UK), 171nn33–34
Pratt, Mary Louise, 8, 76
Prohibition Act of Mixed Marriages (1949), 154n67